Lecture Notes in Computer Science 2193

Edited by G. Goos, J. Hartmanis, and J. van Leeuwen

Springer

Berlin
Heidelberg
New York
Barcelona
Hong Kong
London
Milan
Paris
Tokyo

Fabio Casati   Dimitrios Georgakopoulos
Ming-Chien Shan (Eds.)

Technologies
for E-Services

Second International Workshop, TES 2001
Rome, Italy, September 14-15, 2001
Proceedings

 Springer

Series Editors

Gerhard Goos, Karlsruhe University, Germany
Juris Hartmanis, Cornell University, NY, USA
Jan van Leeuwen, Utrecht University, The Netherlands

Volume Editors

Fabio Casati
Ming-Chien Shan
Hewlett-Packard
1501 Page Mill Road, 1 U-4, Palo Alto, CA 94304, USA
E-mail: {casati, shan}@hpl.hp.com

Dimitrios Georgakopoulos
Telcordia Technologies
106 E. Sixth Street, Littlefield Building 415, Austin, TX 78701, USA
E-mail: dimitris@research.telcordia.com

Cataloging-in-Publication Data applied for

Die Deutsche Bibliothek - CIP-Einheitsaufnahme

Technologies for E-services : second international workshop ; proceedings /
TES 2001, Rome, Italy, September 14 - 15, 2001. Fabio Casati ... (ed.). -
Berlin ; Heidelberg ; New York ; Barcelona ; Hong Kong ; London ; Milan ;
Paris ; Tokyo : Springer, 2001
   (Lecture notes in computer science ; Vol. 2193)
   ISBN 3-540-42565-9

CR Subject Classification (1998): H.2, H.4, C.2, H.3, J.1, K.4.4, I.2.11

ISSN 0302-9743
ISBN 3-540-42565-9 Springer-Verlag Berlin Heidelberg New York

Springer-Verlag Berlin Heidelberg New York
a member of BertelsmannSpringer Science+Business Media GmbH

http://www.springer.de

© Springer-Verlag Berlin Heidelberg 2001
Printed in Germany

Typesetting: Camera-ready by author, data conversion by Christian Grosche, Hamburg
Printed on acid-free paper   SPIN: 10840622   06/3142   5 4 3 2 1 0

Preface

The workshop on Technologies for E-Services (TES) is a forum for the exchange of ideas, results, and experiences in the area of e-services. The first edition of the workshop (TES 2000) was organized in Cairo, Egypt in conjunction with the VLDB conference. Following the success of the first edition and pushed by many requests, we organized a second edition, also in conjunction with VLDB.

TES 2001 took place in Rome, Italy, in the Pontificia Università Urbaniana, a university belonging to the Catholic Church, located in the center of Rome and overlooking St. Peter's Cathedral. The TES workshop began right after VLDB, and lasted two days. It featured the presentation of fifteen papers focused on several aspects of e-services, including e-service description, e-service composition, peer-to-peer execution of e-services, transactional issues in e-services, e-services infrastructures, and e-services for mobile users. In addition, the workshop included overview and discussion papers that presented and summarized the issues that still need to be addressed to realize the e-services vision.

We take this opportunity to thank the many people that contributed to the organization of the workshop. The TES organization was coordinated by Mariagrazia Fugini (TES organization chair), in conjunction with the wonderful support provided by the local VLDB organization. VLDB 2001 officers, and in particular Paolo Atzeni (general chair) and Stefano Ceri (program chair and workshop coordinator), also provided invaluable help and support. We are very grateful to all of them.

We also thank the members of the program committee and the additional reviewers for their thorough work, that greatly contributed to the quality of the final program. A special thank goes to Stefanie Chatelain, who coordinated many aspects of the paper review process. The quality of all the accepted papers was very high, and we are grateful to the authors for submitting their interesting results and innovative contributions to the TES workshop.

We hope that the participants have found the workshop interesting and stimulating, and we thank them for attending the workshop and for contributing to the discussions, despite the many temptations provided by the beautiful city of Rome. We are also confident that the readers of this book will find that the time and money have been well invested.

July 2001

Fabio Casati
Dimitrios Georgakopoulos
Ming-Chien Shan

TES 2001 Organization

Workshop Officers

General Chair
Ming-Chien Shan
Hewlett-Packard
Palo Alto, California, USA

Program Chair
Dimitrios Georgakopoulos
Telcordia Technologies
Austin, Texas, USA

Organization Chair
Mariagrazia Fugini
Politecnico di Milano
Milan, Italy

Program Committee

Gustavo Alonso	ETH Zurich, Switzerland
Alejandro Buchmann	Darmstad University of Technology, Germany
Christoph Bussler	Oracle corp., USA
Fabio Casati	Hewlett-Packard, USA
Andrzej Cichocki	Telcordia, USA
Panos Chrysanthis	University of Pittsburgh, USA
Anindya Datta	Georgia Inst. of Technology, USA
Umesh Dayal	Hewlett-Packard, USA
Claude Godart	LORIA, France
Paul Grefen	University of Twente, The Netherlands
Rick Hull	Lucent Labs, USA
Alfons Kemper	Passau University, Germany
Hong Jun Lu	Honk Kong Univ. of Science and Technology, China
Heiko Ludwig	IBM TJ Watson Research Center, USA
John Mylopoulos	University of Toronto, Canada
Maria Orlowska	University of Queensland, Australia
Tamer Ozsu	University of Waterloo, Canada
Mike Papazoglou	Tilburg University, The Netherlands
Louiqa Raschid	University of Maryland, USA
Hans-Jörg Schek	ETH Zurich, Switzerland
Cyrus Shahabi	USC, USA

Afroditi Tsalgatidou   University of Athens, Greece
Gerhard Weikum   University of the Saarland, Germany
Lizhu Zhou   Tsinghua University, China

Additional Referees

Mariagrazia Fugini   Heiko Schuldt
Ralf Muhlberger   Wijnand Derks

Table of Contents

E-Services: Current Technology and Open Issues

Thomi Pilioura[*] and Aphrodite Tsalgatidou[†]

University of Athens
Department of Informatics & Telecommunications
TYPA Buildings, Panepistimiopolis, Ilisia
GR-157 84, Athens, Greece
{thomi,afrodite}@di.uoa.gr

Abstract. The Internet changes the way business is conducted. It provides an affordable and easy way to link companies with their incorporating trading and distribution partners as well as customers. However, the Internet's potential is jeopardized by the rising digital anarchy: closed markets that cannot use each other's services; incompatible applications and frameworks that cannot interoperate or build upon each other; difficulties in exchanging business data; lack of highly available servers and secure communication. One solution to these problems is a new paradigm for e-business in which a rich array of modular electronic services (called e-services) is accessible by virtually anyone and any device. This new paradigm is currently the focus of the efforts of many researchers and software vendors. This paper presents the e-services architecture, its advantages as opposed to today's applications and gives an overview of evolving standards. It then presents the related technical challenges, the way some of them are addressed by existing technology and the remaining open issues.

1   Introduction

Companies face a number of challenges in choosing and implementing the right software and technology solutions in order to better serve their needs and support their business endeavors. This has become particularly problematic in recent years as companies attempt to leverage existing practices, systems and resources across the Web. Critical to success in this environment is to find an integrated, robust e-business solution that allows a company to leverage existing applications, rapidly adapt to the unique needs of the business, and continually evolve as business requirements change over time.

Nowadays, the current trend in the application space is moving away from tightly coupled systems (e.g. DCOM based business solutions [1]) and towards systems of loosely coupled, dynamically bound components (e.g. Jini [2] or Enterprise Java

---

[*] Ms. Thomi Pilioura is also with the National Bank of Greece, email: tpilioura@nbg.gr.
[†] Corresponding Author.

F. Casati, D. Georgakopoulos, M.-C. Shan (Eds.): TES 2001, LNCS 2193, pp. 1-15, 2001.

Beans [3]). Systems built with these principles are more likely to dominate the next generation of e-business systems, with flexibility being the overriding characteristic of their success.

A new paradigm for e-business [4, 5], called e-services, seems to be able to help in this direction. E-services are self-contained, modular applications that can be described, published, located and invoked over a network. The e-services framework enables an application developer who has a specific need to cover it by using an appropriate e-service published on the Web, rather than developing the related code from scratch.

The e-service architecture is the logical evolution from object-oriented systems to systems of services. As in object-oriented systems, some of the fundamental concepts in e-services are encapsulation, message passing and dynamic binding. The e-service approach can be considered as a component-based approach where components are large and loosely coupled. Furthermore, the e-service approach advances the component-based paradigm a step beyond signatures, since information related to the quality of service and to what it does is also published in the service interface.

The goal of this paper is to give a technology overview of the challenging area of e-services and to draw some conclusions regarding the status, the applicability and the future of e-service technology. It is therefore organized as follows. Section 2 presents the e-services architecture and its anticipated benefits as compared to today's applications. Section 3 gives an overview of evolving standards. Section 4 presents the technical challenges deriving from the e-services architecture, the way some of them are addressed by current technology and the remaining open issues. Finally, we present our concluding remarks.

2   The E-Services Concept

E-services constitute a new model for using the Web. It allows the publishing of business functions to the Web and enables universal access to these functions. The architecture that enables it, is presented in the following paragraphs along with the benefits that this architecture could bring to e-business.

2.1   The E-Services Architecture

Several basic activities need to be supported by any service-oriented environment:
1. An e-service needs to be created and described.
2. An e-service needs to be published to one or more Intranet or Internet repositories for potential users to locate.
3. An e-service needs to be located by potential users.
4. An e-service must be invoked to be of any benefit.
5. An e-service may need to be unpublished when it is no longer available or needed, or may need to be updated to satisfy new requirements.

In addition to these basic activities there are some other activities that need to take place in order to take full advantage of the e-services architecture. Such activities include e-services integration with existing infrastructure, e-services management and maintenance. However, we consider that the e-services architecture requires at least the following basic operations: describe, publish, unpublish, update, discover and invoke, and contains 3 roles: service provider, service requester and service broker [6]. Fig. 1illustrates the e-services architecture.

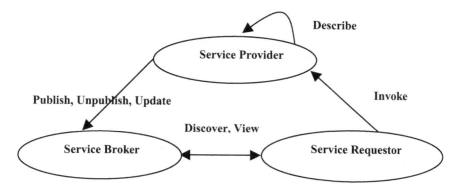

Fig. 1. E-Services Architecture.

Service Provider: A service provider is the party that provides software applications for specific needs as services. Service providers publish, unpublish and update their services so that they are available on the Internet. From a business perspective, this is the owner of the service. From an architectural perspective this is the platform that holds the implementation of the service.

Service Requestor: A requestor is the party that has a need that can be fulfilled by a service available on the Internet. From a business perspective, this is the business that requires certain function to be fulfilled. From an architectural perspective, this is the application that is looking for and invoking a service. A requestor could be a human user accessing the service through a desktop or a wireless browser; it could be an application program; or it could be another e-service. The requestor finds the required services via the Service Broker and binds to services via the Service Provider.

Service Broker: This party provides a searchable repository of service descriptions where service providers publish their services and service requesters find services and obtain binding information for services. It is like telephone yellow pages. Such examples of service brokers are the e-speak E-services Village [7], UDDI (Universal Description, Discovery, Integration) [8], [9], [10] and XMethods [11].

2.2   Anticipated Advantages of E-Services

The following paragraphs focus on the anticipated benefits of e-service approach as compared to today's applications.

Interoperability: Any e-service can interact with any other e-service. This is achieved through an XML-based interface definition language and a protocol of communication. By limiting what is absolutely required for interoperability, interacting e-services can be truly platform and language independent. This means that developers should not be expected to change their development environments in order to produce or consume e-services. Furthermore by allowing legacy applications to be exposed as services, the e-services architecture easily enables interoperability between legacy applications or between e-services and legacy applications.

Just-in-Time Integration: Traditional system architectures incorporate relatively brittle coupling between various components in the system. These systems are sensitive to change. A change in the output of one of the subsystems or a new implementation of a subsystem will often cause old, statically bound collaborations to break down. E-services systems promote significant decoupling and just-in-time integration of new applications and services, as they are based on the notion of building applications by discovering and orchestrating network-available services. This in turn yields systems that are self-configuring, adaptive and robust with fewer single points of failure.

Easy and Fast Deployment: Enterprises using the e-service model are expected to provide new services and products without the investment and delays a traditional enterprise requires. They may utilize the best-in-their-class component services without having to develop them (outsourcing).

Efficient Application Development: Application development is also more efficient because existing e-services can be reused and composed to create new e-services. An e-service can aggregate other e-services to provide a higher-level set of features.

Strong Encapsulation: All components are services. What is important is the type of behavior a service provides, not how it is implemented. This reduces system complexity, as application designers do not have to worry about implementation details of the services they are invoking.

3   Evolving Standards for E-Services

Today there is a lot of activity in the e-services area. We are currently witnessing the rapid development and maturation of a stack of interrelated standards that are defining the e-services infrastructure. In this section we will outline the key standards of WSDL (Web Services Description Language) [12], SOAP (Simple Object Access Protocol) [13] and UDDI (Universal Description, Discovery, Integration) [14, 15]. Each one of these standards supports some of the basic operations of a service-oriented environment, namely describe, publish, unpublish, update, discover and invoke.

3.1   Web Services Description Language (WSDL)

For an application to use an e-service, the programmatic interface of the e-service must be precisely described. In this sense, WSDL plays a role analogous to Interface Definition Language (IDL) used in distributed programming. It is an XML grammar for specifying properties of an e-service such as *what* it does, *where* it is located and *how* to invoke it.

A WSDL document defines *services* as collections of network endpoints, or *ports*. In WSDL, the abstract definition of endpoints and messages is separated from their concrete network deployment or data format bindings. This allows the reuse of abstract definitions: *messages*, which are abstract descriptions of the data being exchanged, and *port types* that are abstract collections of *operations*. The concrete protocol and data format specifications for a particular port type constitute a reusable *binding*. A port is defined by associating a network address with a reusable binding, and a collection of ports defines a service. Hence, a WSDL document uses the following seven elements in the definition of network services:

− *Types:* A container for data type definitions using some type system (such as XSD).
− *Message:* An abstract, typed definition of the data being communicated.
− *Operation:* An abstract description of an action supported by the service.
− *Port Type:* An abstract set of operations supported by one or more endpoints.
− *Binding:* A concrete protocol and data format specification for a particular port type.
− *Port:* A single endpoint defined as a combination of a binding and a network address.
− *Service:* A collection of related endpoints.

3.2   Simple Object Access Protocol (SOAP)

SOAP [13] is a standard for sending and receiving messages over the Internet. It is independent of the programming language, object model, operating system and platform. It uses HTTP as the transport protocol and XML for data encoding. However, other transport protocols may also be used. For example, Simple Mail Transport Protocol (SMTP) can be used to send SOAP messages to e-mail servers.

SOAP defines two types of messages, Request and Response, to allow service requestors to request a remote procedure and to allow service providers to respond to such requests. A SOAP message consists of two parts, a header and the XML payload. The header differs between transport layers, but the XML payload remains the same. The XML part of the SOAP request consists of three main portions:

− The *Envelope* defines the various namespaces that are used by the rest of the SOAP message.
− The *Header* is an optional element for carrying auxiliary information for authentication, transactions, and payments. Any element in a SOAP processing chain can add or delete items from the Header; elements can also choose to ignore items if they are unknown. If a Header is present, it must be the first child of the Envelope.

– The *Body* is the main payload of the message. When SOAP is used to perform an RPC call, the Body contains a single element that contains the method name, arguments, and e-service target address. If a Header is present, the Body must be its immediate sibling; otherwise it must be the first child of the Envelope.

A SOAP response is returned as an XML document within a standard HTTP reply. The XML document is structured just like the request except that the Body contains the encoded method result. The XSI/XSD tagging scheme is optionally used to denote the type of the result.

3.3   Universal Description, Discovery, Integration (UDDI)

UDDI defines a common means to publish information about businesses and services. It can be used at a business level to check whether a given partner offers a particular e-service, to find companies in a given industry with a given type of service, and to locate information about how a partner or intended partner has exposed an e-service in order to learn the technical details required to interact with that service.

The UDDI specifications consist of an XML schema for SOAP messages, and a description of the UDDI APIs specification.

The UDDI XML schema defines four key data structures: business entities, business services, binding templates and tModels. Business entities describe information about a business, including their name, description, services offered and contact information. Business services provide more detail on each service being offered. Each service can then have multiple binding templates, each describing a technical entry point for a service (e.g., mailto, http, ftp, etc.). Finally, tModels describe what particular specifications or standards a service uses. With this information, a business can locate other services that are compatible with its own systems. UDDI also provides identifiers and categories to mark each entity using various taxonomies (related industry, products or services offered and geographical region).

A UDDI Business Registry is itself a SOAP e-Service. IBM, Microsoft, and Ariba are implementing UDDI Registries. Service providers will only have to register at one of the implementations since updates to any are replicated in the others on a daily basis. Each of the business registries provides operations to create, modify, delete, and query each of the four data structures. All these operations can be performed either via a Web site or by using tools that make use of the UDDI API specification.

The UDDI APIs contain messages for interacting with UDDI registries. Inquiry APIs are provided to locate businesses, services, bindings, or tModels. Publishing APIs are included for creating and deleting UDDI data in the registry. The UDDI APIs are based on SOAP.

4   Technical Challenges: Current Technology and Open Issues

For e-services to succeed, there are a number of technical challenges that have to be met, many of which are related to the open and hostile environment in which they have to survive. These challenges are related to:

1. The e-services life cycle, which includes activities such as the description, publishing, discovery, invocation, integration and management of an e-service.
2. Some initial activities that have to be performed by the users before searching for a suitable e-service, e.g. requirements analysis and description of their needs.

The challenges can be split into categories accordingly to three different dimensions: the complexity of the e-services, the indispensability of the operations performed on e-services and the level of the abstraction related to the operations, see Fig. 2.

Services may be simple or composite. Composite services consist of a number of simple services. Operations to simple or composite services may have basic or value-added functionality.

- Basic operations concern functionality necessary to be supported by every e-service environment, namely e-service description, publishing, discovery and invocation.
- Value-added operations bring value-added functionality and better performance to the e-service environment, e.g. e-service management, security and accountability.

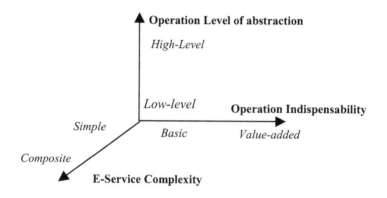

Fig. 2. Dimensions of Technical Challenges for E-Services.

All kinds of operations, either basic or value-added applied either to simple or to composite services are expected to expose their functionality at two different levels:

- At a lower abstraction level, i.e. at a level mainly concerned with the syntactic or implementation aspects of an e-service
- At a higher abstraction level, i.e. at a level where the main focus is on the semantic or conceptual aspects of e-services.

Low level operations are tailored towards the programmers' requirements, while high level operations facilitate the work of business users by shielding off the lower level technical details. It is expected for the e-service paradigm to prevail if all desirable operations are offered at a high abstraction level.

The above three-dimensional categorization results in the eight sub-cubes depicted in Figure 3. Each sub-cube describes a specific category of technical challenges:

1. Techical challenges related to low level (syntactic level) basic operations to simple e-services.

2. Techical challenges related to high level (semantic level) basic operations to simple e-services.
3. Techical challenges related to low level value-added operations to simple e-services.
4. Techical challenges related to high level value-added operations to simple e-services.
5. Techical challenges related to low level basic operations to composite e-services.
6. Techical challenges related to high level basic operations to composite e-services.
7. Techical challenges related to low level value-added operations to composite e-services.
8. Techical challenges related to high level value-added operations to composite e-services.

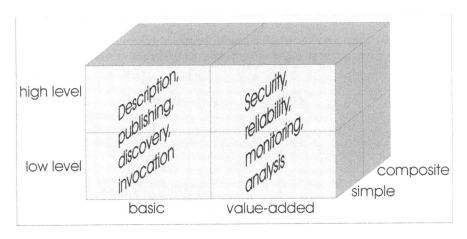

Fig. 3. Cubiform Representation of Technical Challenges for E-Services.

The standards presented in the previous section mainly address the first category of technical challenges, i.e. they provide basic operations to simple services at a low abstraction level, for example the format of messages needed to invoke an e-service.

There are however some other initiatives, research projects and vendor products [16, 17] that offer interesting solutions to the other categories of challenges. In the following paragraphs we examine the challenges for basic and value added operations and how some research projects and software products address them. The first subsection describes the technical challenges for low level or high level *basic* operations performed on simple or composite services. The second subsection describes the technical challenges for low level or high level *value-added* operations performed on simple or composite services.

4.1   Technical Challenges for Basic Operations

Description: The description of an e-service can be at both syntactic and semantic level. The WSDL, analyzed in section 3, describes the syntactic aspects of a service.

Essentially, a WSDL document describes how to invoke a service, and provides information on the data being exchanged, the sequence of messages for an operation and the location of the service. WSDL is not able to sufficiently capture the semantics of the business domain and the structure of the service (e.g. the sub-services, the part of the services).

The Advertisement and Discovery of Services (ADS) protocol specification [19] supports the following three classes of service descriptions: the description of a simple service, the description of a collection of services, the description of a repository of services. ADS uses the service description architecture of WSDL. Therefore, it describes the syntactic aspects of a service.

The Service Description Language (SDL) described in [18], addresses e-service description at both lower and higher level and offers constructs to describe:

- Service properties i.e. service general information (e.g. identification, owner), service access information (e.g. service location-URL, public key certificate) and contact information
- Service ontology i.e. what is the service about and the terminology that is needed to discover the service.
- Service cost i.e. the estimated cost for using the service or the information provided by the service
- Payment i.e. the way the service receives the payment from the customers
- Actors, i.e. the people or organizations using the service. However, SDL does not specify how this is possible if e-services are enacted through a web interface.
- Authorization/security/visibility, i.e. who can see/use what (service contents and functions).
- Service contents: which specifies the content and the structure of the underlying service e.g. the attributes, objects, constraints on use of attributes/objects etc. For example a car information object can have attributes such as brand, model, color and mileage. SDL specifies the data types of the attributes to guarantee type safe orchestration of e-services. However, this violates encapsulation.
- Service capability: which specifies the service structure/components, the conditions of using the service and the order of component invocation.

SDL documents on one hand need to be easily understood by non-technical end-users without the technical details such as network and security information. On the other hand, programmers who are responsible for e-service integration require these last categories of information. Thus they have defined various views of an SDL document: the yellow page view, the white page view and the technical green page view. The first two views particularly aim to inform business users, whereas the last view is tailored towards the requirements of the implementers.

In ebXML [20], the CPP (Collaboration Protocol Profile) [21] describes the service provider, the role it plays, the services it offers and the technical details on how these services may be accessed.

In e-speak [22], e-service providers provide a description of the e-service that consists of attributes specific to that service. The more attributes registered for e-services, the richer users' requests for services can be. Technically speaking, the attributes are meta-data expressed in XML. They have to conform to a specific agreed-upon vocabulary developed for that type of service. Service providers may create their own vocabularies or select a Microsoft BizTalk vocabulary, or use a combination of the two.

Publishing: Publishing is one of the basic operations as it makes a service known and available to be used. Publishing just like description can be at both syntactic and semantic level. The offered solutions include the ones provided by UDDI, e-speak E-services Village, eFlow [23] and ebXML Registry and Repository [24]. E-services Village is an online community for e-Speak developers to register their services. eFlow provides a repository of processes, service nodes and service data type definitions. The repository is organized into a hierarchy dividing the former into groups and simplifying its browsing. The ebXML Registry has schema documents, business process documents and CPP documents. Requestors communicate with the Registry using the ebXML Messaging Service [25].

Given the existence of these registries, the Advertisement and Discovery of Services Protocol (ADS) mentioned above, asks the question "how do I facilitate the building of a crawler that can pull e-services advertisements off the Web, without people having to push advertisements for their services to the registry?" ADS supports two mechanisms that allow service providers to announce the availability of service descriptions: the creation of a file placed in the root directory of their server and the use of a meta tag which can be included in any HTML file to denote the location of the service description.

Discovery: Discovery of services is a basic operation that has to be supported at a high level, as it is important to be able to describe your needs at a conceptual level and to make sure that your needs are matched with what the service provides. Both WSDL and UDDI address this issue only at a low-level. The Service Request Language (SRL) proposed in [26] attempts to tackle this issue at a higher level. SRL is a declarative language for querying and requesting an e-service described using SDL. This language is able to query the system at two levels: metadata level (service location and semantic exploration) and service level (connect to the actual services and use their operations). E-speak also addresses the discovery issue at a conceptual level. In e-speak, users just have to express their service request as a collection of attribute values. Then, e-Speak will automatically discover registered services that have the desired attributes.

Invocation: This operation is mainly addressed at the syntactic level by SOAP and the emerging W3C XML Protocol (XP) [27]. Invocation is also addressed by the ebXML Message Service, which, in contrast to SOAP, provides a Quality of Service (QoS) framework that ensures reliable message delivery. The QoS framework can be extended to support security and transaction semantics.

4.2   Technical Challenges for Value-Added Operations

Composition: Composition refers to the combination of basic e-services (possibly offered by different companies) into value-added services that satisfy user needs. An interesting issue here is to find which architectures, models, and languages can achieve zero latency e-service composition. eFlow [28, 29] supports the dynamic composition of simple e-services at a semantic level. It allows configurable composite services, where different customers select the desired subset of features that this composite service can offer. It also provides dynamic service process modification (ad-hoc changes and dynamic process evolution), to adapt to changes in the business environment. Another solution is provided by the Polymorphic Process Model (PMM) [30] which also enables dynamic composition of e-services at a semantic level by separating the service interfaces from service implementations and defining the service interfaces in terms of service state machines and its input/output parameters. A further advantage of this is the ability to use multiple implementations for the same service without the need to modify the specification of the running process that invokes the service.

Integration: Integration means associating a new e-service with another e-service or other resources such as databases, files, directories and legacy applications. The need of integrating several e-services to perform a business function generates a lot of issues, ranging from understanding and accessing the different APIs with the appropriate communication protocol, to managing the different security requirements, data formats, programming models and transmission models. To further complicate the picture, different e-services often run on top of heterogeneous hardware and software platforms. What we need is easy integration, namely use of e-services without having to write integration code before. A solution to this problem is provided by Enterprise Integration (EAI) platforms. Integrators such as Tibco's ActiveEnterprise and ActiveExchange [31], SeeBeyond's eGate [32] or BEA's eLink [33], WebMethods' solutions [34], ease the daunting task of connecting different applications, by providing uniform access to heterogeneous systems and by offering design tools that help system integrators in appropriately accessing the different applications and managing their results. If fundamental re-implementation of business operational systems is required, it is doubtful how willing all these companies will be to pass from their approach to the e-services approach. At the moment, it seems that standards are useful if you start building an application from scratch. If you already have some applications developed e.g. using an EAI system, it's very difficult to integrate into it e-services using UDDI, as you need to write a lot of integration code, build up some wrapper and so on. In other words, for already deployed applications, the practical solutions used at this moment, seem to be better and simpler than the standards.

Brokering: There may be multiple service providers that offer the same or similar services, i.e., their services can be used to achieve the same or similar objectives. Normally a customer may use the services that offer the most favorable terms in achieving its business objectives. To select the best collection of services, a service integrator may perform dynamic service selection and integration to dynamically construct a new service. This task is heavily dependent on the way the services are modeled and described. There are preliminary research contributions in the area of service quality and automatic service selection via service brokering in the literature [35, 36, 37, 38].

Reliability: Some e-service providers will be more reliable than others. How can this reliability be measured and communicated? What happens when an e-service provider goes off-line temporarily in situations such as temporary outages caused by nightly maintenance or backups? Do you locate and use an alternative service hosted by a different provider, or do you wait around for the original one to return? How do you know which other providers to trust? What happens if you're in the middle of a payment transaction for the acquired e-service? On the other hand, if you are the company that makes direct Web service connections possible, how do you achieve disaster recovery and migration of all your business partners to a backup system? How do you describe reliability and how do you ensure that a service satisfies your needs? How QoS in general (parameters such as the throughput, response time, cost) is expressed in a set of parameters? Preliminary research contribution includes the CMI system that implements CMM model [38]. CMM provides that each service has a set of QoS attributes that provide information on the expected QoS of the service execution. Furthermore, each activity variable in a process type that is bound to a service interface can have a description of the desired QoS. This description can include conditional statements to allow adaptation of the favored QoS to the current situation of the running process. Thus, if there are multiple service providers, the provider that is selected is the one who offers a service that best matches the desired QoS goal.

Security: Some e-services will be publicly available and unsecured, but most business-related services will need to use encrypted communications with authentication. It is likely that HTTP over SSL will provide basic security, but individual services will need a higher level of granularity. Do services need to be able to provide security at the method level? How does an e-service authenticate users? If you sign up with a provider that provides services around the world, how do these services learn about your security privileges? Proposed standards such as XML Key Management Specification (XKMS) [39], XML Signature, XML encryption and OASIS Security services seems to be able to be incorporated into e-services systems.

Transactions: Traditional transaction systems use a two-phase commit approach – all of the participating resources are gathered and locked until the entire transaction completes, at which point, the resources are finally released. This approach works fine in a closed environment where transactions are short-lived, but doesn't work well in an open environment where transactions can span hours or even days. What kind of transaction should be integrated into E-services? It seems that the proposed standards such as XAML [40] and XLANG [41, 42] provide some solutions in these questions. More specifically, XAML has been designed to support current transaction monitors and includes support for commit, cancel, and retry operations. For example, one can ask for commitment among all web services involved in a business transaction. If one fails or refuses to commit, XAML provides the framework for canceling the operation. XAML can ensure transaction integrity and provide a single, complete business transaction to the consumer. XLANG is based on an optimistic model that has been proposed in database research, where actions have explicit compensatory actions that negate the effect of the action. XLANG is a notation for expressing the compensatory actions for any request that needs to be underdone.

Manageability: What kinds of mechanisms are required for managing a highly distributed system [43]? Since the properties of the system are a function of the properties of its parts, do the managers of each of the various e-services need to coordinate in a particular way? Is it possible to "outsource" the management of some e-services to other e-services? Initial research contribution in this aspect is provided by the Common Information Model (CIM) [44] that defines the schema and protocol standards for enabling the design of management e-services.

Accountability: How do you define how long a user can access and execute an e-service? How do you charge for e-services? Will the dominant model be subscription-based, or pay-as-you-go? If you sell an e-service, how do you designate the ownership has changed? Can an e-service be totally consumed on use, or can you reuse the service multiple times as part of your purchase agreement? Standards do not provide any answers to these questions and, to our knowledge, there are yet not any research results.

Testing: When a system is comprised of many e-services whose location and qualities are potentially dynamic, testing and debugging takes on a whole new dimension. How do you achieve predictable response times? How e-services that come from different providers, hosted in different environments and on different operating systems can be debugged? These questions are still open.

E-service Monitoring and Analysis: How service executions can be monitored and how service execution data can be analyzed in order to improve the service quality or efficiency. An answer to this is provided by eFlow [29], as it includes components that allow users to monitor and analyze a service while in execution.

E-Service Contracts: A contract specifies, usually in measurable terms, what services the provider will furnish. Some metrics that contracts may specify include: what percentage of the time services will be available, the number of users that can be served simultaneously, the schedule for notification in advance of changes that may affect users and help desk response time for various classes of problems. In ebXML a Trading Partner Agreement (TPA) [21] is created during an engagement between two parties. It contains information that outlines the service and the process requirements agreed upon by all parties. The TpaML (Trading Partner Markup Language) [45] is an additional specification proposed by IBM to manage conversations between trading partners.

5   Conclusion

E-services is the next stage of evolution for e-business. Perhaps what is the most intriguing about the e-service paradigm is that what it matters is the e-service functionality irrespectively of the technology that has been used to build them. An e-service is accessible over the web, it exposes an XML interface, it is registered and can be located through an e-service registry and it communicates with other services using XML messages over standard Web protocols. Therefore, all web services environments can interoperate – at least in theory.

There are a number of standards, frameworks and tools that support e-services but it seems that they still are in early stages of development. In this paper we have given an overview of evolving standards, such as WSDL, SOAP and UDDI and we examined the various technical challenges and the corresponding research contributions. From this analysis, it became obvious that the examined existing standards approach e-service development bottom-up and provide solutions only to problems at a very low abstraction level. They don't tackle problems existing at a high abstraction level, e.g. how a business user can describe his/her needs? How can s/he select the optimum service from a number of different providers? How can s/he be sure that the selected e-service indeed satisfies his/her needs? We consider that answers to these questions are of first priority as, there is not any use to know the format of messages of an e-service if you don't know if this service satisfies your needs, need. We examined some original research contributions that address the e-service development using a top-down approach in this area e.g. the CMM project [38]. We think that what is needed is a merge between these solutions and the existing standards.

It seems that E-services may be an evolutionary step in designing distributed applications, however, they are some issues that require careful consideration. There are a lot of hurdles and limitations that must be overcome in order for mass adoption to occur. It is important that all initiatives cooperate in the development of universally accepted e-services standards, because one of the key attributes of Internet standards is that they focus on protocols and not on implementations. Otherwise, competing standards from industry heavyweights could prevent widespread adoption of e-services.

References

1. http://msdn.microsoft.com/library/backgrnd/html/msdn_dcomarch.htm
2. http://www.sun.com/jini
3. http://java.sun.com/products/ejb/
4. E-services: Taking e-business to the next level. IBM White Paper, Available at http://www-3.ibm.com/services/uddi/papers/e-businessj.pdf
5. Fingar, P.: Component-Based Frameworks for E-commerce. In Communications of the ACM, Vol. 43 (10), (2000), 61-70
6. Web Services architecture overview: The next stage of evolution for e-business. Available at: http://www-106.ibm.com/developerworks/library/w-ovr/?dwzone=ws
7. http://208.185.204.196/esv/home.htm
8. http://uddi.microsoft.com/
9. https://service.ariba.com/UDDIProcessor.aw
10. http://www-3.ibm.com/services/uddi/
11. www.xmethods.com
12. http://msdn.microsoft.com/xml/general/wsdl.asp
13. http://www.soap-wrc.com/webservices/default.asp
14. http://www.uddi.org
15. http://www.oasis-open.org/cover/uddi.html
16. Kuno, K.A.: Surveying the E-services Technical Landscape. In Proceedings of the 2nd Int. Workshop on Advance Issues of E-Commerce and Web-Based Inf. Systems (WECWIS 2000), IEEE Computer Society, (2000), 99-10. On line proceedings at: http://www.computer.org/proceedings/wecwis/0610/0610toc.htm
17. Pelzt, C.: Interacting with services on the Web: a review of emerging technologies and standards for e-services. Available at: http://devresource.hp.com/devresource/ Topics/

18. van den Heuvel, W.J., Yang, J., Papazoglou, M.P.:Service Representation, Discovery and Composition for E-Marketplaces. To be presented at the 6th Int. Conf. on Cooperative Information Systems (CoopIS 2001), Trento, Italy, September 5-7, (2001)
19. The Advertisement and Discovery of Services (ADS) protocol for Web Services. Available at : http://www.cn.ibm.com/developerWorks/web/ws-ads/index_eng.shtml
20. ebXML – White Paper – Enabling Electronic Business with ebXML. Available at: http://www.ebxml.org/white_papers/whitepaper.htm
21. Collaboration-Protocol Profile and Agreement Specification v1.0, Available at: http://www.ebxml.org/specs/index.htm
22. Kim, W., Graupner, S., Sahai, A., Lenkov, D.: E-speak – a XML Document Interchange Engine for Web-based e-Services. To be presented at the *EC-WEB 2001 Conference*, Munich, Germany, 3-7 Sept. (2001)
23. Hewlett-Packard, eFlow Model and Architecture, version 1.0. (1999)
24. Registry Information Model v1.0, http://www.ebxml.org/specs/index.htm
25. Message Service Specification v1.0, http://www.ebxml.org/specs/index.htm
26. Yang, J., van den Heuvel, W.J., Papazoglou, M.P.: Service Deployment for Virtual Enterprises. In Proceedings of ITVE 2001 Workshop on Information Technology for Virtual Enterprises, Queensland, Australia, Jan. 29-30, (2001)
27. http://www.w3.org/2000/xp/Activity
28. Casati, F. et al: Adaptive and Dynamic Service Composition in *eFlow*. Available at: http://www.hpl.hp.com/techreports/2000/HPL-2000-39.html
29. Casati, F., et al.: eFlow: a Platform for Developing and Managing Composite e-Services. In Proceedings of the Academia/Industry Working Conference on Research Challenges (AIWoRC 2000), Buffalo NY, April 27-29, IEEE Comp. Society, (2000)
30. Schuster, H., Georgakopoulos, D., Cichocki, A., Baker, D.: Modeling and Composing Service-Based and Reference Process-Based Multi-enterprise Processes. In Proceedings of CaiSE 2000. Lecture Notes in Computer Science, Vol. 1789, Springer-Verlag, Berlin Heidelberg New York (2000) 247-263
31. http://www.tibco.com/products/index.html
32. http://www.seebeyond.com/
33. http://www.bea.com/products/elink/index.shtml
34. http://www.webmethods.com/
35. Geppert, A., Kradolfer, M., Tombros, D.: Market-Based Workflow Management. In International Journal of Cooperative Information Systems, Vol. 7 (4), (1998)
36. Bichler, M., Segev , A., Bean, C.: An Electronic Broker for Business-to-Business Electronic e-Commerce in the Internet. In International Journal of Cooperative Information Systems, Vol. 7 (4), (1998)
37. Nodine, M.H., Bohrer, W., Ngu, A.H.H.: Semantic Brokering over Dynamic Heterogeneous Data Sources in InfoSleuth. In Proceedings of ICDE (1999) 358-365
38. Georgakopoulos, D., Schuster, H., Chicocki, A., Baker, D.: Managing process and service fusion in virtual enterprises. In Information Systems, Vol. 24 (6), (1999) 429-456
39. http://xml.coverpages.org/xkms.html
40. http://www.xaml.org/
41. http://entmag.com/displayarticle.asp?ID=11220072307AM
42. http://www.xmlmag.com/upload/free/features/xml/2000/04fal00/sg0004/sg0004.asp
43. Machiraju, V., Dekhil, M., Griss, M., Wurster, K.: E-Services Management Requirements. In Proceedings of Technologies for E-services Workshop, Cairo, Egypt. September (2000)
44. CIM Standards, Available at: http://www.dmtf.org/spec/cims.html
45. TpaML Specification, Available at: http://www.oasis-open.org/cover/tpa.html

The Role of B2B Protocols in Inter-Enterprise Process Execution

Christoph Bussler

Oracle Corporation, Redwood Shores, CA 94065, U.S.A.
Chris.Bussler@Oracle.com

Abstract. One of the myths of inter-enterprise process execution is that work-flow management systems (WFMSs) deployed in enterprises can achieve the collaboration between enterprises across networks and that there is "one process across enterprises". The reality is that important model primitives are missing in WFMSs required to achieve inter-enterprise process collaboration. WFMSs were not designed to deal with executing message protocols across networks. In contrast, business-to-business (B2B) protocols address all the required functionality to exchange messages reliably between enterprises across networks and are not concerned about enterprise internal processes. In that sense, B2B protocols expose the "public" (i. e. externally visible) processes whereby WFMSs implement the "private" (i. e. internal) processes of an enterprise. With this approach many of the inter-enterprise collaboration management requirements can be addressed like public process description, advertisement, discovery, selection, composition, delivery, monitoring and contracts. The contribution of this paper is to introduce an approach to bind public and private processes implemented as B2B protocols and workflow types as well as show an approach of inter-enterprise collaboration management.

1   Introduction

In order to make inter-enterprise processes work, each involved enterprise has to implement not only its internal processes ("private processes"), but also its external behavior ("public processes"). A public process is the definition and execution of a formal message exchange so that messages can be exchanged with other enterprises in a pre-defined sequence and with pre-defined message formats over networks.

The public processes of two enterprises have to match in order to allow inter-enterprise processes to work. For example, if one enterprise sends a purchase order (PO) then the other enterprise must be able to receive the PO in the format sent over the same network. The exact definition of matching public processes is called business-to-business (B2B) protocols. Several efforts are ongoing [4] that define B2B protocols so that enterprises do not have to mutually agree on proprietary B2B protocols but instead can follow a given defined standard.

Once an enterprise has defined its public processes, they have to be managed. This includes the advertisement (how to make public processes available and in which formal language), the discovery (how to find enterprises with matching processes), the selection (which enterprise to contact), the monitoring (in which state of execution

F. Casati, D. Georgakopoulos, M.-C. Shan (Eds.): TES 2001, LNCS 2193, pp. 16–29, 2001.

are public processes) as well as contracts (how to establish a legal binding between enterprises based on public processes).

The technology of choice to implement enterprise private processes is workflow management systems (WFMSs) [19]. This technology allows not only to define workflow types but also to execute workflow instances. During execution human interaction is facilitated (to gather data or to approve actions) as well as non-human interaction with back end application systems like enterprise resource planning systems (ERPs). However, it is not required to use a WFMS to implement private processes. Depending on the complexity, any software that allows to implement the necessary functionality is sufficient.

It is a myth that the private processes and the public processes are "distributed" processes across enterprises in the sense of a distributed workflow. A distributed workflow means that there is one workflow instance whereby its different parts (like subworkflows or data flows) are managed by different instances of WFMSs. In addition, it would require a common workflow modeling environment. Especially across enterprises this is impossible to achieve since no two WFMSs of different vendors share common workflow semantics let alone the requirement to synchronize the WFMSs over unreliable public networks like the Internet. In case of an enterprise implementing private processes with software different from WFMSs this approach is impossible altogether.

Implementing distributed workflows across enterprises is not desirable for enterprises even if they had the technology available to do it. It would mean that enterprises would have to agree on one workflow type definition that implements the whole distributed workflow. This encompasses the private processes of the enterprises involved as well as the public process between them. At the same time the enterprises involved had the problem to hide the private portion of a distributed workflow since due to competitive reasons they do not want to share internal processing which is usually showing the competitive advantage. Furthermore, any change in the private portion would require to revise the whole distributed workflow since the implementation is one complete workflow type. That would affect all enterprises involved.

An alternative approach that does not cause all the problems mentioned is to model the private process with a workflow, the public process with a B2B protocol and define a binding to relate both. In this approach, which is suggested in this paper, the two companies only have to agree on the public processes that have to be externally visible by definition. The implementation of the private processes are completely independent of the public processes and each enterprise can manage the private processes completely independent from each other. The binding between the private process and the public processes provides isolation and independence. Any revision of a private process might require a change in the binding. But that binding is within the enterprise and does not affect the other enterprises.

The contribution of this paper is the development of a method to clearly separate private and public processes and use public processes as the means of the externalization of enterprise behavior for management issues like advertisement and discovery. Sect. 2 will discuss the method of separating private and public processes. Sect. 3 will briefly discuss the management of public behavior of enterprises. Sect. 4 discusses related work and Sect. 5 summarizes.

2   Binding of Public and Private Processes

Inter-enterprise process management consists of three parts that are discussed next. First, public processes have to be defined (B2B protocols). Second, enterprise internal processes have to be defined (workflow types). Once this is achieved, both have to be bound such that messages incoming through a B2B protocols can be consumed by corresponding workflow types. The binding of B2B protocol to workflow types is the third part that is required for inter-enterprise message exchange.

2.1   Public Processes

B2B protocols like RosettaNet [24] are specifically designed for inter-enterprise message exchange. B2B protocols are outward focused in the sense that they are concerned about the message exchange between enterprises. Their concern is not to implement the private processes of an enterprise. In general, the concepts of B2B protocols are

- **Message format**. The message format defines the business content of messages. For example, each business document like a purchase order or invoice is described as an XML DTD [38].
- **Activities for sending and receiving of messages**. Messages have to be sent to enterprises as well as received from enterprises. Distinct steps in B2B protocols define when a message is to be received and when a message must be sent. Activities are typed (by referring to the message type to be sent or to be received). This allows to check if two public processes from two different enterprises match.
- **Business messages and acknowledgment messages**. One type of message contains business content whereas other types of messages contain acknowledgments. For example, a message can acknowledge that a message with business content was received.
- **Time-out and retry logic**. B2B protocols have to achieve reliable messaging over unreliable networks. Time-outs defined on messages as well as retry logic allow to handle failures. For example, a time-out can specify that an acknowledgment message has to be received within two hours of sending a business message. If no acknowledgment message is received within two hours it is assumed that the business message was lost and it will be re-sent.
- **Duplicate check and avoidance**. B2B protocols also have to implement an exactly once message transfer. This ensures that messages are received as well as are received exactly once. Due to the time-out and retry requirement it might be the case that the same message is sent twice (e. g. when the message was not really lost but the acknowledgment was late). In this case the duplicate must be eliminated.
- **Roles**. A B2B protocol has two "halves", one for each enterprise involved. The behavior of both has to match so that the B2B protocol has the correct sequencing and message formats in both of its parts. The way this is achieved is that a B2B protocol definition contains two parts that are related. Each part is called a role in order to distinguish the two parts. Example roles are buyer and seller and imple-

ment the buyer and seller behavior. A buyer sends purchase orders whereby a seller receives purchase orders.

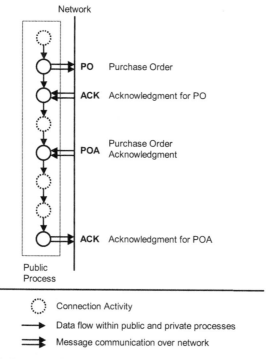

Fig. 1. Sample Public Process: The Buyer "half".

Fig. 1 shows a graphical representation of a public process that implements the behavior of a buyer. It defines the messages being exchanged as well as the sequence of steps involved in the exchange. This public process sends a purchase order (PO) and expects an acknowledgment afterwards (ACK). Then it expects a purchase order acknowledgment message (POA) and sends an ACK. This example of a public process will later on be bound to a private process. The dashed activities are connection activities used for the binding with private processes.

In order to implement these B2B protocol concepts additional functionality has to be in place. This is transport like HTTP in order to transport the messages, security to encrypt/decrypt as well as to sign messages, packaging in order to encapsulate the business content of messages with header and trailer data for transport purposes. This functionality is not relevant for the topic of this paper and is discussed in [4].

All the above mentioned functionality is necessary to successfully implement and execute B2B protocols. It is important to mention that not all B2B protocols implement all the functionality discussed above. Many define only a part of all functionality necessary to fully implement B2B protocols. For example, OAGIS [21] only defines the message formats. RosettaNet [24] in contrast is completely defined. In case of partially defined B2B protocols the enterprises that plan to exchange messages have to complement the B2B protocol in order to complete it. Each functionality not defined by the B2B protocol is subject to bi-enterprise agreement and understanding. For example, in the case of OASIS' message formats companies could decide to use all of the RosettaNet functionality except the message formats as defined by Rosetta-Net.

2.2   Private Processes

The discussion of private processes of enterprises is intentionally kept short in the following. Workflow technology is known for quite some time and its use within enterprises is accepted. Several products exist and are readily available for use [1, 2, 6, 13, 14, 16, 17, 22, 25, 27, 31].

Relevant for the following discussion of binding public to private processes are the following workflow concepts:
- **Workflow steps**. Workflow steps represent the activities of a workflow type, i. e. which functionally is executed during workflow execution. For example, an authorization step is used to approve a particular purchase order.
- **Control flow**. Control flow defines the order in which workflow steps are going to be executed during workflow execution. For example, a purchase order extraction step is executed before an authorization step. This is turn is executed before sending the approved purchase order to another enterprise.
- **Data flow**. Data flow defines how data "flow" from workflow step to workflow step. For example, the extracted purchase order is passed to the authorization step and then passed on to the workflow step sending it to another enterprise.

Current workflow technology can model private processes within enterprises with the supported workflow concepts.

2.3   Binding of Public and Private Processes

Since public processes are outward focused and private processes are inward focused it is necessary to bind both so that the isolation is preserved while allowing the data to flow from within the enterprise to other enterprises across networks. In order to achieve this the concept of "connection activities" is introduced. Connection activities are activities dedicated to the communication between private and public processes. They are used in public processes as well as private processes to "hand-over" messages from a private process to a public process and vice versa. Connection activities in context of workflow management are specialized workflow steps with the sole purpose of communicating with public processes. In context of public processes connection activities are specific activities solely designed for communication with private processes.

Fig. 2 shows a private process that deals with an enterprise internal purchasing process and a public process that exchanges POs and purchase order acknowledgments POAs as well as their corresponding ACKs (see Fig. 1). The connection activities shown are typed and have a direction. A connection activity is related to a message type and can only deal with this one message type. The direction indicates if the message is sent from the private process to the public process or vice versa. The private purchasing process itself connects to an enterprise resource management system (ERP).

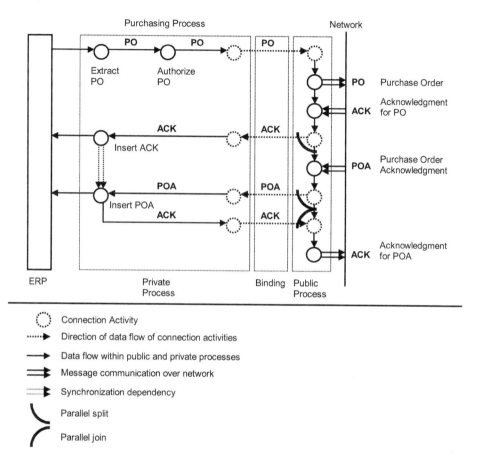

Fig. 2. Private Purchasing Process with Public Process Containing Acknowledgments.

The control flow and the data flow connecting the internal activities of public and private processes are different from those going across private and public processes. This is indicated in Fig. 2 by different connecting arrows. The reason for this is that the flow of data crosses the boundary from a publicly visible state to an invisible state. An enterprise sees from the outside only that the message is going to be sent to a private process but has no visibility of the private process itself.

The control flow between a public process and a private process happens in general in parallel to any ongoing control flow within the public process or within the private process. For example, in Fig. 2 the receiving and the subsequent processing of the first ACK in the private process happens in parallel to the receiving and subsequent processing of the POA. The parallel split within the public process to send the ACK to the private process never joins back the public process. In that sense it is not a parallel branching in the traditional sense but a real parallel split within the public process (see Sect. 2.6 below for discussion). Also, the parallel join combines two independent control flows without them both originating at the public process.

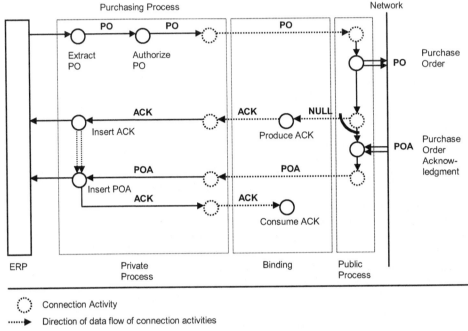

Fig. 3. Binding of Same Private Process to Alternative Public Process.

The dashed double arc within the private process indicates a dependency between the "insert ACK" and "insert POA" steps. This synchronization makes sure that the ACK is inserted into the ERP before the POA (necessary from a business logic viewpoint). This is necessary because the ACK as well as the POA processing are truly in parallel as discussed before. Otherwise, it could happen that the POA is inserted before the ACK. That would violate business data consistency within the ERP.

2.4   Dynamic Binding of Public Processes

The same enterprise can exchange messages with several other enterprises. That does not mean that all follow the same public process. For example, Fig. 2 shows the behavior similar to RosettaNet from a buyer side. However, if the other enterprise does not implement RosettaNet, but EDI, then the public process looks different. Fig. 3 shows this case.

As shown in Fig. 3 the public process does not send acknowledgments. However, the private process is the same purchasing process as before. This means that the binding from the public process to the private process needs to be modeled differently than the one shown in Fig. 2. Acknowledgments have to be created and consumed by the binding itself to make up for the difference. The NULL document sent from the public to the private process indicates the successful sending of the PO. Only then can an ACK be generated and passed on to the private process.

The binding must be flexible enough to bridge the differences between the public and the private process in such a way that the private process can stay unchanged for different public processes. Binding is therefore extended with additional modeling capability that allows to add steps. Fig. 3 shows that the acknowledgment is generated and consumed during the binding. The binding steps are indicated with dotted circles to show that those belong to the binding and neither to the private nor to the public process.

This extended binding mechanism makes sure that different enterprises with different public processes can be bound to the same private processes.

2.5   A Note on B2B Protocol Implementation

Enterprises that implement private processes with WFMSs ask if this technology could be used to implement public processes, too. Unfortunately, WFMSs do not provide all required functionality for this. For example, the complete message handling functionality is missing. WFMSs do not have the notion of messages, security (encryption, decryption, non-repudiation, signing) or trading partner management. All this is necessary for the transmission of messages across networks.

WFMSs provide workflow steps, control flow and data flow capabilities. That allows the definition of the internal part of public process behavior (like shown in Figs. 1, 2 and 3). Not all WFMSs support the parallel split or the parallel join as discussed in Sect. 2.6 below.

Workflow technology does not have the concepts of dynamic binding of public and private processes. WFMS assume that a workflow instance executes in isolation. If two workflow instances are related by the WFMS itself, one must be a subworkflow of the other one. Two top level workflow instances cannot be related by current WFMSs since no modeling concepts are available for this functionality.

This brief discussion shows clearly that WFMSs must be augmented with functionality like message handling and public/private process binding. This way a complete system can be built having workflow technology as a subcomponent that allows to model and to execute public processes.

Another important aspect of B2B protocol implementation is that the software executing public processes at the different enterprises can be from different vendors. Key in inter-enterprise message exchange is that the message exchange itself conforms to the public process definition. As long as the behavior of the messages is compliant to the public process the message exchange works. This can be achieved with different software implementations.

2.6   A Note on the Parallel Split and Parallel Join Concept

As indicated in Figs. 2 and 3, a parallel split is required that allows a public process to continue its execution while at the same time the execution of the binding and eventually of the private process continues. For example, in Fig. 2, once the first ACK is received, the public process needs to send the ACK through the connection activity to the private process while continuing its own processing and executing the step waiting for the POA.

The significance of the parallel split is that the control flow splits and continues the parallel processing within the public process without the parallel executions ever joining back in the public process. Basically, it is like executing a traditional parallel split step without ever executing a join step during the workflow execution.

If a WFMS does not provide this functionality, this behavior needs to be implemented as a workflow step itself. One possibility would be that the workflow step invokes a program that hands over the document to the binding (like the ACK in the example discussion before). In this case the workflow step behaves from a WFMS's viewpoint like a normal workflow step. The WFMS is not aware of the fact that a parallel split happened. One implication of this "workaround" is that a workflow monitoring tool cannot show the step as a parallel split step but shows it as a normal step.

The fundamental underlying issue that requires a parallel split concept is that there are two types of control flow going on at the same time. One control flow is within a public process that executes the public process itself. In Fig. 2 this is indicated by the vertical control flow arcs within the public process not crossing any boundary. In Fig. 1 this is shown even more clearly. At the same time there is control flow and data flow between the public process and the private process (vertical flows). These flows cross the boundaries of the public and the private process. Both types of flows are concurrently executed resulting in the need for a parallel split concept.

A similar discussion can take place for the parallel join concept where the parallel control flows being joined do not originate in the public process previous to the join. In this case the parallel join combines a control flow from within the public process as well as from within the private process. The parallel join has to wait for both control flows to be executed for it to continue. For example, in Fig. 2 the second last step in the public process joins two control flows. If a WFMS does not support this concept, one possibility is to implement the functionality in a program and use a normal workflow step to invoke this program. This is the same approach as described above for the parallel split.

3   Public Process Management

Establishing public processes is only one step in achieving inter-enterprise process execution. The other important step is to find other enterprises that want to engage in inter-enterprise process execution while making business sense. There are two ways to find trading partners. One is to select trading partners that are already enabled for inter-enterprise process execution using public processes or those that are willing to implement those. The other way is to advertise publicly the public processes that are entertained and have potential trading partners discover those. The latter one is the more challenging approach. All what is involved in a public "advertisement and discovery" environment is discussed briefly in the following.

- **Public process description**. In order for the public to understand the meaning of public processes a formalized representation of public processes is required. Given a formal language for public process definitions potential trading partners can understand their meaning. Several proposals for languages are available. ebXML [8] as well as RosettaNet [24] provide representations of public processes. In contrast, WSDL [37] provides a language for defining signatures of individual functions but not processes.
- **Advertisement**. Once public processes are defined their definition has to be stored in a place that is accessible by potential trading partners for search. This requires a publicly known location and access interface for retrieving public process information. UDDI [29] is an effort to provide a public registry that allows an enterprise to advertise public processes. ebXML [11] defines a registry mechanism. Unlike UDDI it does not address making one available for the public.
- **Discovery**. Given a public registry an enterprise can browse in this registry and find matching public processes. Those indicate a possibility to establish inter-enterprise process execution. However, the fact that two enterprises can exchange purchase order does not mean a collaboration makes sense. A major important detail is that the business data to be exchanged match on a business level. For example, an enterprise that wants to buy computer disks has to find a supplier that sells computer disks. This means that in addition to public processes (like exchange of POs and POAs) an ontology has to be attached to the public process that defines the data content of message exchanged in order to make the match complete (like that computer disks are sold and not chairs).
- **Selection**. If an enterprise finds several potential trading partners through the discovery process it has to select one. The selection is usually based on qualities of the business behavior rather than on the fact that an enterprise can participate in inter-enterprise process execution. However, these qualities like credit rating, reliability, quality are not publicly available. The selection process therefore involves some manual work to select appropriate trading partners (like talking to existing trading partners about a potential one exchanging experiences).
- **Composition**. An enterprise can execute inter-enterprise processes with several trading partners at the same time. It has to make sure that it sends and receives messages from its trading partners according to the public processes of each of them. In this case the enterprise composes the public processes of all its trading partners. An example is the request for quotation process (RFQ) before buying a

product. The RFQ process usually contacts several suppliers for quotes according to their individual public processes.

- **Delivery**. When public processes are executed quality of service is key for success. Public processes have to be executed completely according to their description. All reliability and security definitions have to be followed so that both trading partners involved can safely depend on each other. It is also expected that trading partners do not misuse public processes for spamming their competition with bogus messages.

- **Monitoring**. At any point in time the trading partners involved in the inter-enterprise process execution want to know the status of the collaboration. Since the public processes are public both trading partners know exactly at any point in time the state of execution of the public process. Each trading partner knows if the other one needs to send back a message or if the trading partner waits for one. Furthermore, each trading partner knows the state of the private process at any point in time. The only more complicated case is where a trading partner wants to know the state of the other trading partner's private process. This can be achieved by either a monitoring tool that directly access the trading partners private process execution environment or by introducing another public process that defines monitoring messages exchanged. The latter approach is preferable since an enterprise can decide which state information to expose and which not. This is important for keeping internal competitive knowledge private.

- **Contracts**. A fundamental requirement is that a legally enforceable contract is in place before inter-enterprise process execution takes place. Otherwise arbitrary disputes will take place because all interaction is based on good will. Initial steps are taken by ebXML [10] for defining trading partner agreements that define allowed message exchanges. However, legally enforceable electronic contracts are still not readily available [35].

The big caveat of the public process approach is security. If a public process is made available in a registry for discovery it should not be possible at this time to send message to the enterprise that exposed the public process. Otherwise, if the network addresses would be known at this point in time, spamming would be easy to achieve. The challenge here is that the physical addresses to effectively exchange message do not become known until a contract is in place. In this case the misuse of the public process can be enforced.

A special note on the discovery and selection is in order here. Marketplaces are environments where two enterprises "find" each other by various matchmaking approaches like supply/demand matching, auctions, and that like. In this case the matchmaking starts on a business level and has to be supported by the technical infrastructure.

4   Related Work

Two examples of standards addressing public processes are RosettaNet [24] and ebXML [8]. RosettaNet pre-defines specific public processes called Partner Interface Processes (PIPs) whereby ebXML allows to define arbitrary public processes through

Collaborations. This means that in case of RosettaNet two enterprises can interoperate by virtue of being RosettaNet compliant. In the case of ebXML two enterprises have to agree on a definition of their public processes first. This is facilitated by Collaboration Partner Agreements (CPAs) [10]. Standards like EDI [12] are neither defining public processes nor providing a mechanism to define public processes. In this case enterprises need to borrow the mechanism from e. g. ebXML to define public processes. None of the standards addresses the interplay between public and private processes.

Crossflow [15] is concerned about a methodology to establish and to maintain contracts between enterprises. Furthermore, a system is proposed to enforce the contracts. However, the system is not built do deal with arbitrary public processes and no standard definition language and semantics is provided for the enforcement of contracts between two enterprises. All enterprises involved are required to use the same software for contract enforcement.

Web services [34] are currently being defined. From [34] can be derived that the concept of web services is not well-defined yet. However, efforts in registries like UDDI [29] and description languages like WSDL [37] show that the current thinking in this space is more along the lines of remote function calls than public process descriptions. With WSDL an elaborate scheme is given to define signatures of remote functions as well as their binding to physical locations. However, public process descriptions are impossible to define due to missing activity, control flow and data flow concepts.

WSFL [36] is concerned about a flow language describing web services composition (very similar to the workflow definition language of [17]). It is not concerned about the definition of public processes.

Products of vendors like [3, 7, 18, 20, 23, 28, 32, 33] support inter-enterprise message exchange following specific selected standards. However, it is impossible to derive from the data made available by the vendors how the internal implementation would support the approach proposed in this paper.

5   Summary

The clear separation between private and public processes is key to provide the necessary isolation and abstraction between enterprise internal processes and processes across enterprises. The flexible binding between public and private processes as discussed in this paper is achieving this separation. Furthermore, with the self-contained definition of public processes it is possible to publicly advertise an enterprises' message exchange capability in public registries. This supports trading partner discovery and selection in an automated fashion.

References

1. Action Technologies. http://www.actiontech.com.
2. BEA Process Integrator.
   http://www.bea.com/products/weblogic/integrator/index.shtml.
3. BEA Collaborate.
   http://www.bea.com/products/weblogic/collaborate/index.shtml.
4. Bussler, C.: B2B Protocol Standards and their Role in Semantic B2B Integration Engines. In: Bulletin of the Technical Committee on Data Engineering. IEEE Computer Society, Vol. 24, No.1 (2001) .
5. Casati, F.; Shan, M.-C.: Models and Languages for Describing and Discovering E-Services. 2001 SIGMOD International Conference on Management of Data. Santa Barbara, CA, USA, May 2001.
6. COSA Workflow. http://www.ley.de/_englisch/cosa/index.htm.
7. Cyclone Commerce. http://www.cyclonecommerce.com/.
8. ebXML. http://www.ebxml.org.
9. ebXML Business Process Specification Schema. Version 1.01. May 2001. http://www.ebxml.org.
10. ebXML Collaboration-Protocol Profile and Agreement Specification. Version 1.0. May 2001. http://www.ebxml.org.
11. ebXML Registry Services Specification. Version 1.0. May 2001. http://www.ebxml.org.
12. EDI. http://www.x12.org.
13. Foro. http:// http://www.foro-wf.com/web/default.html.
14. Fujitsu I-Flow. http://www.i-flow.com/.
15. Hoffner, Y.; Field, S.; Grefen, P.; Ludwig, H.: Contract-Driven Creation and Operation of Virtual Enterprises. Research Report, RZ 3328, #93374, Computer Science, IBM Research, February 2001.
16. Hewlett-Packard Process Manager. http://www.ice.hp.com/cyc/af/00/.
17. IBM MQ Series Workflow. http://www-4.ibm.com/software/ts/mqseries/.
18. IONA Netfish XDI. http://www.iona.com/products/.
19. Jablonski, S.; Bussler, C.: Workflow Management. Concepts, Architecture and Implementation. International Thomson Publisher (1995) .
20. Microsoft Biztalk Server. http://www.microsoft.com/biztalkserver.
21. OAGIS. http://www.openapplications.org/.
22. Oracle Workflow.
    http://technet.oracle.com/docs/products/oracle8i/doc_library/817_doc/oi s.817/a85440/wf/wftop.htm.
23. Peregrine B2B Integration Platform. http://www.peregrine.com.
24. RosettaNet. http://www.rosettanet.org.
25. Staffware 2000. http://www.staffware.com.
26. The XML Cover Pages. http://www.oasis-open.org/cover.
27. Tibco TIB/Inconcert. http://www.tibco.com/products/in_concert/index.html.
28. Tibco Active Exchange. http://www.tibco.com/products/activeexchange.
29. UDDI: Universal Description, Discovery and Integration. http://www.uddi.org.
30. VAN. http://www.edi-info-center.com/html/vans.html.
31. Versata Integration Server. http://www.versata.com.
32. Vitria Business Ware.
    http://www.vitria.com/products/businessware/overview.html.
33. Webmethods B2Bi.
    http://www.webmethods.com/content/1, 1107,B2BiSolutions,FF.html.
34. W3C Web Services Workshop. http://www.w3c.org/2001/03/wsws-program.

35. Winn, J.: The Emperor's New Clothes: The Shocking Truth About Digital Signatures and Internet Commerce. March 2001. http://www.smu.edu/~jwinn/shocking-truth.htm .
36. WSFL. Web Services Flow Language. Version 1.0. IBM Software Group, May 2001. http://www-4.ibm.com/software/solutions/webservices/pdf/WSFL.pdf .
37. WSDL. Web Services Description Language. Version 1.1. Ariba, IBM, Microsoft. January 2001. http://msdn.microsoft.com/xml/general/wsdl.asp .
38. XML. http://www.w3c.org/xml .

Conversations + Interfaces = Business Logic

Harumi Kuno[1], Mike Lemon[1], Alan Karp[1], and Dorothea Beringer[2]

[1] Hewlett-Packard Laboratories
1501 Page Mill Road, MS 1U-14
Palo Alto, CA 94304 USA
[2] Hewlett-Packard Co.
19320 Pruneridge Avenue, MS 49b-26
Cupertino, CA 95014 USA
{harumi_kuno,mike_lemon,alan_karp,dorothea_beringer}@hp.com

Abstract. In the traditional application model, services are tightly coupled with the processes they support. For example, whenever a server's process changes, existing clients using that process must also be updated. However, electronic commerce is moving toward e-service based interactions, where corporate enterprises use e-services to interact with each other dynamically, and a service in one enterprise could spontaneously decide to engage a service fronted by another enterprise. We clarify here the relationship between currently developing standards such as UDDI, WSDL, and WSCL, and propose a conversation controller mechanism that leverages such standards to direct services in their conversations. We can thus treat services as pools of methods, independent of the conversations they support. Even method names can be decided on independently of the conversations. Services can spontaneously discover each other and then engage in complicated interactions without the services themselves having to explicitly support conversational logic. The dynamism and flexibility enabled by this decoupling is the essential difference between applications offered over the web and e-services.

1 Introduction

Electronic commerce is moving towards a model of e-service based interactions, where corporate enterprises use e-services to interact with each other dynamically [1]. For example, a procurement service in one enterprise could spontaneously decide to engage a storefront service fronted by another enterprise. These services can communicate by exchanging messages using some common transport (e.g., HTTP) and message format (e.g., SOAP).

However, suppose that the storefront service expects the message exchanges to follow a specific pattern (conversation), such as the conversation depicted in Figure 1 (shown from the perspective of the storefront service). Service developers must now address several issues. How does the client service know what conversations the storefront service supports? Does the storefront service developer have to code the conversation-controlling logic directly into the service? If

F. Casati, D. Georgakopoulos, M.-C. Shan (Eds.): TES 2001, LNCS 2193, pp. 30–43, 2001.

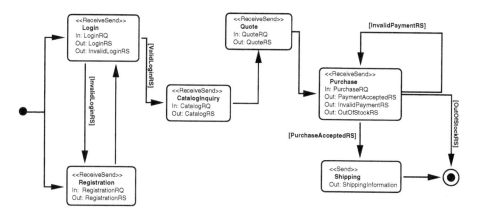

Fig. 1. An Example Conversation Depicted as a UML Activity Diagram. Interactions are represented as action states.

so, do developers have to re-implement the client and storefront services each time a new message exchange is added to the supported conversation?

A model of dynamic service interactions thus imposes the following requirements:

1. Services must be able to describe themselves, and clients must be able to discover them.
2. A service must be able to describe its abstract interfaces and protocol bindings so that clients can figure out how to invoke it.
3. A service must be able to describe the kinds of interactions (conversations) that it supports (e.g., that it expects clients to login before they can request a catalog) so that clients can engage in complex exchanges with the service.

The Universal Description Discovery and Integration (UDDI) [2,3,4] specifications address the first problem by defining a way to publish and discover information about Web services. The Web Services Description Language (WSDL) [5] addresses the second problem, defining a general purpose XML language for describing the interface and protocol bindings of network services. The Web Services Conversation Language (WSCL)[1] [6,7] addresses the last problem, providing a standard way to model the public processes of a service, thus enabling network services to participate in rich interactions. Together, UDDI, WSDL, and WSCL enable developers to implement web services capable of spontaneously engaging in dynamic and complex inter-enterprise interactions.

In this paper, we describe how these standards enable us to separate interface logic from conversation logic. We begin by discussing our perspective of e-services as pools of functional endpoints that can be composed using conversations (Section 2). In Section 3 we provide a brief overview of UDDI, WSDL, and WSCL,

---

[1] WSCL was originally named the *Conversation Definition Language* (CDL).

and describe how they enable the creation of specifications describing service endpoints and conversations. We have implemented a prototype conversation controller that leverages service interface descriptions and conversation specifications expressed using WSCL and WSDL, which we describe in Section 4. We present related work in Section 5, and summarize our conclusions and discuss future directions in Section 6.

2   Approach

E-services are much more loosely coupled than traditional distributed applications. This difference impacts both the requirements and usage models for e-services. E-services are deployed on the behalf of diverse enterprises, and the programmers who implement them are unlikely to collaborate with each other during development. However, the primary function of e-services is to enable business-to-business interactions. Therefore, e-services must support very flexible, dynamic bindings. E-services should be able to discover new services and interact with them dynamically without requiring programming changes to either service. This distinction is what separates e-services from applications delivered over the web.

In our model, e-services interact by exchanging messages. Each message can be expressed as a structured document (*e.g.*, using XML) that is an instance of some document type (*e.g.*, expressed using XML Schema). A message may be wrapped (nested) in an encompassing document, which can serve as an envelope that adds contextual (delivery or conversation specific) information (*e.g.*, using SOAP).

We define a conversation to be a sequence of message exchanges (interactions) between two or more services. We define a *conversation specification* (also known as a *conversation policy*) to be a formal description of "legal" message type-based conversations that a service supports. Our goal is to enable e-services developed by different enterprises to engage in flexible and autonomous, yet potentially quite complex, business interactions (conversations).

We advocate a service-centric perspective that separates service interfaces from conversation specifications. This approach allows us to treat services as pools of interfaces that can be specified by individual participants and then later composed using separate conversation specifications. We can then create conversation controller services that can use conversation and interface specifications to direct services in their interactions, thus freeing service developers from having to explicitly program conversational logic. Such a single third-party conversation controller could leverage "reflected" XML-based specifications to direct the message exchanges of e-services according to protocols without the service developers having to implement protocol-based flow logic themselves. The conversation controller can assume responsibility for the conversation logic, leaving service developers free to focus on service-specific logic. For example, the controller would handle exceptions due to message type errors, while the service would be responsible for handling exceptions related to message content.

The advantage of this approach is that it enables services to be easily and flexibly composed with a minimum of programming effort. In order to participate in a given conversation type, a service need only to be able to accept and produce messages of the appropriate types. This allows services and clients to discover each other and interact dynamically using published specifications.

That is to say, because the conversation policies are not service-specific, services and clients can interact even if they were not built to use precisely matching conversation policies, as long as both parties are capable of sending and receiving appropriate messages. Furthermore, because the service interfaces and the conversation policies are decoupled, different instances of a service could name their methods independently, e.g., a client could use the same conversation specification to talk to two different book-selling services, despite the fact that one service supports a Login method while the other uses a corresponding Sign-on method.

Finally, this approach gives us a scalable mechanism for handling the versioning (evolution) of conversation policies. Services would not necessarily have to be updated in order to support new or modified conversation policies. For example, suppose that the conversation in Figure 1 were updated to allow the client to send a quote request before it has requested a catalog. We could effect this change by simply updating the conversation specification; we would not have to modify either the storefront or the procurement services' code.

3   Currently Developing Standards for Service Communication Specifications

The prevalent model for e-service communication is that e-services will publish information about the specifications that they support. UDDI facilitates the publication and discovery of e-service information. The current version of WSDL (1.0) is an XML-based format that describes the interfaces and protocol bindings of web service functional endpoints. WSDL also defines the payload that is exchanged using a specific messaging protocol; SOAP is one such possible messaging protocol. However, neither UDDI nor WSDL currently addresses the problem of how a service can specify the sequences of legal message exchanges (interactions) that it supports. (We use the term "conversation" to refer to a legal sequence of message exchanges.)

The Web Services Conversation Language (WSCL) addresses this issue, providing an XML schema for defining legal sequences of documents that e-services can exchange. WSCL and WSDL are highly complimentary – WSDL specifies how to send messages to a service and WSCL specifies the order in which such messages can be sent. The advantage of keeping the two distinct is that doing so allows us to decouple conversational interfaces (represented by WSCL) from service-specific interfaces (represented by WSDL). This means that a single conversation specification can be implemented by any number of services, independent of the protocols supported by the various implementations.

3.1   UDDI Registries

A UDDI business registration is an XML document that describes a business entity and its web services. The UDDI XML schema defines four core types of service information: *business information* (such as business name and contact information), *business service information* (general technical and business descriptions of web services), *binding information* (specific information needed to invoke a service), and *service specification information* (associating a service's binding information with the business service information it implements).

Programmers and programs can use the UDDI Business Registry to locate technical information about services, such as the protocols and specifications that they implement. More importantly, the UDDI Business Registry also serves as a registry for abstract (service-independent) specifications. Services can refer indirectly to the UDDI registrations for specifications they implement, which makes it straightforward to identify the business service information that represents a given service.

The UDDI *tModel* is a meta-data construct that uniquely identifies reusable service-related technical specifications for reference purposes. A service publishes tModelInstanceDetails, which is a list of tModelInfo elements that refer to the tModels that the service supports. A UDDI tModel data structure includes a unique key (*tModelKey* attribute), a *name* element, an optional description, and an overviewDoc element in which we can store a URL for the actual specification document.

For example, suppose we wanted to register a WSCL specification of the "storefront" conversation depicted in Figure 1 in a UDDI registry. We would create a tModel entry within the UDDI registry that referred to the actual WSCL specification document in its *overviewDoc* element. Figure 2 shows a UDDI tModel reference for a WSCL specification for a service conversation.

```
<tModel authorizedName="XXXX" operator="YYYY" tModelKey="ZZZZ">
    <name>storefrontConversation</name>
    <description xml:lang="en">
  WSCL description of a simple storefront conversation
    </description>
    <overviewDoc>
<description xml:lang="eng">WSCL source document.</description>
<overviewURL>http://foo.org/specs/storefrontWSCL.xml</overviewURL>
    </overviewDoc>
</tModel>
```

Fig. 2. A UDDI tModel Referencing a WSCL Specification.

This "storefront conversation" tModel can now be referenced by the tModelInstanceInfo of any service that implements that conversation type (Figure 3.

```
<businessService>
  (. . .)
  <bindingTemplates>
    <bindingTemplate>
      (. . .)
      <accessPoint urlType="http">http://www.foo.com/</accessPoint>
      <tModelInstanceDetails>
      <tModelInstanceInfo tModelKey="ZZZZ">
          (. . .)
        </tModelInstanceInfo>
      </tModelInstanceDetails>
      (. . .)
    <bindingTemplate>
      (. . .)
  <bindingTemplates>
</businessService>
```

Fig. 3. A tModelInstanceInfo Referencing a Conversation tModel.

3.2 Web Service Conversation Language

WSCL addresses the problem of how to enable services (often called web services or e-services in this context) from different enterprises to engage in flexible and autonomous, yet potentially quite complex, business interactions. It adopts an approach from the domain of software agents, modeling protocols for business interaction as *conversation policies,* but extends this approach to exploit the fact that Service messages are XML-based business documents and can thus be mapped to XML document types. Each WSCL specification describes a single type of conversation from the perspective of a single participant. A service can participate in multiple types of conversations. Furthermore, a service can engage in multiple simultaneous instances of a given type of conversation or even conversations of different types.

WSCL specifies the public interface to web-services, but does not specify how the conversation participants will handle and produce the documents received and sent. A conversation definition is thus service independent, and can be used by any number of services with completely different implementations. A conversation developer (e.g. a vertical standards body) can create a WSCL description of some conversation, and publish it in a UDDI directory. A service provider who wanted to create a service that supported that conversation description could create and document service endpoints that support the messages specified by the WSCL document. Any software developer who wants to create an application using the published web-service can download the WSCL files describing the conversations supported, and implement the necessary methods accordingly. Ideally, software developers creating and using web-services will be supported by tools that allow them to map easily and quickly from the interactions outlined in the conversation definition to any existing applications and back-end logic, while separating cleanly between the public and the private processes. Without any formal definition of the conversations, such tool support will not be possible.

Figure 1 depicts a UML diagram of a simple purchase conversation definition from the perspective of the seller. A service that supports this conversation definition expects a conversation to begin with the receipt of a LoginRQ or a RegistrationRQ document. Once the service has received one of these documents, it answers with a ValidLoginRS, a InvalidLoginRS, or a RegistrationRS, depending on the type and content of the message received. Although this conversation is defined from the perspective of the seller, it can be used to determine the appropriate message types and sequences for both the seller and the buyer. The buyer simply derives his conversation definition by inverting the direction of the messages' halves of a conversation.

There are four elements to a WSCL specification:

- *Document type descriptions* specify the types (schemas) of XML documents that the service can accept and transmit in the course of a conversation. The schemas of the documents exchanged are not specified as part of the WSCL specification document; the actual document schemas are separate XML documents and are referenced by their URL in the interaction elements of the conversation specification.
- *Interactions* model the actions of the conversation as document exchanges between conversation participants. WSCL currently supports four types of interactions: *Send* (the service sends out an outbound document), *Receive* (the service receives an inbound document), *SendReceive* (the service sends out an outbound document, then expects to receive an inbound document in reply), and *ReceiveSend* (the service receives an inbound document and then sends out an outbound document).
- *Transitions* specify the ordering relationships between interactions. A transition specifies a source interaction, a destination interaction, and optionally a document type of the source interaction as additional condition for the transition.
- The *Conversation* element lists all the interactions and transitions that make up the conversation. It also contains additional information about the conversation like its name, and with which interaction the conversation may start and end. A conversation can also be thought of as being one of the interfaces or public processes supported by a service. Yet in contrast to interfaces as defined by CORBA IDE or Java interfaces, conversations also specify the possible ordering of operations, i.e. the possible sequences in which documents may be exchanged.

Although WSCL specifies the valid inbound and outbound document types for an interaction, it does not specify how the conversation participants will handle and produce these documents; it only specifies the abstract interface, the public process. The WSCL specification of a conversation is thus service-independent, and can be used (and reused) by any number of services. We can use the *tModel* structure to register WSCL conversation specifications in UDDI registries (as illustrated above).

Table 1. Comparison of Aspects of WSDL and WSCL.

		WSDL	WSCL
Abstract	choreography	*out of scope*	Transition
Interfaces	messages	Operation	Interaction
Protocol Bindings		Binding	*out of scope*
Concrete Services		Service	*out of scope*

3.3 Web-Service Definition Language (WSDL)

As noted before, WSCL specifications are conversation-specific. WSCL describes the structures (types) of documents a service expects to receive and produce (by either explicitly including or else by referring to the document type definitions), as well as the order in which document interchanges will take place, but does not specify how to dispatch received documents to the service. This is partially addressed by WSDL. WSDL documents describe the abstract interface and protocol bindings of a network service. WSDL specifications that describe abstract protocol interfaces are reusable and thus are registered as UDDI tModels.

A reusable WSDL document consists of four components: document type, message, portType (named set of abstract operations and messages involved with those operations), and binding definitions (define message format and protocol details for a specified portType's operations and messages). For example, the "storefront" conversation shown in Figure 1 requires that a service implementing the "Start" interaction provide some sort of endpoint that can accept a *LoginRQ* or *RegistrationRQ* document and output either a *LoginRS* or a *RegistrationRS* document.

3.4 Mapping between WSDL and WSCL

We identify three main aspects of web services. The *abstract interface* (public process, business model) describes the messages or documents (business payload) a service can exchange, as well as the order in which they are exchanged. The *protocol binding* represents the protocols used for exchanging documents. Finally, the *service* itself consists of a particular location that implements a set of abstract interfaces and protocol bindings.

Table 1 shows how these three different aspects are covered by WSDL and WSCL. We can map the corresponding terminology used by WSDL and WSCL to describe operations and interactions as shown in Table 2. It is evident that the only overlap between WSDL and WSCL exists in the specification of the documents being exchanged.

There are a number of ways that we could extend WSDL or WSCL to make explicit the mapping between WSDL port types/operations and WSCL interactions. For example, we could add protocol bindings in WSDL that refer to WSCL conversation specifications or we could add choreography to WSDL port type descriptions. However, to do so by extending WSDL or WSCL would couple these specifications. Instead, we advocate that services should use other methods

Table 2. Comparison of Terminology of WSDL and WSCL.

WSDL	WSCL
Port Type	Conversation
Operations:	**Interactions:**
One-way	Receive
Request-response	ReceiveSend
Solicit-response	SendReceive
Notification	Send
Input	InboundXMLDocument
Output, Fault	OutboundXMLDocument
Names of Operation, Input, Output, Fault	ID of Interaction, InboundXML Document OutboundXMLDocument
Message	URL of XML schema (WSCL delegates the specification of the payload entirely to an external XML schema, whereas WSDL directly uses XML data types)

of mapping between the WSDL and WSCL specifications that they support. For example, one option is that when a service populates its UDDI *businessService* entry, it creates *tModelInstanceInfo* records for the WSDL and WSCL specifications that it supports. The mappings between these specifications can then be deduced by document type (mapping WSDL input message types to WSDL InboundXMLDocument schemas). Alternatively, a separate mapping document could be created to map explicitly between WSCL interactions and WSDL operations and port types.

4   Dynamic Conversation Controller for E-Services

Thus far we have shown how WSDL and WSCL can be used to specify the conversational and functional interfaces of e-services. We have implemented a prototype conversation controller that leverages these specifications to direct services in their conversations. (This prototype is described more fully in [8].) We exploit the fact that e-service messages are XML-based business documents and can thus be mapped to XML document types. Our conversation controller can act as a proxy to an e-service, and track the state of an ongoing conversation based on the types of messages exchanged. Specifically, the Conversation Controller requires two pieces of information: a specification of the structure of the conversations supported by the service (interactions, valid input and output message types of interactions, and transitions between interactions), and a specification of the service's interfaces, mapping document types to appropriate service entry points (for given interactions).

Our Conversation Controller is designed to act as a proxy to a service. Once it has received a message on behalf of an e-service, the Conversation Controller can dispatch the message to the appropriate service entry point, based on the state of the conversation and the document's type.

When forwarding the response from the e-service to the client, the Conversation Controller includes a prompt indicating valid document types that are accepted by the next stage of the conversation. This prompt can optionally be filtered through a transformation appropriate to the client's type. In addition, if the client requests it and provides a specification of its interfaces, the Conversation Controller can also direct the client's side of the conversation. Thus neither the service nor the client developer must explicitly handle conversational logic in their code.

Each time the Conversation Controller receives a message on behalf of the service, it will identify the current stage of the conversation and verify that the message's document type is appropriate; if not, then it will send an exception. If the message type is valid, then the Conversation Controller will invoke the service appropriately. It will then identify the document type of the response from the service, identify the new state and the valid input documents for that state, and format an appropriate response for the client. The Conversation Controller can also pass the response through an appropriate transformation, if requested by the client. (For example, if the client is a web browser and has requested form output, then the Conversation Controller may transform the response into an HTML form prompting for appropriate input.)

Moreover, if the client is another service that can return a specification of its own service entry points, then the Conversation Controller could automatically send the output message to appropriate client entry points; if a valid input document for the new state is returned, the Conversation Controller could then forward it to the service, thus moving the conversation forward dynamically. As a result, the Conversation Controller can help a client and service carry out an entire conversation without either the client or the service developer having to implement any explicit conversation control mechanisms. This means that the client developer does not need complete knowledge of all the possible conversations supported by all the services with which the client might interact in the future. For example, each time the Conversation Controller receives a message on behalf of a service, it could implement the pseudo-code listed below.

1. Look at the message header and determine the current state of the conversation. (Ask the service for specifications, if necessary.)
2. From the conversation specification, get the valid input document types for the current state.
3. Verify whether the current message is of a valid input document type for the current state.
4. If the received message is of a valid type, then look up the inbound document in the dispatch specification and dispatch the message to an appropriate service entry point. If more than one appropriate service entry point exists, then dispatch it to each entry point (in order specified by the service) until the service produces an output document of a valid document type. If no entry point exists or no valid output document is produced, then inform the client, also prompting for valid input document types.

5. From the conversation specification, calculate the conversation's new state, given the document type of the output document returned by the service. Look up the valid input documents for this new state.
6. Format the output document in a form appropriate to the client type, also prompting for the input document types that are valid in the new state.

4.1   Client Automation

An argument can be made that developers implementing e-service clients will not want a conversation controller to direct their part of the conversation, both because they expect to hard-code the client parts of the conversation and also because they will find the idea of using a third-party to control the conversation foreign[2]. However, decoupling conversation logic from business logic on the client side greatly increases the flexibility of a client by allowing it to interact dynamically with services even if their conversation policies do not match exactly. For example, the same client code could be used to interact with two services that support different conversation policies but common interfaces.

In order for a conversation controller to direct the client's part of a conversation, the controller must be able to dispatch messages the client receives from the server in order to generate documents that the server requests. This means that the client must be able to communicate its service interfaces to the Conversation Controller. For example, we can extend the process described in the previous section to allow the Conversation Controller to direct both the server and client sides of the conversation, producing the pseudo-code listed below.

1. Look at the message header and determine the current state of the conversation. (Ask the service for specifications, if necessary.)
2. From the conversation specification, get the valid input document types for the current state.
3. Verify whether the current message is of a valid input document type for the current state.
4. If the received message is of a valid type, then look up the inbound document in the dispatch specification and dispatch the message to the appropriate service entry point; otherwise, inform the client that the message is not a valid type and prompt for the input document types that are valid in the new state.
5. From the conversation specification, calculate the conversation's new state, given the document type of the output document returned by the service. Look up the valid input documents for this new state.
6. If the client wishes to be treated as a browser, then format the output document in an appropriate HTML form, also prompting for the valid input document types for the new state.
7. If the client wishes to be directed by the Conversation Controller and there are valid input documents for the new state, then look up outbound document types in the client's dispatch table, and invoke the appropriate client methods that could produce valid input documents.

---

[2] Conversation with Kevin Smathers, 1/4/2001.

8. If the client produces a valid input document, then send it to the service, invoking it through the Conversation Controller (recursion takes place here).
9. If the client does not produce any valid input documents, or if there were no valid input documents in the new state, then format and return the output document in an appropriate HTML form, also prompting for the new state.

4.2   Conversation Controller State

The Conversation Controller that we have outlined above does not include any performance management, history, or rollback mechanisms. If one subscribes to the idea that intermediate states of an e-service's conversation are *not* transactional, and one also supposes that Conversation Management functionality (including performance history, status of ongoing conversations, etc.) is distinct from Conversation Control functionality, then the Conversation Controller can operate in a stateless mode.

5   Related Work

In his survey of agent systems for E-Commerce, Griss [9] notes that researchers in the agent community have proposed a number of agent communication systems over the past decade, and indeed agent-based e-commerce systems seem like a natural model for the future of e-services. Griss identifies several kinds of agent systems appropriate for E-Commerce, including personal agents, mobile agents and collaborative/social agents. Griss then lists seven properties that represent dimensions of agent-like behavior: adaptability, autonomy, collaborations, intelligence, mobility, persistence and personality/sociability. We believe that although e-services exhibit some of these properties, e-services are not necessarily adaptable, intelligent or anthropomorphic (they are not required to exhibit personality/sociability). However, since agents dynamically communicate via message exchanges that conform to specified protocols/patterns, agent-based conversations are recognized as an especially appropriate model for e-service interactions.

Several existing agent systems allow agents to communicate following conversational protocols (or patterns). However, to the best of our knowledge, all of these are tightly coupled to specific agent systems, and require that all participating entities must be built upon a common agent platform. For example, the Knowledgeable Agent-oriented System (KaoS) [10] is an open distributed architecture for software agents, but requires agent developers to hard-wire conversation policies into agents in advance. Walker and Wooldridge [11] address the issue of how a group of autonomous agents can reach a global agreement on conversation policy; however, they require the agents themselves to implement strategies and control. Chen, et al. [12] provide a framework in which agents can dynamically load conversation policies from one-another, but their solution is homogeneous and requires that agents be built upon a common infrastructure.

Our Conversation Controller is unique in that we require only that a participating service produce two XML-based documents – 1) a specification of the conversational flows it supports and 2) a specification of the service's functionality (describing how the service can be invoked).

A few E-Commerce systems support conversations between services. However, these all require that the client and service developers implement matching conversation control policies. RosettaNet's *Partner Interface Processes* (PIPs) [13] specify the roles and required interactions between two businesses. *Commerce XML* (cXML) [14] is a proposed standard being developed by more than 50 companies for business-to-business electronic commerce. cXML associates XML DTDs for business documents with their request/response processes. Both RosettaNet and CommerceXML require that participants pre-conform to their standards. Our work is completely compatible with such systems, but is also unique in that we allow a service's clients to share the service's Conversation Controller dynamically – without having to implement the client to the specifications of the service.

Insofar as they reflect the flow of business processes, e-service conversations also resemble workflows. However, as the authors of the Web Services Conversation Language (WSCL) [6] observe, workflows and conversations serve different purposes. Conversations reflect the interactions between services, whereas workflows delineate the work done by a service. A conversation models the externally visible commercial interactions of a service, whereas a workflow implements the service's business functionality. In addition, workflows represent long-running concurrent fully integrated processes, whereas e-service conversations are loosely coupled interactions.

6   Conclusions / Future Work

E-services pose a new set of requirements and usage models for service interactions. E-services must enable business-to-business interactions without requiring intensive collaboration between service developers. Therefore, we advocate a service-centric perspective that separates service interfaces from conversation specifications. Distinguishing between conversation logic and service functionality allows us to treat services as pools of interfaces that can be described using service specifications and composed using conversation specifications.

In this paper, we have sketched how to use WSDL to create specifications describing service interfaces and how to use WSCL to create abstract conversation specifications. We have discussed how these standards relate to each other and how we can use them to compliment each other. We also described how services can refer to the WSDL and WSCL specifications they support in their UDDI registrations. We have built a prototypical conversation controller service that leverages these specifications to direct services in their interactions. This third-party conversation controller uses "reflected" XML-based specifications to direct the message exchanges of e-services according to protocols without the service developers having to implement protocol-based flow logic themselves. The advantage of this approach is that it treats services as pools of methods that can be easily and flexibly composed with a minimum of programming effort.

In the future, we plan to investigate more sophisticated uses of conversation policies. For example, we would like to provide a model for the explicit support of deciding conversation version compatibility. We would also like to explore how to support both nested conversations and multiparty. Finally, we hope to address how to exploit document type relationships when manipulating message documents. For example, we would like to use subtype polymorphism to establish a relationship between a document type accepted as input by an interface specification and a corresponding document type in a conversation specification.

References

ˈ1. Kuno, H.: Surveying the E-Services Technical Landscape. In: International Workshop on Advanced Issues of E-Commerce and Web-Based Information Systems (WECWIS). (2000)
2. Boubez, T., Hondo, M., Kurt, C., Rodriguez, J., Rogers, D.: UDDI Data Structure Reference V1.0. Technical report (2000)
3. Boubez, T., Hondo, M., Kurt, C., Rodriguez, J., Rogers, D.: UDDI Programmer's API 1.0. Technical report (2000)
4. Ariba, Inc. and International Business Machines Corporation: UDDI Technical White Paper. Technical report, Ariba, Inc. and International Business Machines Corporation and Microsoft Corporation (2000)
5. Christensen, E., Curbera, F., Meredith, G., Weerawarana, S.: Web Services Description Language (WSDL) 1.0. Technical report (2000)
6. Banerji, A., Bartolini, C., Beringer, D., Chopella, V., Govindarajan, K., Karp, A., Kuno, H., Lemon, M., Pogossiants, G., Sharma, S., Williams, S.: Web Services Conversation Language (WSCL) 1.0. Technical report, Hewlett-Packard Web Services Organization (2001)
7. Beringer, D., Kuno, H., Lemon, M.: Using WSCL in a UDDI Registry 1.02: UDDI Working Draft Best Practices Document. Technical report, Hewlett-Packard Company (2001)
8. Kuno, H., Lemon, M.: A Lightweight Dynamic Conversation Controller for E-Services. In: International Workshop on Advanced Issues of E-Commerce and Web-Based Information Systems (WECWIS). (2001)
9. Griss, M.: My Agent Will Call Your Agent . . . But Will It Respond? Software Development Magazine (2000)
10. Bradshaw, J.M.: KAoS: An Open Agent Architecture Supporting Reuse, Interoperability, and Extensibility. In: Knowledge Acquisition for Knowledge-Based Systems Workshop. (1996)
11. Walker, A., Wooldridge, M.: Understanding the emergence of conventions in multi-agent systems. In: First International Conference on Multi-Agent Systems. (1995)
12. Chen, Q., Dayal, U., Hsu, M., Griss, M.: Dynamic Agents, Workflow and XML for E-Commerce Automation. In: First International Conference on E-Commerce and Web-Technology. (2000)
13. Web page: (http://rosettanet.org)
14. Web page: cxml.org. (http://www.cxml.org)

Compatibility of *e*-Services in a Cooperative Multi-platform Environment

Massimo Mecella[1], Barbara Pernici[2], and Paolo Craca[1]

[1] Università di Roma "La Sapienza"
Dipartimento di Informatica e Sistemistica
Via Salaria 113, 00198 Roma, Italy
mecella@dis.uniroma1.it, p.craca@usa.net
[2] Politecnico di Milano Dipartimento di Elettronica e Informazione
Piazza Leonardo da Vinci 32, 20133 Milano, Italy
barbara.pernici@polimi.it

Abstract. Dynamic composition and reconfiguration of *e*-Services in cooperative processes involving several organizations requires mechanisms for ensuring that each cooperative process is guaranteed to evolve correctly against its specification. The cooperative process is specified and deployed as a set of cooperating *e*-Services, each with specific interfaces and evolution, and the concept of compatibility between *e*-Services is defined, based on their external behavior. An algorithm for checking compatibility is proposed and a tool provides support both at design-time and at run-time. A run-time architecture supporting the execution of *e*-Services in a multi-platform environment is discussed, based on a repository storing all *e*-Service and process specifications.

1 Introduction

The more and more widespread use of Internet is pushing the evolution of current *e*-Business systems into *e*-Services or Web-Services. As regards the features of an *e*-Service, many definitions are proposed in the literature; in this work we focus on *e*-Services as dynamically composable components provided by an organization with the following characteristics [11]:

- *open*: independent, as much as possible, of specific platforms and computing paradigms;
- *developed* not only for intra-organization applications, but also *for inter-organizations applications*, to be assembled and reused in a distributed, Internet-based cooperative environment;
- *easily composable*: assembling and integrating the *e*-Service in an inter-organization application does not require the development of complex adapters.

An *e*-Application is a distributed application which integrates in a cooperative way the *e*-Services offered by different organizations. The dynamic integration of different *e*-Services into cooperative *e*-Applications requires the development of a complex platform in which the *compatibility* of different *e*-Services is defined. The definition and development of such a cooperative platform requires:

F. Casati, D. Georgakopoulos, M.-C. Shan (Eds.): TES 2001, LNCS 2193, pp. 44–57, 2001.
© Springer-Verlag Berlin Heidelberg 2001

- the definition of a common *conceptual component model* for *e*-Services, map-pable on different technological component models. A conceptual component model allows the definition of interfaces for *e*-Services and to specify their behavior without considering the specific technologies in which *e*-Services are deployed;
- the definition and development of a *repository* in which both the conceptual specifications of different *e*-Services and running instance data can be stored. The repository should be accessible to all cooperating organizations;
- the definition of *compatibility rules* and the development of *algorithms* for the verification of relationships among *e*-Services and to evaluate their dynamic and adaptive substitution in complex *e*-Applications;
- the development of a suite of *tools for cooperative architects and designers*, to be used for the management of the different *e*-Services and their assembling;
- the definition and deployment of a *run-time architecture* for *e*-Applications.

On the technological side, the availability of different cooperative platforms and technologies (e.g., OMG CORBA, SUN Enterprise JavaBeans, Microsoft Enterprise .NET, Web technologies such as SOAP, XMLP, servlets and server side script pages, XML, and so on) enables the effective development of such a platform, and its deployment on open architectures. On the modeling side, the OMG Unified Modeling Language (UML) as a de facto standard for soft-ware specifications pushes towards its use for the definition of an open common conceptual component model.

The aim of this work is to present an ongoing work towards the development of a platform for dynamically composable *e*-Applications in a multi-platform environment, based on a common conceptual component model for *e*-Services. The goal of this paper is to define the concept of compatibility for *e*-Services and to propose an algorithm for checking if an *e*-Service can be substituted with another in an *e*-Application.

The remainder of this paper is as follows. In Section 2, the conceptual com-ponent model for *e*-Services is described; Section 3 describes the proposed plat-form for *e*-Services in a cooperative multi-platform environment. In Section 4, the notion of compatibility between *e*-Services is given and an algorithm for its verification is presented. Section 5 presents related relevant research work and Section 6 concludes the paper by remarking which other elements need to be realized.

2   Conceptual Component Model for *e*-Services and Cooperative Processes

A *cooperative process*, also referred to as *macro process* or *multi-enterprise pro-cess* [?], [16], is a complex business process involving different organizations. Unlike traditional workflow processes where all the activities concern the same enterprise or enterprises using a predefined platform, in a cooperative process the activities involve different organizations, either because they form together a virtual enterprise, or since they exchange services and information in a coordinated way. Each organization may have its internal processes supported by different technologies.

A cooperative process can be abstracted and modeled as a set of e-Services exported by each organization involved. This allows hiding the details of process execution in each of the cooperating organizations: internals of each organization processes are not exposed to public domain, platform-dependent characteristics are hidden. As a result, the cooperative process description is more understandable by designers, since it hides details which are not necessary for cooperation. The e-Services define both the structure of data exchanged among the cooperating organizations, and the behavioral aspects that specify which interactions are allowed among them and possible sequences of interactions.

A cooperative process specification is a set $\mathbb{W} = \{\mathbb{C}_1, \ldots, \mathbb{C}_n\}$ *where* $\mathbb{C}_i$ *is an e-Service specification.*

The global cooperative process control and evolution is guaranteed both by the correct evolution of each of the e-Services, including exception handling, and by the e-Application coordinating them.

The definition of a cooperative process as set of e-Services constitutes a reference schema for the cooperation among organizations, that is the e-Services defined during this specification step are binding for the different organizations. An e-Service represents a "contract" on which an organization involved in the cooperative process agrees; if later the same organization, or also a different one, proposes a new e-Service in place of the agreed one, the compatibility of the new e-Service needs to be verified. Compatibility means that the behavior of the new e-Service can be restricted to the behavior specified in the old one; the details will be discussed in the following of this paper.

All e-Services are compliant to a conceptual component model; each e-Service is described through a conceptual specification consisting of a UML Class Diagram for the structural part and of UML Statechart Diagrams for the behavioral aspects [12].

In the class diagram, each class is stereotyped with <<flat>>, <<active>> and <<event>>, to represent respectively structured data, characterized by properties/attributes only, the main functionalities provided by the e-Service, and the events raised/reacted to by active classes. The services an e-Service exports are described as events, including both the ones the e-Service reacts to and the events it produces; events are not only simple primitive signals, but they carry parameters (i.e., structured data); parameters can be optional and the types of parameters are either basic types or are specified through flat classes. Data provided as input to the e-Service and the ones it provides as output are therefore represented as flat classes. Active classes are the abstraction of the business logic of the e-Service; at least one active class needs to be defined in an e-Service, but an e-Service can also include the definition of several active classes.

For each active class, a statechart diagram is specified, which describes how objects are constrained to evolve during the flow of the cooperative process the e-Service participates in, that is the correct sequences of events processed by the e-Service. Statechart diagrams are a graphical representation of active class state machines, which are used for specifying the order (i.e., sequence) in which services (i.e., events) can be invoked. Different active class state machines of the same e-Service are concurrent and independent.

An e-Service is a tuple $\mathbb{C} = \langle \Phi, \mathcal{E}, \Delta, \Psi \rangle$ *where* Φ *is a set of flat classes,* $\mathcal{E}$ *is a set of input and output events,* Δ *is a non-empty set of active classes (i.e.,* cardinality(Δ) ≥ 1 *) and* Ψ *is a set of active class state machines. In an e-Service there are as many state machines as active classes, i.e.,* cardinality(Δ) = cardinality(Ψ).

An active class state machine is a tuple $\mathbb{SM} = \langle \Sigma, \Gamma, \mathcal{E}, s_0, s_f \rangle$ *where* Σ *is the set of states,* Γ *is the set of transitions,* $\mathcal{E}$ *is the set of input and output events,* $s_0 \in \Sigma$ *is the initial state and* $s_f \in \Sigma$ *is the final state.*

An event $\alpha(p_1, \ldots, p_n)$ *consists of a name* α *and a set of parameters* p_i , $i = 1 \ldots n$; ε *is the empty event and it is a valid event. The type of a parameter is either a basic type or a flat class. All or some of the parameters may be optional.*

A guard condition σ *is a boolean formula consisting of terms, that is:*

- true *and* false *are terms;*
- *a term is an expression* < property > < operator > < value >; *property is an attribute of an event or of a flat class,* operator *can be* $=, <, >, \leq$ *or* $\geq$, *and* value *is defined in the domain of the type of* property;
- *if* F *and* G *are term, also* (F), NOT (F), F AND G, F OR G *are terms.*

A transition $s \xrightarrow{\alpha[\sigma]/\beta} t$ *consists of a source state* $s \in \Sigma$, *a target state* $t \in \Sigma$, *an input event* $\alpha \in \mathcal{E} - \{\varepsilon\}$, *a guard condition* σ *and an output event* $\beta \in \mathcal{E}$. σ *(which may be omitted, meaning it consists of the only term* true*) is the condition under which, upon the receiving of* α, *the transition takes effectively place;* β *may be the empty event, in this case no output event is raised during the transition.*

By using such a component model, only the external interfaces (input/output data and offered services) of each e-Service are described, and the protocol (i.e., sequences of operations to be invoked) for interacting with it.

As an example, in Figure 1 the specification of a generic "Buyer Payment" e-Service is shown; it consists of a class diagram of 11 classes (1 active class, 7 event classes and 3 flat classes), of which the active class PaymentManager is associated to a statechart diagrams representing the corresponding state machine.

The conceptual component model is the abstraction of technological component models; each e-Service is provided by organizations as a *component*. The interface of such component can be generated from the e-Service specification, and implementations for it need to be provided. Different running instances of

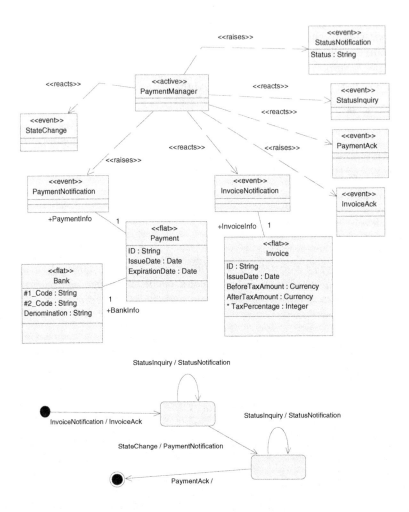

Fig. 1. An *e*-Service Specification: The class diagram and the statechart diagram of the active class `PaymentManager` (from [12]).

the component (possibly several instances for each possible implementation) exist in a cooperative environment.

The use of different component models, one at the conceptual level (i.e., *e*-Service) and many at technological level (i.e., component as CORBA object, or EJB, or servlet, etc.) is due to the coexistence of different cooperative technologies and to the opportunity, in a multi-organization environment, of integrating all these components by adopting a conceptual, i.e., technology-independent, component model for them, not focusing only on static interface issues (as current component models do) but also on behavioral issues.

In this paper the technological base for components will be no further addressed; a general discussion of the approach and of some issues that need to be solved for its effective adoption is provided in [12]. Conversely the focus on this paper will be on the e-Service level.

3   A Platform for Cooperative Processes

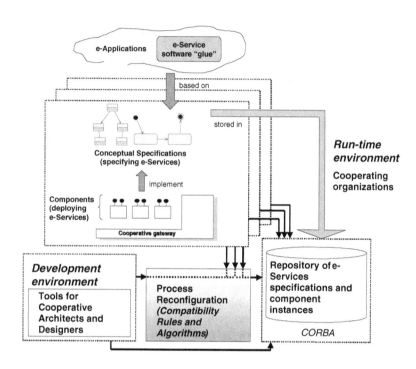

Fig. 2. A Platform for e-Service Composition and Reconfigurable Cooperative Processes.

A platform for e-Service composition and cooperative processes is shown in Figure 2. e-Services are deployed as components on different cooperative gateways, which are the computing server platforms of the various cooperating organizations which host components [?].

An e-Application provides the coordination of different e-Services forming a cooperative process, by realizing the "glue" interconnecting and orchestrating the different components; such a "glue" needs to be based on the cooperative process specification and therefore on the "contracts" implied by the different e-Services. Currently we are investigating different solutions for the deployment of such a "glue".

A repository in which to store both e-Service specifications and component instance information is central to the platform. A prototype has been developed for the repository, which allows managing specifications both through an application programming interface (CORBA invocations) and through XML documents [12].

On top of the repository several tools for cooperative architects and designers can be built, e.g., graphical user interfaces for specifying, storing and retrieving both process and e-Service specifications and instance information. They constitute the development environment for designing e-Applications.

Initially, e-Services are specified and deployed as components when different organizations decide to automatize cooperative processes they are involved in (e.g., a supply chain, a procurement process, etc.). Later it is possible to register new e-Services in the repository and to specify if they are compatible with other e-Services, with respect to the specified cooperative processes. As an example, the reader should consider the case of cooperative processes for procurement, in which a new competitor enters into the market and wants to be part of the processes as a supplier; the same competitor might be interested in entering with the same e-Service in several cooperative processes, adapting the e-Service to the specific characteristics of each process and restricting its behavior for compatibility with the various specifications of the processes.

Let $\mathbb{C}$ and $\mathbb{D}$ be two e-Services, and $\mathbb{W}$ a cooperative process in which $\mathbb{C}$ takes part. $\mathbb{D}$ is compatible with $\mathbb{C}$ with respect to $\mathbb{W}$ (referred to as $\mathbb{D} \rhd_{\mathrm{W}} \mathbb{C}$) if the behavior of $\mathbb{D}$ can be restricted to the behavior of $\mathbb{C}$ with respect to $\mathbb{W}$, according to the definitions presented in Section 4.

Restricted behavior in a cooperative process means that the new e-Service $\mathbb{D}$ is able to react to the same incoming events of the e-Service $\mathbb{C}$ it is compatible with, with the same behavior; possible new events raised by the new e-Service $\mathbb{D}$ (and/or additional event parameters) will be not considered in the cooperative process; in such a way, all the additional behavior presented by the new e-Service is not used in the current cooperative process.

If the e-Service specification $\mathbb{D}$ is compatible with the e-Service specification $\mathbb{C}$, then a component instance $\mathcal{D}$ implementing $\mathbb{D}$ can replace instances of $\mathbb{C}$ in the e-Application (i.e., in the cooperative process).

This substitution is possible only under certain constraints, that is that the e-Service instance $\mathcal{C}$ to be substituted, implementing $\mathbb{C}$, is not running yet. More precisely, an e-Service can be in one of several *activation states* (similar to the ones proposed in [?]): not_instantiated, ready, running, suspended, finished, as shown in Figure 3. The substitution is possible if $\mathcal{C}$ is not_instantiated or ready. When $\mathcal{C}$ enters into the ready state, it means that all the corresponding active class state machines $\mathbb{C}.\mathbb{SM}_i$, $i = 1 \ldots n$, are in the initial state, whereas the finished state means that all the the corresponding active class state machines $\mathbb{C}.\mathbb{SM}_i$ are in the final states. In the other activation states $\exists i$, $i = 1 \ldots n : \mathbb{C}.\mathbb{SM}_i$ is in some intermediate state.

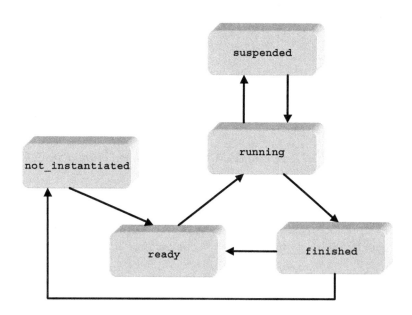

Fig. 3. Activation States of an e-Service.

4   Compatibility of e-Services

As discussed in Section 3, the goal of this paper is to define a notion of compatibility between e-Services, which preserves the behavior with respect to a cooperative process specification. An algorithm for checking compatibility between e-Services is proposed.

An e-Service $\mathbb{D}$ can restrict its behavior to the one specified by the e-Service $\mathbb{C}$ if it reacts to compatible event sequences in the same way as $\mathbb{C}$. In general, $\mathbb{D}$ could react also to different events, but the cooperative process specification in which $\mathbb{C}$ is involved guarantees such events will not be raised; therefore the cooperative process is correctly executed also with $\mathbb{D}$; simply the additional services offered by $\mathbb{D}$ are not exploited in this cooperative process.

The starting point for defining compatibility between e-Services is to provide the notion of compatibility among basic elements. Given two elements of the form < name > : < type > (such as a parameter of an event, or an attribute/property of a flat class) we assume it is possible to define they are compatible through the interactive intervention of the human designer or by using thesaurus techniques [3] (as for example to decide that an attribute Name : String in a flat class Person in $\mathbb{D}$ is similar to FirstName : String in the flat class Person in $\mathbb{C}$). In this paper we do not further address such problem, but we assume to have the operator compatibility $\triangleright$ among such basic elements.

An input event $\alpha'(p'_1, \ldots, p'_n, o'_1, \ldots, o'_m)$ *in* $\mathbb{D}$ *is compatible with an input event* $\alpha(p_1, \ldots, p_n)$ *in* $\mathbb{C}$ *(* $\alpha' \triangleright \alpha$ *) if* $\forall i = 1 \ldots n$ *,* $p'_i \triangleright p_i$ *and* $\forall j = 1 \ldots m$ *,* o'_j *is defined as optional.*

An output event $\beta'(p'_1, \ldots, p'_n, o'_1, \ldots, o'_m)$ *in* $\mathbb{D}$ *is compatible with an output event* $\beta(p_1, \ldots, p_n)$ *in* $\mathbb{C}$ *(* $\beta' \triangleright \beta$ *) if* $\forall i = 1 \ldots n$ *,* $p'_i \triangleright p_i$ *; no conditions are required on* o'_j *,* $j = 1 \ldots m$ *.* ε *is compatible only with itself, whereas every output event is compatible with* ε *.*

A guard condition σ' *in* $\mathbb{D}$ *is compatible with a guard condition* σ *in* $\mathbb{C}$ *(* $\sigma' \triangleright \sigma$ *) if the following are satisfied:*

- *the syntax structures of the two formulas are equal;*
- *Given two correspondent terms* < property' > < operator > < value > *in* σ' *and* < property > <operator > < value > *in* σ, *it holds* < property' > $\triangleright$ < property >; < operator > *and* < value > *are the same.*

A transition $s' \xrightarrow{\alpha'[\sigma']/\beta'} t'$ *in* $\mathbb{D}$ *is compatible with a transition* $s \xrightarrow{\alpha[\sigma]/\beta} t$ *in* $\mathbb{C}$ *(* $s' \xrightarrow{\alpha'[\sigma']/\beta'} t' \triangleright s \xrightarrow{\alpha[\sigma]/\beta} t$ *) if* $\alpha' \triangleright \alpha$ *and* $\beta' \triangleright \beta$ *and* $\sigma' \triangleright \sigma$ *. No conditions are required on the source and target states.*

By defining transition compatibility, we are able to compare the services offered by an e-Service with respect to the ones offered by another; the compatibility of the offered services is only a static aspect (i.e., e-Service interfaces are compatible) but there are not guarantees that the two e-Services behave in the same way when triggered in a cooperative process. The following step is to compare service request protocols "understandable" by the two e-Services; in order to ensure that two compatible e-Services follow the same protocol in participating in a cooperative process, we introduce the following definitions.

Let $\mathbb{SM}$ *be the active class state machine of an e-Service* $\mathbb{C}$ *. A trace* $\chi = \langle s_0, \ldots, s_{n+1} \rangle$ *is a finite sequence of states:*

- $s_i \in \Sigma$, $i = 1 \ldots n + 1$;
- s_0 *is the initial state and* $s_{n+1} = s_f$ *is the final state;*
- $\forall i = 1 \ldots N$ *,* $s_i \xrightarrow{\alpha_i[\sigma_i]/\beta_i} s_{i+1}$ *is a transition* $\in \Gamma$ *.*

Let $\chi' = \langle s'_0, \ldots, s'_{n+1} \rangle$ *be a trace in* $\mathbb{D}.\mathbb{SM}$ *and* $\chi = \langle s_0, \ldots, s_{m+1} \rangle$ *a trace in* $\mathbb{C}.\mathbb{SM}$ *.* χ' *is compatible with* χ *(* $\chi' \triangleright \chi$ *) if the following are satisfied:*

- $m = n$;
- $\forall i = 1 \ldots n$ *,* $s'_i \xrightarrow{\alpha'_i[\sigma'_i]/\beta'_i} s'_{i+1} \triangleright s_i \xrightarrow{\alpha_i[\sigma_i]/\beta_i} s_{i+1}$.

Traces represent possible computations (i.e., sequences of events) an e-Service is involved in. We propose a notion of compatibility between e-Services that requires that all the possible traces the e-Service $\mathbb{C}$ can execute when involved in a cooperative process $\mathbb{W}$ can be executed also by the e-Service $\mathbb{D}$.

An active class state machine $\mathbb{SM}'$ *of an e-Service* $\mathbb{D}$ *is compatible with an active class state machine* $\mathbb{SM}$ *of an e-Service* $\mathbb{C}$ *($\mathbb{D}.\mathbb{SM} \triangleright \mathbb{C}.\mathbb{SM}$) if* $\forall \chi$ *in* $\mathbb{C}.\mathbb{SM} : \exists \chi' \triangleright \chi$ *in* $\mathbb{D}.\mathbb{SM}$.

Let $\mathbb{C}$ *an e-Service involved in a cooperative process* $\mathbb{W}$, *and* $\mathbb{D}$ *an e-Service.* $\mathbb{D}$ *is compatible with* $\mathbb{C}$ *with respect to* $\mathbb{W}$ *($\mathbb{D} \triangleright_{\mathrm{W}} \mathbb{C}$) if* $\forall \mathbb{SM}$ *in* $\mathbb{C} : \exists \mathbb{SM}' \triangleright \mathbb{SM}$ *in* $\mathbb{D}$.

Based on such notions, an algorithm to verify e-Service state machine compatibility is proposed. The algorithm checks if every possible trace in the e-Service $\mathbb{C}.\mathbb{SM}$ state machine has a compatible one in the e-Service $\mathbb{D}.\mathbb{SM}'$ state machine. The algorithm uses two stacks, one for each state machine, in order to "visit" and check all the states; at each cycle two states (one for each state machine) are popped from the stacks and all the transitions starting from them are compared with respect to compatibility, by taking into account special cases such as loop transitions (source and target states are equals) and final transitions (i.e., with the final state as target state). If there are compatible transitions, the target states of such transitions are pushed into the respective stacks, otherwise the algorithm returns with failure; the algorithm returns with success when all the possible states have been checked, that is the two stacks are empty. The pseudo code of the algorithm is presented in the following page.

INPUT PARAMETERS ($\mathbb{C}.\mathbb{SM}$, $\mathbb{D}.\mathbb{SM}'$)
OUTPUT VALUE (*check* : Boolean)   // *check* = TRUE iff $\mathbb{D}.\mathbb{SM}' \triangleright \mathbb{C}.\mathbb{SM}$

```
{
    var stack_C : STACK;
    var stack_D : STACK;
    var loop_C : Boolean;
    var loop_D : Boolean;
    var check : Boolean;
    var ss : State;
    var tt : State;

    check := TRUE;
    stack_C.push(C.SM.s₀);
    stack_D.push(D.SM'.s'₀);

    WHILE ( ( check == TRUE ) AND ( NOT  stack_C.isEmpty() ) )
    DO {
        ss := stack_C.pop();
        tt := stack_D.pop();
        FOREACH ss  ᵅ⁽ᵅ⁾/ᵝ  xx in C.SM
            IF ( check == TRUE )
```

```
                    THEN {
                        loop_C := FALSE;
                        loop_D := FALSE;
                        IF ( xx <> C.SM.s_f )
                        THEN IF ( xx == ss )
                                THEN loop_C := TRUE;
                                ELSE stack_C.push(xx);
                        IF ( NOT ∃ tt →^{α'[σ']/β'} yy in D.SM'
                                compatible with ss →^{α[σ]/β} xx )
                        THEN check := FALSE;
                        ELSE IF ( yy <> D.SM'.s_f )
                                THEN {
                                    IF ( yy == tt ) THEN loop_D := TRUE;
                                    IF ( loop_C )
                                    THEN check := loop_D;
                                    ELSE stack_D.push(yy);
                                }
                    }
        }
        IF ( NOT stack_D.isEmpty() ) THEN check := FALSE;
        return check;
}
```

The test of compatibility for two e-Services with respect to a cooperative process in which the first one takes part is given by the following algorithm:

INPUT PARAMETERS ($\mathbb{C}$, $\mathbb{D}$)

OUTPUT VALUE ($check$: Boolean) $//$ $check$ = TRUE iff $\mathbb{D} \rhd_W \mathbb{C}$

```
{
    var check : Boolean;

    check := TRUE;
    FOREACH SM ∈ C
        check := check AND ( ∃ SM' ∈ D compatible with C.SM );
}
```

The test of compatibility between e-Services is currently implemented in a prototype using recursion in the main program and some helper functions for checking compatibility among events and guard conditions. The compatibility between basic elements is defined by the cooperative designer. The e-Service specifications are retrieved from the repository. This prototype is based on Java and on CORBA for accessing the repository.

5   Related Work

The problem of inter-organization processes has been studied in order to provide a flexible technological infrastructure not adopting a strictly coordinated system for inter-organization cooperation [6].

In the workflow community, much attention has been paid to adaptive and extensible systems and to the separation of concern between interface and implementation of a process and/or activity. The eFlow system [4] is a process management system that supports adaptive and dynamic service composition, by separating the concepts of process schema, service node and service process instance, all of them described through an XML-based description language. In [16], different activities of a multi-enterprise process are decoupled into activity interfaces and activity implementations, the former ones being modeled as state machines that include application-specific operations and states, and have input/output parameters.

Process Brokers [9], [14] are an extension of the Message Broker technologies, in which the middle layer not only interconnects the different cooperating applications, but also encapsulates the process logic for connecting them.

The cooperative platform proposed in this work is based on the separation between e-Service specification and component implementation, thus extending previous work to a cooperative multi-organization and multi-platform environment. A similar multi-platform approach has been recently adopted in Casati et al. 2001, where the specific issue of composing basic e-Services is addressed, and an e-Service definition language is presented.

UDDI is an initiative for defining an XML schema to publish and discover services on the Web. The UDDI Business Registry stores different types of information about a service, that is business contact information ("white pages"), business category information ("yellow pages") and technical service information ("green pages") [17]. The component model described in this paper and the repository described in [12] are not restricted to static information about e-Services, but also behavioral aspects are considered.

As regards the notion of compatibility between e-Services, several papers [13], [7], [8], [15] have been devoted to define notions such as inheritance, substitutability, polymorphism, etc. among components based on behavioral aspects modeled as statechart diagrams and state machines. In this paper we use a simplified version of statechart diagrams and state machines, as they represent a conceptual model of the behavior of an e-Service and not the design of an implementation object.

In [2] and [1] it is defined how it is possible to generate a new and more specific workflow component which can substitute a previous and more general one, based on a Petri Net representation of the workflow component. The notion of compatibility proposed in this paper is aimed at checking if already defined e-Services are compatible, therefore it is not a generative notion but it aims at a-posteriori verification of compatibility and substitutability.

6   Concluding Remarks and Future Work

In this paper a platform for cooperative processes and e-Service composition has been proposed; the central element is the separation among e-Service specifications, described according to a component model based on a particular tailoring of UML, and components, based on technological component models, which deploy such e-Services. A notion of compatibility among e-Services and an algorithm for checking it have been described.

A repository for publishing, storing and managing cooperative process schemas, e-Service specifications and instance information has been developed as first element of such a platform. Based on the algorithm proposed in this paper, tools for reconfiguration, both at development- and run-time, are being developed.

Some issues need to be solved, such as precise techniques for generating components targeted to a given technological component model starting from e-Service conceptual specifications, and for checking if a given component is compliant with an e-Service specification. The coordination of different e-Services composing a cooperative process need to be investigated, in order to address problems such as deadlocks, dependability, etc., and the design of such a coordination "glue" need to be provided, being the ultimate goal the definition of a complete platform for cooperation among organizations based on e-Services in a multi-platform environment.

References

1. van der Aalst, W.M.P.: How to Handle Dynamic Change and Capture Management Information: An Approach Based on Generic Workflow Models. International Journal of Computer Systems, Science & Engineering, vol. 15, no. 5, 2001.
2. van der Aalst, W.M.P., Weske, M.: The P2P approach to Interorganizational Workflows. Proceedings of the 13th International Conference on Advanced Information Systems Engineering (CAISE'01), Interlaken, Switzerland, 2001.
3. Beneventano, D., Bergamaschi, S., Castano, S., Corni, A., Guidetti, R., Malvezzi, G., Melchiori, M., Vincini, M.: Information Integration: The MOMIS Project Demonstration. 26th Very Large Data Bases Conference (VLDB 2000), Cairo, Egypt, 2000.
4. Casati, F., Ilnicki, S., Krishnamoorthy, V., Shan, M.C.: Adaptive and Dynamic Service Composition in eFlow. Proceedings of the 12th International Conference on Advanced Information Systems Engineering (CAISE 2000), Stockholm, Sweden, 2000.
5. Casati, F., Sayal, M., Shan., M.C.: Developing E-Services for Composing E-Services. Proceedings of the 13th International Conference on Advanced Information Systems Engineering (CAISE'01), Interlaken, Switzerland, 2001.
6. Grefen, P., Aberer, K., Hoffner, Y., Ludwig H.: CrossFlow: Cross-Organizational Workflow Management in Dynamic Virtual Enterprises. International Journal of Computer Systems Science & Engineering, vol. 15, no. 5, 2001.
7. Harel, D., Gery, E.: Executable Object Modeling with Statecharts. IEEE Computer, vol. 30, no. 7, July 1997 (also, Proceedings of 18th International Conference on Software Engineering (ICSE '96), Berlin, Germany, 1996).

8. Harel, D., Kupferman, O.: On the Behavioral Inheritance of StateBased Objects. Proceedings of the 34th International Conference on Component and Object Technology, Santa Barbara, CA, 2000.
9. Johannesson, P., Perjons, E.: Design Principles for Application Integration. Proceedings of the 12th International Conference on Advanced Information Systems Engineering (CAISE 2000), Stockholm, Sweden, 2000.
10. Mecella, M., Batini, C.: Enabling Italian e-Government Through a Cooperative Architecture. In Elmagarmid, A.K., McIver Jr, W.J. (eds.): Digital Government. IEEE Computer, vol. 34, no. 2, February 2001.
11. Mecella, M., Pernici, B.: Designing Wrapper Components for e-Services in Integrating Heterogeneous Systems. To appear in VLDB Journal, 2001 (A preliminary version also in Proceedings of the 1st VLDB Workshop on Technologies for E-Services (VLDB-TES 2000), Cairo, Egypt, 2000).
12. Mecella, M., Pernici, B., Rossi, M., Testi, A.: A Repository of Workflow Components for Cooperative e-Applications. Proceedings of the 1st IFIP TC8 Working Conference on E-Commerce/E-Business, Salzburg, Austria, 2001.
13. Nierstrasz, O.: Regular Types for Active Objects. In Nierstrasz O., Tsichritzis D. (eds): Object-Oriented Software Composition. Prentice Hall, 1995.
14. Process Broker Consortium: A Process Broker Architecture for Systems Integration. White paper, 1999. Available on line: http://www.dsv.su.se/~pajo/arrange/Publications/publications.html.
15. van Rein, R.: Specifying Processes with Dynamic Life Cycles. Proceedings of the 12th International Conference on Advanced Information Systems Engineering (CAISE 2000), Stockholm, Sweden, 2000.
16. Schuster, H., Georgakopoulos, D., Cichocki, A., Baker, D.: Modeling and Composing Service-based and Reference Process-based Multi-enterprise Processes. Proceedings of the 12th International Conference on Advanced Information Systems Engineering (CAISE 2000), Stockholm, Sweden, 2000.
17. UDDI.org: UDDI Technical White Paper, 2001. Available on line: http://www.uddi.org/pubs/lru_UDDI_Technical_Paper.pdf.

Beyond Discrete E-Services: Composing Session-Oriented Services in Telecommunications

Vassilis Christophides[1], Richard Hull[2], Gregory Karvounarakis[1,2],
Akhil Kumar[2], Geliang Tong[2], and Ming Xiong[2]

[1]Institute of Computer Science, FORTH
Vassilika Vouton, P.O. Box 1385, GR 71110, Heraklion, Greece
{christop,gregkar}@ics.forth.gr
[2]Bell Laboratories, Lucent Technologies, Murray Hill, NJ 07974
{hull,akhil,tong,xiong}@research.bell-labs.com

Abstract. We distinguish between two broad categories of e-services: *discrete* services (e.g., add item to shopping cart, charge a credit card), and *session-oriented* ones (teleconference, collaborative text chat, streaming video, c-commerce interactions). Discrete services typically have short duration, and cannot respond to external asynchronous events. Session-oriented services have longer duration (perhaps hours), and typically can respond to asynchronous events (e.g., the ability to add a new participant to a teleconference). When composing discrete e-services it usually suffices to use a process model and engine that composes the e-services as relatively independent tasks. But when composing session-oriented e-services, the engine must be able to receive asynchronous events and determine how and whether to impact the active sessions. For example, if a teleconference participant loses his wireless connection then it might be appropriate to trigger an announcement to some or all of the other participants. In this paper we propose a process model and architecture for flexible composition and execution of discrete and session-oriented services. Unlike previous approaches, our model permits the specification of scripted "active flowcharts" that can be triggered by asynchronous events, and can appropriately impact active sessions. We introduce here a model and language for specifying process schemas (essentially a collection of active flowcharts) that combine multiple e-services, and describe a prototype engine for executing these process schemas.

1 Introduction

The use of web-accessible e-services will revolutionize the way that many e-commerce and consumer software applications are provided. Until now, much of the research (e.g., see [3,6,7,18,24]) and emerging infrastructure (e.g., IBM's Web services Toolkit, Sun's Open Net Environment and JiniTM Network technology, HP's e-speak, Microsoft's .Net and Novell's One Net initiatives[3]) in e-services has been focused on the composition of *discrete*, *short-running* tasks such as "add an item to a

---

[3] See http://www.alphaworks.ibm.com/tech/webservicestoolkit, http://www.sun.com/sunone, http://developer.java.sun.com/developer/ products/jinni, http://www.e-speak.hp.com, http://www.microsoft.net/net, and http://www.novell.com/news/onenet, respectively.

F. Casati, D. Georgakopoulos, M.-C. Shan (Eds.): TES 2001, LNCS 2193, pp. 58-73, 2001.
© Springer-Verlag Berlin Heidelberg 2001

shopping cart", "charge a credit card" or "check the availability of tickets". While the APIs of such services may include several methods that can be invoked, they are typically *unresponsive* or *unaware* of *asynchronous events* arising from other e-services or from external applications. In contrast, there are several kinds of *session-oriented* e-services that do need to respond to asynchronous events during their life-cycle. Such e-services arise in telecommunications, c-commerce [4], and cross-organizational workflows [16]. We use the term "responsive" for e-services that need to respond to asynchronous events in their environment, and "insular" for e-services that can be isolated from such events. This paper introduces the AZTEC framework, which uses a new process model and architecture that enables highly flexible, scripted handling of asynchronous events in composite e-services involving responsive sessions.

Many e-services for telecommunication applications, such as voice calls, teleconferences, internet-based multimedia chat or collaboration, single- or multi-participant streaming video sessions and interactive games, are session-oriented and responsive. For example, all of them need to respond (by shutting down) if they are used in conjunction with a pre-paid billing account that runs out of money. It may be desirable to impact a teleconference if a participant drops out (e.g., because they move out-of-range of wireless connection), perhaps by informing the other participants. Another class of examples arises when using "presence" services, which generate messages when someone becomes present on a network (e.g., by turning on their cell phone, or typing something on a keyboard). Presence information could be used to automatically connect an invited participant into a teleconference, or to alert viewers of a streaming video that an interested friend has just become present.

Moreover, the notion of collaborative commerce (c-commerce) is focused on supporting all aspects of electronic communication and interaction between the (human and automated) participants in commercial transactions. Many of these interactions have long duration (ranging from a phone call to a catalog-sales company to the month-long process of obtaining a home mortgage), and are impacted by events generated by the involved participants, and by external applications. As just one example, it may be useful to automatically monitor customer sessions at a web-based storefront and proactively intervene, by enabling a sales person or product expert to join into the session [2]. Finally, in the context of cross-organizational workflows, sub-workflows are usually packaged as outsourced e-services. Then, an execution of a sub-workflow may both generate and respond to multiple events [16].

To provide a framework for assembling, executing, and monitoring insular (discrete) and responsive (session-oriented) e-services we combine elements of the workflow and event paradigms. This combination permits a loosely coupled process definition environment. More specifically, workflow-style constructs can be used for specifying how to respond to a given event type, but the specifications of these responses do not need to be embedded into a single workflow schema. This allows a modularization of the specification of a composite e-service, in which the event responses can be considered as logical building blocks. This is consistent with the increasing autonomy between activities (e.g., outsourced e-services) that a web-enabled distributed architecture can provide.

Our contribution in this paper is a model, a language and an engine for creating composite e-services involving sessions. We propose an *Active Flowchart Model*, supporting the specification of process schemas (that define a composite e-service) essentially as a collection of "active flowcharts", i.e., flowcharts coupled with the event types that can trigger them. The language used to define active flowcharts is called XASC (XML-based Active Service Composition). It is XML-based in two ways: the active flowcharts are themselves specified in XML, and the interfaces between the flowcharts and e-services are based on SOAP XML messages [21]. The engine is event-driven, supports explicit prioritizations between flowchart enactments, as well as simultaneous execution of multiple process enactments. The engine forms one component of the AZTEC system, which also provides the means for automatic generation of process schemas using higher-level specifications.

Since the main focus of this paper is on the process model and runtime execution engine for composite e-services involving sessions, we do not address issues such as publishing, registering, or selecting atomic or composite e-services using emerging technologies like UDDI (Universal Description Discovery and Integration), and WSDL[4] (Web Services Description Language). We note that AZTEC builds on top of standards for accessing session-based telecommunications services (e.g., SIP, Parley), and that Lucent and other providers are currently developing technologies (e.g., SoftSwitch, PacketIN, Flexant) that enable invocation and interaction with session-oriented telecommunications services programmatically, i.e., as e-services.

The paper is organized as follows. Section 2 identifies key issues raised when composing session-oriented e-services, and motivates the various elements of our approach. Section 3 presents the Active Flowchart Model, including a high-level specification of the XASC language and its semantics. Section 4 describes the architecture and run-time environment of AZTEC, including both the execution engine and the components for automated generation of process schemas. Section 5 discusses related research, and Section 6 presents our ideas for future work.

2   Motivation and Approach

This section examines more closely the fundamental issues that arise in composing responsive, session-oriented e-services, and then describes the key components of the approach taken by AZTEC. We introduce a representative class of composite e-services involving sessions to provide grounding for the discussion. The example is called "(Design your own) Smart Teleconference", and comes from telecommunication applications. Similar needs are also exhibited in the context of collaborative commerce and cross-organizational workflows.

With existing technology it is possible to request that a phone-based audio teleconference be set up, to run from a start time to an end time, with a given number of ports (i.e., participants). This kind of teleconference supports a very limited set of automated functions – people can join the teleconference or exit it, and perhaps the group can request extensions of the teleconference (e.g., add 15 minutes). The charge for the teleconference is based on the maximum number of ports requested not the number of ports used. Adding more ports typically requires operator intervention.

---

[4] See http://www.w3.org/TR/SOAP, http://www.uddi.org, and
http://www-106.ibm.com/developerworks/library/ w-wsdl.html, respectively.

Based on emerging technologies in the telephony network it will soon be possible to dynamically assemble and invoke much richer forms of teleconferencing. In our hypothetical Smart Teleconference application, a user will be able to request that a multimedia teleconference be established with a given start and end time, a given set of invited participants, a set of different interaction formats (e.g., audio bridge, internet-based text chat, internet-based collaborative web browsing, shared view of video streams), the use of presence services, and guidelines concerning quality of service, costs, and billing model (e.g., pre-paid or account-based). As a particular example, Rick may request that a smart teleconference involving an audio bridge and possibly a text-chat bridge be set up to run between 10 AM and 12 noon, involving five participants, namely Akhil, Geliang, Gregory, Ming, and Vassilis. A presence service is to be used, both to identify whether an active participant loses their wireless connection, and to automatically connect an invited participant if he/she has not been active but becomes present on a network (e.g., by turning a wireless device on). Also, the teleconference will be charged to Rick's pre-paid account (which happens to have $25 in it), and the overall expected cost is to be minimized.

In this example, during execution, there will be four sessions in operation, each potentially interacting with the others. For example, if a participant drops from the audio conference then the other participants might be notified through the text-chat session. Likewise, the presence server may lead to the automated connecting of new participants. Finally, the billing session may receive periodic updates about the services being rendered by the other sessions, and may impact the other sessions (by shutting them down) if the account runs dry.

In the AZTEC framework we view the sessions as being wrapped, to form *session objects* with an API that includes synchronous function calls and generated events. The wrappers would typically translate between the internal representation of functions and events and the SOAP interface [21] supported by the e-service realizing the session. The wrappers can also transform asynchronous function calls into synchronous function calls (e.g., to yield a synchronous function that asks the telephony network to place a phone call and then give as a return value information about whether the call was answered, busy, or rang until a time-out occurred).

A primary purpose of a process schema composing multiple session objects is to specify how these objects are to interact. We identify three challenges of managing these interactions:

1) Knowing *what* is interacting: Inquiring about the explicit state of external session objects is not always possible. From a requester viewpoint the objects might have to be treated as black boxes supporting a well-defined but limited interaction interface.

2) Knowing *how* the session objects should impact each other: The impact of one session object on another will be application dependent, i.e,. depending on the goals of a specific composition of e-services. In addition, the logic used when reacting to events generated by session objects will depend on the state of other session objects and the state of the overall process enactment.

3) Knowing *when* the interactions will take place: Interactions with autonomous session objects can't be specified statically, since the service requester has a limited ability to supervise the session object, and the session object may be reacting to multiple non-deterministic events not directly visible through its interface.

The AZTEC framework responds to items (1) and (2) by permitting the use of flowcharts to specify how to respond to a given session-object event. In particular, these flowcharts can probe the session objects as to their current state, and then impact one or more of the session objects. The flowcharts provide many of the advantages of workflow models (e.g., separation of control logic from tasks performed), but also support lower-level data manipulation constructs (e.g., to restructure or merge data from different events). As will be seen below, constructs are provided in AZTEC so that one flowchart enactment may launch another one.

One implication of item (3) is that it cannot be predicted in advance when or how frequently a given session object event will occur. This is the fundamental motivation for incorporating the event-driven paradigm into our model, rather than attempting to extend any of the commonly used workflow models, so that all the flowcharts could be combined into a single workflow schema.

We note that the enactment of a single flowchart may involve numerous requests against external session objects (and perhaps databases, etc.), and may thus take hundreds of milliseconds or even multiple seconds or minutes to execute. This is in marked contrast with the approach taken by action algebras based on situation calculi. In those models, the action taken when an event is received is viewed as atomic and instantaneous [20]. The potential for long-running enactments and for events to arrive soon after one another leads to the potential for interleaved flowchart enactments, which is another implication of item (3). In some cases there may need to be some prioritization and/or interaction between two or more flowchart enactments. In AZTEC, we provide both priorities and also the ability for one flowchart enactment to suspend, examine, modify and resume another.

Finally, one could naturally ask: Why use flowcharts, as opposed to a full-fledged programming language, as in Java beans? One motivation concerns the need for some flowchart enactments to access, and perhaps manipulate, the state of another enactment. Since flowcharts have restricted flow-of-control logic that is easily accessible, they are easier to reason about and manipulate than unrestricted code blocks. The other motivation stems from an important goal of AZTEC, which is to enable the automated construction of process schemas, i.e., composite e-services, to achieve some high-level requirements. Although automated assembly is not the focus of this paper, we make a few remarks about how AZTEC will support this process in Subsection 4.3.

3   The Active Flowchart Model

A key focus of the AZTEC platform is to support session-oriented services, responsive to asynchronous events. A key design criterion for AZTEC is to enable the specification of highly customized and/or personalized reactions to asynchronous events coming from external e-services. To this end, we introduce a process model for active flowcharts i.e., flowcharts that can be invoked asynchronously whenever a matching event occurs (in the style of Event-Action rules [25]). To illustrate how the

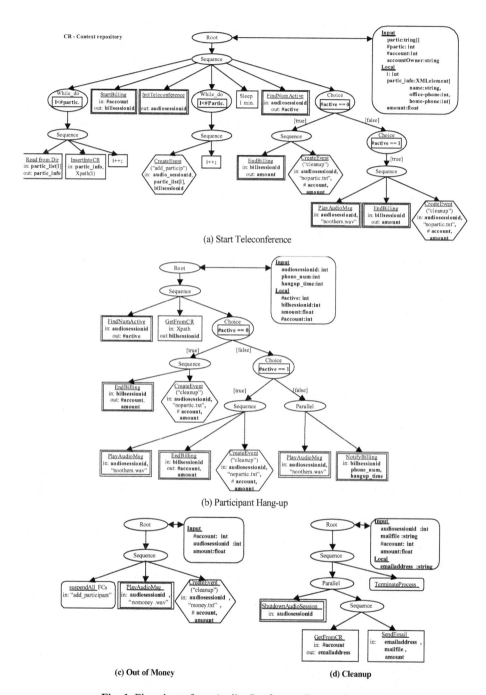

(a) Start Teleconference

(b) Participant Hang-up

(c) **Out of Money**

(d) **Cleanup**

Fig. 1. Flowcharts from Audio-Conference Process Schema.

Active Flowchart Model and the AZTEC platform can support a smart teleconference we rely in the rest of the paper on a simplified example with only audio conferencing, and a pre-paid billing model. In our example, we consider an event-based interaction with two session-oriented e-services appropriately wrapped as session objects using SOAP [21]: (a) the *audio_conf_service*, that can initiate audio conferences, add participants to it, and monitor when participants have hung up; and (b) the *billing_service*, that maintains pre-pay accounts, can keep track of how much money is being used during an audio conference, and generate an event if the account runs out of money. Five active flowchart schemas need to be defined for this example: (1) **Start_audio_conference**, (2) **Add_participant**, (3) **Participant_hang_up**, (4) **Out_of_money**, and (5) **Clean_up**. We are giving below the abstract syntax of the XASC language, used to define these flowchart schemas, and we will explain its various constructs using the graphical representation of our flowcharts in Figure 1 (a concrete XML syntax is forthcoming).

An XASC process schema (e.g. Smart Teleconference) consists of a set of active flowchart schemas, an identified root flowchart, and an XML Schema [22] for the Context Repository. For each active flowchart, the enactment-priority indicates the priority with which the flowchart should be executed, if invoked by the specified event type.

<process-schema>   :== <active-flowchart>$^+$<root-flowchart-name><CR-schema>
<active-flowchart> :== <event-name><flowchart-name><enactment-priority>

In our example, executing the XASC process schema causes the root **Start_audio_conference** flowchart to be launched. This collects participant profile data (including office and home phone numbers), initiates an audio conference, notifies the billing service about the new audio conference, and then launches an enactment of **Add_participant** for each invited participant. The latter flowchart attempts to add one participant to the audio conference, first by ringing their office phone and if no answer then ringing their home phone. If the participant answers, then the billing service is notified. Although not illustrated in our simplified example, the **Add_participant** flowchart might also be invoked in the middle of the audio conference. If a participant hangs up then the audio_conference service generates an event, which in turn launches the **Participant_hang_up** flowchart not presented here. If at least two participants remain, then the flowchart enactment simply informs the billing service that one participant dropped; if zero or one participant remains then the flowchart enactment invokes the **Clean_up** flowchart. The **Out_of_money** flowchart is launched if the billing service generates an event indicating that the account against which the audio conference is being charged has run out of money. This flowchart plays a message to the participants telling them that the account is out of money, and then invokes the **Clean_up** flowchart. Importantly, the **Out_of_money** flowchart also suspends the operation of all flowchart enactments of type **Add_participant**. Finally, the **Clean_up** flowchart has the job of requesting the *audio_conf_service* to end the conference.

Before continuing we note that our model supports four *modes of interaction* between flowchart enactments: (1) by generating events that launch other flowchart enactments; (2) by sharing data in the Context Repository; (3) by querying the status of other flowchart enactments, and even suspending and subsequently altering the activity of other enactments; and (4) by using priorities to enforce a certain execution order between steps of flowchart enactments. More details are presented below.

Active flowcharts essentially subscribe to various event types in order to be asynchronously notified by external e-services (session objects), or other flowcharts. Both events (i.e., messages) and flowcharts (i.e., processes) are first-class citizens in our model. Despite the fact that in our example there is a one-to-one correspondence between event types and flowchart schemas, an XASC design choice was to favor modularity of definitions. Thus, different process schemas may reuse both event types related to specific session objects (e.g., in case of new flowcharts using the same e-services) and flowchart schemas (in case of new e-services composed using the same flowcharts).

```
<event>        :== <event-name><event-arg>*
<event-arg>    :== <parm-name><parm-type>
<parm-type>    :== <XMLSchema-Type>
```

Event types are defined by their name, and the name and the type of their input parameters. These parameters are used for passing data from a session object to an active flowchart enactment and vice versa (i.e., the data flow), as well as, from one flowchart enactment to another. XASC event and flowchart parameter values are XML data, typed according to a process-specific XML Schema.

```
<flowchart>            :== <flowchart-signature> <flowchart-body>
<flowchart-signature>  :== <flowchart-name> <flowchart-arg>*
<flowchart-arg>        :== <parm-name> <parm-type>
<flowchart-body>       :== start <flowchart-var>* <subflow> finish
<flowchart-var>        :== <parm-name> <parm-type>
<subflow>              :==  begin-seq <subflow>⁺ end-seq
                          | begin-parallel <subflow>⁺ end-parallel
                          | begin-choice <condition> <subflow>+ end-choice
                          | begin-loop <condition> <subflow>⁺ end-loop
                          | task
<condition>            :== <condition-var>⁺ <literal>
<condition-var>        :== <parm-name> <parm-type>
<task>                 :==  <task-input-arg>* <task-output-arg>*
                          ( <external-task>
                          |<internal-task>
                          |<event-task>  )
<task-input-arg>       :== <parm-name><parm-value>
<task-output-arg>      :== <parm-name><parm-value>
<parm-value>           :== <XMLSchema-Instance>
                          |<parm-name>
```

Flowchart signatures state their name and input parameters. Note that the signature of enabling events should subsume the signature of the flowcharts. This can be statically checked during an XASC process schema compilation [17]. The body of a flowchart is defined using a structured workflow language introduced in [15], although extended to permit input parameters and local variables. One motivation for using this model is the relative ease of querying flowchart enactments about their state [10]. For **Start_audio_conference** the input variables are an array of participants (names), the size of the array, an account number to be billed, and the conference "sponsor", which will be notified about status and completion of the audio conference. It also uses local variables, which are private to a single flowchart enactment. These enactments can also access the Context Repository, which enables sharing of information between flowchart enactments.

Each flowchart has a unique root task (delimited by start and finish) and the control constructs (seq, parallel, choice, loop) are properly nested (matching respective begin and end tags). For instance, the **Start_audio_conference** flowchart performs seven sequential tasks: (a) insert participant profile information into the Context Repository, (b) initialize the billing session, (c) start the audio conference session, (d) add participants into the audio conference, (e) sleep for a short period (say, 1 minute), (f) get the number of active participants, and (g) check whether the audio conference was successfully launched. Boolean conditions of the choice and loop control tasks are evaluated against flowchart input arguments or local variables. In **Start_audio_conference** we can see the while-do loop condition ($i<$#$part$) for finding participant info (office and home phone numbers) from a directory, as well as the choice branches (#$active=0$, #$active=1$) for ending the teleconference when the number of active participants is not sufficient. Additionally, in the **Clean-Up** flowchart we can see the parallel construct used to shutdown the audio session while notifying the teleconference sponsor about the total cost.

Various kinds of XASC tasks exist with corresponding input and output parameters. External tasks (represented with double squares) make synchronous function calls to session-oriented and discrete e-services, while internal tasks (represented with simple squares) use available AZTEC functions/operations. For example, in the **Start_audio_conference** flowchart, the second and third sequence tasks are synchronous calls to the *billing* and the *audio_conf* e-services in order to initialize the corresponding sessions and obtain respectively the billing and audio session id. Internal processing tasks implement various operations, including manipulations of literal data and accesses to the Context Repository, namely insert (creating new values), set (replacing values) and get operations (reading values). Each time an XASC process schema is executed, the Context Repository is initialized as a new XML document, instance of an XML Schema specified by the application programmer. For instance, the second sequence task of the first while-do in **Start_audio_conference**, inserts into the created context repository the participant information (name, office and home phones) that will be used by an enactment of the **Add-Participant** flowchart to attempt to add a participant into the teleconference.

Last but not least, tasks may be used to explicitly generate events (represented with hexagons). In **Start_audio_conference**, the first sequence task of the second while-do loop will create an **Add-Participant** event, having as input parameters the participant name (*partlist[i]*), as well as, the initialized audio and billing session ids. Each occurrence of such event has the effect of invoking an **Add_participant** enactment asynchronously. Furthermore, in the seventh task (choice), when only one person is detected to be active (since presumably no other participant had been reached) a voice message is played, the billing session is closed, and an event to is generated to launch the **Clean_up** flowchart. This appropriately closes the audio session, and sends an e-mail to the teleconference sponsor. The last task of **Clean_up** will terminate the entire process enactment, including the cancellation of any extant flowchart enactments, logging anything important from the Context Repository and then freeing up that memory.

A special category of internal XASC tasks (represented with rounded squares) enable to directly suspend, resume or cancel the execution of tasks of a running flowchart enactment, as well as, to examine the current state of an enactment (e.g., using techniques of [10]). The first kind of task is illustrated in the **Out-of-Money** flowchart, which will be launched when the pre-pay billing account runs out of money. Since the objective of this flowchart is to shutdown the entire teleconference, its first task will suspend the tasks of all running enactments of type **Add-Participant**. Clearly, we will not continue attempts to add a participant if the audio conference is being cancelled. The third task of the flowchart will, as previously discussed, launch the **Clean_up** flowchart.

We close this section by commenting on the final mode of interaction between flowchart enactments, namely the use of priorities. For example, the **Out_of_money** flowchart may be given priority over the **Add_participant** and **Participant_hang_up** flowcharts. The prioritization can also be used to favor certain flowchart enactments during periods of heavy load. For example, **Add_participant** enactments might be given higher priority than **Participant_hang_up** ones, because it is important to quickly connect people to the audio conference; delays in clerical updates to the billing session can also be delayed.

4   The AZTEC Platform

This section provides a brief introduction to the AZTEC platform for composing and executing discrete and session-oriented e-services that is currently being developed at Bell Labs. The overall architecture of the system is described in Subsection 4.1. Subsection 4.2 describes how the AZTEC platform executes schemas specified in this process model. Finally, Subsection 4.3 describes how AZTEC supports dynamic changes to process schemas.

4.1 Overall Architecture

The AZTEC platform provides support for service selection and assembly, and for executing the resulting composite service. Note that assembly and execution can be performed as two distinct phases, or can be interleaved, thereby supporting a form of dynamic service selection and assembly. Figure 2 illustrates the main components of the AZTEC platform (shown as the large rounded-corner square), along with an Administration component (upper left) and access to web-services, the telephony network, and the wireless network (across the bottom).

In the upper right of Figure 2, we can see the **Assembly component**, that performs service selection, creation of process schemas, and if needed, the dynamic revision of process schemas. Under typical usage, when a request for a composite service (e.g., a smart conference with various characteristics) is presented to the AZTEC platform, then the Assembly component will analyze the requirements and build a process schema that can support the requested composite service. In the current design, AZTEC's Assembly component uses a form of hierarchical planning [11], that starts by selecting a high-level "template" process schema which may have "slots" that need to be filled in, and then progressively fills in the slots with more detailed templates or grounded schemas (i.e., schemas with no slots). The templates and slot fillers are stored in the **Templates and Fillers Library**, shown in the upper left of the AZTEC platform. For more details on service assembly and the splicing technique used, readers are referred to [9].

The process schema assembly performed by the Assembly component is traditionally viewed as a "design-time" activity. In contrast, the **Execution component** in the bottom center of the AZTEC platform is charged with the "run-time" activity of executing the process schemas. This execution engine is event driven. It interprets the process schemas, and interacts with web-services, telephony services, and wireless services through a collection of **Wrappers** (provided as part of this component) and gateways (provided by emerging products from telephony equipment manufacturers including Lucent).

The final component of AZTEC is for (dynamic) **Schema Management**. This component is used to load process schemas into the Execution component, and more importantly, to enable modifications and refinements (via the Assembly component) to process schemas in the middle of executing on a process schema. In particular, this supports the "design-time" activity of process schema assembly in the midst of "run-time" activity of process schema execution.

As with database mediators [23], humans will have an important role in the creation, maintenance, and monitoring of a running AZTEC platform. Through the **Administration component**, programmers will develop the templates and fillers that are used to support the hierarchical planning process for automated service assembly. Programmers will also specify the policies to be used when building (or modifying) process schemas for satisfying requests for composite services. Finally, humans may choose to monitor the status of service executions, and perhaps directly manipulate the process schema of a running composite service.

4.2 Execution of XASC Process Schemas

We now describe how an XASC process schema is executed by the Execution component of the AZTEC platform. A process enactment gets started by an *init* event generated by the system. Referring to Figure 2, this event is received by the **Event Listener** and passed - through the **Event Queue** - to the **Task Dispatcher**. The Task Dispatcher then assigns a thread from its Thread Pool to initiate the process enactment. This is a predefined procedure for all process enactments, comprising the generation of a unique process identifier for this enactment, the initialization of a **Context Repository** document, which will be used for data passing across flowcharts within this process enactments and, finally, enacting the root flowchart of this process schema. This enactment is represented internally as a DOM tree and placed into the working space of the **Flowchart Logic Server**. Note that due to the structured nature

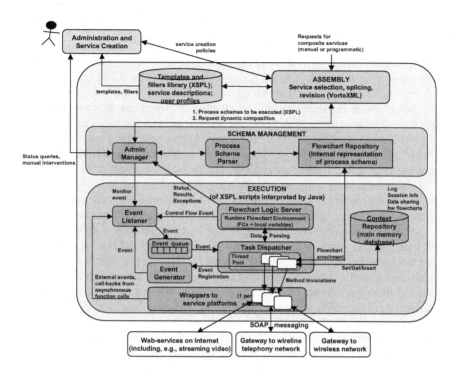

Fig. 2. AZTEC Framework for Assembly and Execution of Session-Oriented E-Services.

of the flowcharts, the order of execution of tasks is equivalent to a depth-first traversal of this tree representation. At this point, the flowchart is ready for execution.

More generally, in the middle of executing a process enactment the Flowchart Logic Server will be executing zero or more flowcharts in parallel. In our running example, in the middle of the teleconference there might be two flowchart enactments running to handle participants who are attempting to join the teleconference and another that deals with a participant who has just hang-up his telephone. Note also that there might be more than one process enactment running at the same time; in this case, however, flowcharts from different process enactments are not allowed to interact with each other - sharing data through different Context Repository documents and having different process identifiers.

For each one of these flowcharts, the Flowchart Logic Server maintains information about their execution state (e.g., which task is currently running) which can also be queried through internal functions. Then, for instance, whenever a task has finished the Flowchart Logic Server will generate a Control Flow Event which - when dispatched – will result to the execution of the appropriate (i.e., the next one in a sequence) task, and send it to the Event Listener module, which will place it in the Event Queue. Finally, the Task Dispatcher has the role of invoking individual tasks in response to events that it gets from the Event Queue. In order to allow for several tasks to be executed concurrently, the invocation of the tasks itself is handled by a set of threads (Thread Pool) coordinated by the Task Dispatcher. When capable of doing more work, i.e. when there are available threads in its Thread Pool, the Task Dispatcher will ask the Event Queue for an event. The Task Dispatcher may also decide to expand its Thread Pool if no threads are available, if, for instance, most of the threads are waiting for results and do not consume much of their CPU time.

A key feature of AZTEC in the execution of multiple flowcharts is the rich flexibility that is given for deciding the priorities with which the steps of different flowcharts should be executed. In AZTEC the prioritization is managed explicitly by separating the Flowchart Logic Server, the Event Queue and the Task Dispatcher. Clearly, when handing the next event to the Task Dispatcher for execution, the Event Queue can easily employ a scheduling algorithm to pick the event with the higher priority. Thus, events with a higher priority are processed sooner that events with a lower priority. Events with the same priority are processed in a FIFO order.

The individual tasks will primarily be function calls to wrapped e-services that are resident on the web, the telephony network, or the wireless network.). In cases when a service will need to send an asynchronous event back to AZTEC (i.e. when a participant has hang-up), this event will be trapped by the wrapper. The wrappers can fill-in application specific information and send the event into the system through the Event Listener, in an appropriate internal representation. When a response is obtained, the Flowchart Logic Server is informed that the task has completed and also receives the returned values of the task (if any).

Finally, this architecture facilitates explicit control on the execution state of flowcharts. For instance, suspending a flowchart is be implemented by just *annotating* the flowchart instance in the Flowchart Logic Server's internal working space as *suspended*. As long as a flowchart is marked as suspended, the Flowchart Logic Server does not send any more events for the execution of its tasks. Moreover, when the Event Queue is asked to give the highest priority event to the Task Dispatcher, it can bypass events that have been produced by flowcharts which are marked as *suspended*. For tasks of a flowchart which are already running, when the *suspend* command arrives, we allow them to finish their execution normally, in order to avoid inconsistencies.

4.3 Loading and Modifying Process Schemas

We now turn to the Schema Management component of AZTEC, which supports the delivery of process schemas into the Execution component, and dealing with dynamic process schema modification and refinement. If a new process schema is created by the Assembly component, then it can be passed into the Admin Manager. This in turn passes the schema to the Process Schema Parser, which parses the XASC specification into an internal DOM representation. If the parsing is successful then the result is placed into the Flowchart Repository, otherwise, an error message is sent back to the Admin Server.

In some cases the Assembly component will provide an incompletely specified process schema to the Execution component. For example, the particular choice of an e-service might be omitted, or in fact a larger portion of a flowchart might be left unspecified. This will permit dynamic selection of e-services and/or refinement of the process schema. How do the empty slots get filled in? The basic approach is that the Flowchart Logic Server will come to a point of the flowchart that is unspecified and notify the Admin Server. The Admin Server in turn will gather appropriate information (e.g., about the current sessions and states of active flowchart instances) and send a request to the Assembly component to fill in the needed parts of the process schema. When this comes back, the Admin Manager gives it to the Process Schema Parser, which in turn produces an internal representation for the flowchart, including a marker indicating where processing should start. Finally, the Admin Manager will send an event into the Event Scheduler indicating that the process schema has been refined and is ready to go.

It should be stressed that in order for the Admin Manager to access the Context Repository, it must go through the Event Scheduler and Task Dispatcher. This design decision is motivated primarily to keep the number of data and control flow paths to a minimum. The Assembly component might also get involved with schema execution if there is a significant exception to a running process schema. In this case, the exception can be passed to the Admin Manager, which can request the Assembly component to create a repair. The Admin Manager is also involved if a human, through the Administration and Service Creation component, wants to examine the runtime status of an XASC process enactment.

5   Related Work

Several proposals for workflow systems attempt to combine the technology of active database   systems with event-based systems.   Some examples of event-driven distributed workflow engines are WIDE [5] and EVE [13]. The main modules in EVE are: an event detection and logging module, rule execution module and service execution module. Upon detection of a primitive or composite event, this module will activate the appropriate rule in the rule execution module. The latter consists of ECA rules. When a rule is activated, it will check the associated condition, and if it is true, the corresponding action is performed. The ction part of the rule will in turn generate events, which are fed into the event detection module. In comparison with AZTEC, EVE has more sophisticated support for events; however, EVE does not have a notion of sessions like AZTEC. Moreover, the action part of the ECA rules in EVE cannot mimic all of the flexibility that the AZTEC flowcharts offer.

Citation [19] describes an event based approach for dynamic modifications of running workflow instances using rules and predicates such as drop, replace, check, delay and process. This approach is especially useful for semantic exception handling. The AZTEC model can also support adaptability in a somewhat different way by changing the contents of the context repository during a running instance. Another interesting service-oriented model for inter-organizational workflows is given by the Crossflow project [16]. This model provides mechanisms for selection and invocation of services, and controlling and monitoring an external service. However, all these models fail to recognize the notion of a session, the only exception being the Caltech Infospheres project [8], where sessions are entities that can be explicitly specified, supported and reasoned with.

6 Future Work

We foresee several areas of further research in connection with the AZTEC framework. One such area relates to further refinement of the active flowchart model, that supports hierarchical and modular constructs for specifying active flowcharts and their interactions, including priorities and data sharing. It is also necessary to perform some kind of global consistency checking for all the flowcharts in an application to ensure that their interactions are "safe". Another research area is performance, since telecommunications applications typically require sub-second responses to most events (such as when a participant is dropped). Hence, we plan to model the performance implications of our architecture in order to ensure that it can meet stringent performance goals. Since multiple flowcharts can run in parallel and generate events simultaneously, priority assignment policies must be compatible with the real-time performance requirements. Although our discussion of the framework has focused on the running of a single enactment (e.g., to control a single multimedia teleconference), in practice the execution engine must support at least hundreds of enactments running at the same time. In such a context, it is important to study issues resulting from the interactions between concurrently running enactments. There are also performance issues related to assignment of priorities to enactments and scheduling of enactments. Finally, it is important to support recovery in our framework so that session-oriented composite e-services can be recovered from failures.

References

1. W.M.P. van der Aalst and A. Kumar, "XML Based Schema Definition for Support of Inter-organizational Workflow", Information Systems Research (accepted).
2. V. Anupam, R. Hull and B. Kumar, "Personalizing E-commerce Applications with On-line Heuristic Decision Making ", *Proceedings of Tenth Intl. World Wide Web Conference*, June 2001.
3. B. Benatallah, B. Medjahed, A. Bouguettaya, A. Elmagarmid and J. Beard, "Self-Coordinated and Self-Traced Composite Services with Dynamic Provider Selection", Technical Report, University of New South Wales, March 2001 (Available at http://sky.fit.qut.edu.au/ ~dumas/selfserv.ps.gz).
4. R. Breite, P. Walden and H. Vanharanta, "C-Commerce Virtuality – Will it work in the Internet?", Proc. of International Conf on Advances in Infrastructure for Electronic Business, Science, and Education on the Internet (SSGRR 2000), http://www.ssgrr.it/en/ssgrr2000/proceedings.htm.
5. F. Casati, P. Grefen, B. Pernici, G. Pozzi, and G. Sanchez. WIDE workflow model and architecture. Technical report, University of Twente, 1996.
6. F. Casati, S. Sayal, M. Shan, "Developing e-services for composing e-services", *Proceedings of CAISE 2001*, Interlaken, Switzerland, June 2001.
7. F. Casati and M. Shan, "Dynamic and adaptive composition of e-services", *Information Systems*, to appear 2001.
8. K. Mani Chandy and Adam Rifkin, "Systematic Composition of Objects in Distributed Internet Applications: Processes And Sessions", Conference Proceedings of the Thirtieth Hawaii International Conference on System Sciences (HICSS), Maui, Volume 1, January 1997, pp. 395-404.

9. V. Christophides, R. Hull, A. Kumar, J. Simeon, "Workflow mediation using VorteXML, " *IEEE Data Engineering Bulletin* 24(1), March 2001, pp. 40-45.

10. V. Christophides, R. Hull, A. Kumar, "Querying and Splicing of Workflows," *CoopIS '02*, September 2001 (forthcoming).

11. K. Erol, J. Hendler, and D. Nau, "Semantics for hierarchical task network planning", Tech. Report CSTR3239, CS Department, Univ. of Maryland, 1994.

12. P. Fankhauser, M. Fernandez, A. Malhotra, et al., "The XML Query Algebra ", W3C Working Draft, 15 February 2001, http://www.w3.org/TR/query-algebra/.

13. A. Geppert and D. Tombros, "Event-based distributed workflow execution with EVE," Technical Report Technical Report 96.5, University of Zurich, 1996.

14. R. Hull, F. Llirbat, E. Simon, et al., "Declarative Workflows that Support Easy Modification and Dynamic Browsing, " *Conference on Work Activities Coordination and Collaboration (WACC)*, San Francisco, February 1999, pp. 69-78.

15. B. Kiepuszewski, A. ter Hofstede and C. Bussler, "On Structured Workflow Modelling", *Proceedings of CAISE 2000*, Stockholm, Sweden.

16. J. Klingemann, J. Wasch and K. Aberer, "Adaptive Outsourcing in Cross-organizational Workflows, GMD Report 30, August 1998.

17. G. Kuper and J. Siméon, Subsumption for XML Types, International Conference on Database Theory (ICDT'2001), January 2001,London, UK.

18. S. A. McIlraith, T. Cao Son, and H. Zeng, "Semantic Web Services", *IEEE Intelligent Systems*, March/April – 2001.

19. R. Muller and E. Rahm, E., "Rule-Based Dynamic Modification of Workflows in a Medical Domain," Proc. Datenbanksysteme in Bro, Technik und Wissenschaft (BTW'99), Freiburg, March 1999, pp. 429-448.

20. R. Reiter, "KNOWLEDGE IN ACTION: Logical Foundations for Describing and Implementing Dynamical Systems". Book in preparation. http://www.cs.toronto.edu/cogrobo/.

21. Simple Object Access Protocol (SOAP) 1.1, W3C Note 08, May 2000, http://www.w3.org/TR/SOAP/.

22. H.S. Thompson, D. Beech, M. Maloney, and N. Mendelsohn. "XML schema part 1: Structures", W3C Recommendation, October, 2000.

23. G. Wiederhold, "Mediators in the Architecture of Future Information Systems" *IEEE Computer*, Volume 25, Number 3, 1992, pp. 38-49.

24. G. Weikum, (Special Issue Editor), *Bulletin of the Technical Committee on Data Engineering*, IEEE Computer Society, Vol. 24, No.1, March 2001.

25. Widom J. and, Ceri S. (Eds.). Active Database Systems: Triggers and Rules For Advanced Database Processing. Morgan Kaufmann, 1996.

View-Based Contracts in an E-Service Cross-Organizational Workflow Environment

Eleanna Kafeza[1], Dickson K.W. Chiu[1], and Irene Kafeza[2]

[1]Department of Computer Science, Hong Kong University of Science and Technology
Clear Water Bay, Kowloon, Hong Kong
[2]Department of Law, City University of Hong Kong, Kowloon, Hong Kong
kafeza@cs.ust.hk, kwchiu@ieee.org, irene.k@plink.cityu.edu.hk

Abstract. In an e-service environment, workflow involves not only a single organization but also a number of business partners. Workflow inter-operability is therefore an important issue for workflow enactment in such an environment. In this paper, we introduce a novel concept of workflow views as a fundamental support for E-service workflow inter-operability and for controlled visibility by external parties. Furthermore, we develop a contract model based on workflow views and demonstrate how management of contracts can be facilitated, with an Internet start-up E-service inter-organization workflow example.

1 Introduction

Workflow is the computerized facilitation or automation of a business process. A business process is a set of one or more linked procedures or activities, which collectively realize a business objective or policy goal. Workflow Management Systems (WFMSs) can assist in specification, decomposition, coordination, scheduling, execution, and monitoring of workflows. In this paper, we use the term workflow to refer to this more general notion of process management. Besides streamlining and improving routine business processes, WFMSs can help in documenting and reflecting upon business processes. Traditional WFMSs often can only coordinate workflows and their enacting agents (often limited to software processes) within a single organization.

The Internet has recently become a global common platform where organizations and individuals communicate among each other to carry out various commercial activities and to provide value-added services. E-service refers to services provided via the Internet. Therefore, there is an impending need for supporting cross-organizational workflows to these activities, especially because many organizations may have already been employing some kind of workflow technologies. Advanced WFMSs are now web-enabled and recent researchers in workflow technologies are exploring cross-organizational workflows to model these activities. In addition, advanced WFMSs can provide various services such as coordination, interfacing, process repository, process (workflow) adaptation and evolution, match-making, exception handling, data and rule bases, etc, with many opportunities for reuse.

F. Casati, D. Georgakopoulos, M.-C. Shan (Eds.): TES 2001, LNCS 2193, pp. 74-88, 2001.
© Springer-Verlag Berlin Heidelberg 2001

We have some preliminary work [4] to demonstrate the feasibility of modeling and enacting composite E-service as workflow extensions, so that we can build E-service agents (i.e., a system that provides E-service as delegated by users), and the system for supporting them quickly, with all the desirable features provided by the underlying WFMS. Furthermore, we have proposed a novel concept of workflow view in [5] for supply-chain management in a cross-organizational workflow environment. As follow-up work, we detail in this paper how composite E-services can be modeled as cross-organization workflow, with respect to our E-ADOME workflow engine extended with various agent interface. In addition, we apply a promising novel approach using workflow views for contract modeling and enforcement. Views help balance trust and security, i.e., only information necessary for the process enactment, enforcement and monitoring of the contract is made available to both parties, in a fully control and understandable manner. Moreover, each party only needs minor or even no modification to its own workflow, but can successfully arrive at a commonly agreed and interoperable interface. This kind of adaptation (fully support by E-ADOME [4,7]) is only required upon their first contract, and reusable subsequently, unless their workflows are changed drastically. Because an organization is probably making lots of contracts with many other different organizations, different views of a workflow can be presented to different organizations according to different requirements. Thus, inter-organization workflows can be developed fast and managed adequately, together with e-contracts, since the E-service arena is very competitive.

The contribution and coverage of this paper are as follows: (i) a cross-organization workflow viewpoint of a composite E-service with a novel concept of workflow views, (ii) a contract model based on workflow view, (iii) illustrates how workflow views facilitate e-contract management, such as process adaptation for interoperability and contract enforcement.

The rest of our paper is organized as follows. Section 2 presents a motivating example to illustrate a novel concept of workflow views in an E-service cross-organizational workflow environment. Section 3 presents our view-based model for e-contracts. Section 4 illustrates how workflow views facilitate e-contract management, and how two organizations can arrive at an e-contract with verification. Section 6 compares related work. Finally, we conclude the paper with our plans for further research in Section 6.

2   Workflow Views

In a B-to-B e-commerce environment, a business process usually involves many participating organizations, i.e., such a business process involves several inter-operating and interacting workflows from different organizations. This is known as cross-organizational workflow. To support workflow inter-operability, one of the basic requirements is a mechanism to let authorized external parties access and make use of only the related and relevant parts of a workflow, while maintaining the privacy of other unnecessary/unauthorized information. Motivated by views in federated object databases, we propose the use of workflow views as a fundamental mechanism for cross-organization workflow interaction. A workflow view can be either regarded as a structurally correct subset of a workflow definition (as in [17]) or a structurally correct composition of workflow definitions.

Workflow views are also useful in providing access to business processes for external customers or users, including B-to-C e-commerce and e-service. For example, external customers or users may want to check the progress or intermediate results of the business processes that they are participating. They may be required to provide additional information or make decisions during business processes. Even within an organization, workflow views are useful for security applications, such as to restrict accesses (like the use of views in databases).

We propose the use the concept of workflow views (which is detailed in the next section) to help advanced interactions among WFMSs and allow them to inter-operate in a white box mode (i.e., they can access some internal information of each other). In particular, we allow execution of another workflow in the same E-ADOME system to handle a task, as a form of dynamic reuse. For example, the task "Detailed Homepage Work" may be contracted out to an outside company as a workflow in another system. Alternatively, the task may be assigned to an in-house team as an extra workflow in the same E-ADOME system (cf. [4]).

Since ADOME-WFMS is event-driven, events and messages from other WFMS are intercepted by the E-ADOME layer and then presented to the ADOME-WFMS. As presented in the example in the following subsection, an event from a workflow of another organization (e.g., an inquiry from a customer) can trigger the start of a workflow in the local ADOME-WFMS, or used for synchronization purposes (e.g., deposit payment triggers ordering of a leased line). Similarly, an event from the local ADOME-WFMS (e.g., an inquiry to a supply) can trigger the start of a workflow in another organization, or used for synchronizing tasks in another organization (e.g., an order triggers delivery from another organization). As such, cross-organization workflow interactions can be facilitated.

2.1   Internet Startup E-Service: Cross-Organization Workflow Viewpoint

In [4], we presented an E-service workflow example based on the Internet Startup Service of Dickson Computer Systems. This workflow actually involves many parties: end-users who need the service, Dickson Computer Systems as a value-added service-provider, and the vendors / basic-service providers of Dickson Computer Systems. In order to explore more detailed interactions among these parties, we proceed to present a cross-organizational workflow view among these parties. We present a multi-party example to illustrate E-service provision chains. This is a novel approach and a significant step forward from our previous work [4] in E-services.

In order to out-source a leased-line based Internet startup project, the end-user undergoes a requisition workflow (cf. Fig. 1(a)). First, quotation inquiries are sent to a number of E-service providers. The received quotations with service details are evaluated. An order form is sent to (filled in through a web interface) the selected E-service provider, say Dickson Computer Systems, with deposit payment. The leased-line and the web server are then installed. The end-user then participates in negotiation and approval of the detail homepage design work and eventually accepts the finished web site. Finally, the balance payment is arranged for.

An E-service provider's workflow starts when an enquiry is received. Fig. 1(b) depicts a workflow based on the Internet startup service Dickson Computer Systems in [4]. The additional required steps are to compile a quotation from update inquiries from its vendors the prices of a server PC and a leased line. It should be noted that multiple PC vendors and multiple leased-line providers might be contacted for selection. After order confirmation, the more accurate action upon the exception "domain name in use by others" is to inform the end user for immediate amendment. The order of a leased line is only triggered until the deposit payment, because leased-line installation charges are not refundable even upon order cancellation, while PC servers are most probably reusable for other customers. Furthermore, there are probably long lasting interactions in the step "detailed homepage work" for design negotiations. Finally, after receiving the payment, the workflow also ends.

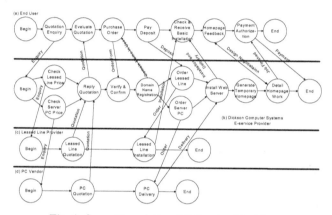

Fig. 1. Cross-Organiztional E-Service Workflow.

A leased-line provider's and a PC vendor's workflow also start when an enquiry is received. Assuming this is the end of the E-service provision chain, the vendors have all necessary information to quote the price. B-to-B orders on standard service packages are usually performed together with payment arrangements. It should be noted that the lease-line provider directly installs the lease line at the end-user's site and therefore directly triggers their "check and receive basic installation" step, without the need to go through Dickson Computer System. These two workflows end after the leased line is installed and after the PC is delivered, respectively.

In this example, The workflow view of the *end-user* presented to the system integrators has the following requirements: (i) The end-user's company profile and other background information are made available on request so that the system integrators can design more personalized proposals. (ii) Changes in delivery requirement, lease-line installation date, or payment arrangement should notify the E-service provider. (iii) In particular, the enquiry process is concealed so that the E-service provider can bid fairly and independently.

The workflow view of the *Dickson Computer Systems* presented to the *end-user* has the following requirements: (i) The company profile of Dickson Computer Systems and specifications service packages are made available on request so that the end-user can evaluate our proposals and quotations more accurately. (ii) Changes in any delivery schedule (hardware or services) should be notified to the end-user. (iii) The progress "Internet Startup Service" and other sub-workflows are available to the end-user so that the user can further monitor the progress of the job and estimate the delivery date. (iv) However, some trade secrets, such as the source and price of services and products, are not presented to the end-user to prevent them from purchasing directly from the vendors. (v) Updated quotation (price) is sent to the end-user upon a significant aggregated price change in hardware or service items with event-triggering mechanism during the evaluation process of the end-user.

The workflow views of the *product or service vendors* (e.g. PC, leased-line) presented to Dickson Computer Systems should have the following requirements: (i) Price for the services or products is updated with event-triggering mechanism. (ii) Technical specifications and related information for the services and products are made available upon request. (iii) Updates in software drivers and service configurations should notify Dickson Computer Systems using event-triggering mechanism (which in turn can notify the end-users). (iv) Changes in lead-time should also be notified. (v) Dickson Computer Systems can monitor the progress of leased line vendor in arranging their installation and web-page designer in the contract-out work so that this information is indirectly available to the customer.

2.2   A Model for Workflow Views

Formally, based on Workflow Management Coalition (WfMC) workflow definitions [21], a workflow is described by $W = (T, A, J, F, X, V, E)$ where T is the set of tasks, $A \in T \times T$ is the set of arcs in the transition graph, J is a Boolean function determines whether there is a join immediately before every task in T, F is a Boolean function determines whether a fork occurs immediately after every task in T, X is the condition function associating every element of A a condition, V is the set of variables, and E is the set of events[1].

A *workflow view* is a structurally correct subset of a workflow definition. Formally, a workflow restriction view $W' = (T', A', J', F', X', V', E')$ is based on $W = (T, A, J, F, X, V, E)$ such that $T' \subseteq T$, $J' \subseteq J$, $F' \subseteq F$, $X' \subseteq X$, $V' \subseteq V$, $E' \subseteq E$, and $\forall (a, b) \in A'$, $\exists n, \forall i, 1 \leq i \leq n, (t_i, t_{i+1}) \in A$ where $t_1 = a$, $t_n = b$ (the transitions in the view W' is based on any valid paths in W).

The components of a workflow include the process flow graph, input/output parameters, objects, rules, events, exceptions and exception handlers associated with the workflow.   Thus a view for a workflow instance also contains these components. Though every component is modeled as objects in most advanced object WFMS, we discuss them separately because each of them has different semantics. Fig. 2 depicts a simple workflow view definition language.

---

[1] Rules are modeled as objects; and exceptions are events [6,7].

```
view v of workflow w begin
    {process p1 view v1 ...}
    {process p2 renames p3 ...}
    {transistion t renames p4 to p5 ...}
    {object o1(=expression1), o2(=expression2)...
        (write) (input) (output) ...)
    (attribute a1,a2,...,an write | read | denied ...}
    {event e1=expression1, e2=expression2, ...}
    {exception e1=expression1, e2=expression2, ...}
    {rule r1=expression1, r2=expression2, ....}
end
```

Fig. 2. Workflow View Definition Language.

Process Flow Graph - Most contemporary WFMSs use a hierarchical composition approach, i.e. a process (workflow) is composed of sub-processes and so on down to leaf-nodes of atomic tasks. This provides a good granularity for providing views of the process flow graph. If a workflow view is to be made available, a fundamental provision is the topmost level process flow graph. However, the detail composition of individual sub-process may be concealed. Thus a process in the flow graph can be presented in one of the following ways. A white-box sub-process is specified with a sub-workflow view by a statement "process p1 view v1", i.e., the details of the sub-process is further visible and subject to the restriction of a sub-workflow view. A black-box sub-process (e.g., "Quotation Enquiry" in Fig. 1) is limited from further details of its further internal composition. Unless a view is specified for the sub-process, it is a black box. A gray box where some sub-processes are visible while other sub-processes are concealed (e.g., the whole end-user procurement process). Furthermore, since the name of a sub-process or a transition label may reveal some information, it can be renamed with a rename statement. The statement "process p2 rename p3" renames a process p3 to p2 while the statement "transition t renames p4 to p5" renames the transition from process p4 to process p5 as t.

Objects Associated with a Workflow Instance - An object associated with a workflow instance need not be presented completely in a workflow view. Some attributes can be hidden from the view, some can be read only, some are presented with write access, while composite attributes can further be composed of attributes of different access. Moreover, derived objects specified with object-SQL can be presented in a view. Input / output parameters are also objects specified for the interaction of the user. These parameters are actively received from or presented to the user upon interaction or certain events, with other regular objects in a workflow view are available only upon user's request. The "object" statement in Fig. 4 presents an object in a view. The optional expression is used to specify a derived object. The write option grants write access to the view user. The output option specifies the content of the object to be actively sent to the user. The input option specifies the object to be updated from the user. When the access of some attributes of an object are different from the default read or write access specified by the "object" statement, it can be overridden by the "attributes" statement, where explicit read, write or denied access can be specified.

Events and Exceptions - When events and exceptions are presented in a view, a mechanism, such as a corresponding message, should notify the view user upon their occurrences. This is particularly useful in providing cross-organizational process synchronization and constraint enforcement. Events and exceptions are specified with "event" and "exception" statements, respectively. In addition, the view provider should support user-specified events based on all their accessible objects and process states. In this way, the user need not poll on their interested objects and thus increase the efficiency. For example, the end-user may specify that changes in the delivery date be an event so that the user can be notified when the delivery is earlier or later then expected.

Rules and Exception Handlers - Rules are presented in a view so that a user can be aware of some of the actions taken by the provider upon certain events or exceptions. This is useful because the process flow graph cannot specify workflow actions that are taken in an asynchronous or event-driven manner. Some of these actions are exception handlers in the view provider. In this way, the user can avoid duplicating some error handling procedures if the errors have already been taken care of. Rules are specified with the "rule" statement, where they can be specified in (Event, Condition, Action) form or any composition of existing rules. In addition, constraints can be specified in the form of rules. Especially, rules can be used as integrity or semantic constraints in views. We are investigating in this direction and further details are beyond the scope of this paper.

3   An E-Contract Model Based on Workflow Views

An e-contract is an abstract of an agreement between two parties. Every contract has some basic information to be captured by an information system. In our e-contract model a *contract description D* is a set of attributes whose values describe the necessarily information in order to form a contract. Example attributes of the describe list are: *D={Accept, Offer, Goal, Schedule, Payment, Documents, QoS, Exception_Rules, Commit, ...}* where *Offer* and *Accept* denotes the organizations that offers and accepts the contract respectively; *Goal* is the objective why the contract is formed; *Schedule* is a set of dates and items to be carried out, including that the contract starts, finish, and any milestone of progress; *Payment* is a set of rules and values for payment; *Documents* is a set of documents that have to be available to both parties before forming the contract; *QoS* is a set of attributes for the required quality of service; *Exception_rules* is set of event-condition-action (ECA) rules to specify anticipated exceptions and their consequences; and *Commit* denotes whether the parties are committed to the contract or not. Since different countries and organizations may pose different requirements for creating a contract, and because of domain-specific requirements, there might be other attributes depending on the case as well.

When forming a contract, besides the description part, the two parties have to agree on the task assignment. For example, in Fig. 1 we have a contract between Dickson Computer Systems and the leased line provider. Each party has its own internal workflow. In order to cooperate, each party must be able to view a subset of the workflow of the other party that will specify the tasks that is obliged to perform. The issue is that in every contract we have to balance two concepts: trust and security. When two parties are forming a contract we assume that there is trust between them and that information necessary for the specification, enforcement and monitoring of the contract is available to both parties. At the same time, for security reasons no party wants to reveal more than it is necessary to the other party. In our e-contract model, the balance is achieved though a workflow view mechanism. Each party specifies a view of its internal workflow that is accessible to the other party. For example, the end-user specifies at the view that the task *evaluate quotation* becomes visible to the Dickson Computer Systems. At the same time details (i.e. the sequence of tasks) that describe how the quotation is evaluated are not disclosed since the user does not want the other party to know the internal evaluation procedure.

Although we may assume a mechanism that enforces the flow of control in each party's workflow, the control flow has to be augmented with inter-organizational communications in order to support the specific contract. These communications are useful for information exchange, control exchange, synchronization, and exception handling.

In our e-contract model, cross-organizational control flow information is specified within *communicating tasks* and their associated *communication links*. In each view, there are some tasks, called *communicating tasks*, through which two parties communicate. For example in Fig. 1, the *Payment authorization* of the End-User's workflow has to interact with the *End* node of Dickson Computer Systems and send the *Payment*. It has also to interact with the *Detail Homepage work* and wait for the *Job finish* message. The communicating tasks of the views of the two parties exchange messages through cross-organizational communication links. Each communicating task receives and sends a set of messages.

When specifying a contract, the order in which these messages occur is crucial. For example, the *Payment* should be sent only after the *job finish* is received. Therefore, with every communicating task we associate a partial order on the messages that has to send/receive. Moreover, we say that two messages are related through a "*strong*" order if and only if a reverse order execution has as a result the breach of contract.

Definition: Let V_i and V_j be the two views of two parties that have formed a contract. We call tasks of the view V_i and V_j that has interaction *communicating tasks*, and we associate with these tasks a set of messages M, and a partial order on $M <$, that imposes an order on the messages.

For example, *pay deposit* is a communicating task of the end-user, while *order leased line* is a communicating task of Dickson Computer Systems. When the *pay deposit* task is executed, a deposit should be paid to Dickson Computer Systems. Therefore, we define a communication link as an arc from the *pay deposit* task to the *order leased line* task. The direction of the communication link specifies which party is responsible for initiating the communication. We call a task responsible for initiating the communication a *performance* task. We also associate the message as a label of the communication link.

There are two different types of communication links, *simple* and *obligatory*. When forming a contract the parties have to specify which cases give ground to breach of the contract, i.e., where one party does not *perform* as it should. The *performance* in our

E-contract model contract is represented by the communication links. If a communication link is characterized as *obligatory*, but the party responsible for the communication fails to do so, then the other party has the right to terminate the contract or take appropriate measurements. For example, if the user in the (*pay deposit, order leased line*) communication link does not pay the deposit within a given deadline, Dickson Computer Systems has the right to terminate the contract.

It should be noted that the contract is in a negotiation state and does not formally starts before the first performance link, i.e., in this example before the order form is sent. We define the communication part of the contract that spans between two different organizations as a bipartite graph and completes our definition for an e-contract as follows:

Definition: Let $t_i \in V_1$ and $t_j \in V_2$ be two communicating tasks from two the workflow views V_1 and V_2. We define a *communication link* from t_i to t_j as a tuple $(t_i, t_j, M, type)$ where t_i is the task to initiate the interaction between the two workflows by sending a message to t_j, M is the message specification ant *type* specifies whether this is a *simple* or *obligatory* link.

Definition: Let V_1 and V_2 be the two workflow views that participate in a contract and T_1 and T_2 the set of communicating tasks respectively. A *cross-organizational communications graph E* is a bipartite graph between T_1 and T_2, where each edge of the graph is a communication link.

Main Definition: An *e-contract* is a tuple (V_1, V_2, E, D) where V_1 and V_2 are workflow views that participate in the contract, E is a *cross-organizational communications graph* between V_1, V_2, and D is a *contract description* of the e-contract based on V_1, V_2.

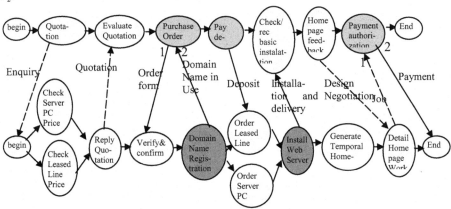

Fig. 3. An E-Contract Communication Graph.

In our graphical representation as depicted in Fig. 3, *simple* links are represented in dashed lines, while the partial order $<$ on the messages of each communicating task is represented by number labels at the end/start of each arc. We extract the messages associated with every communicating task by the labels of the bipartite graph. A performance task has a *send* message while the corresponding task *receives* message. We use light/dark gray color to represent the communicating tasks of the End-User/Dickson Computer System workflow views respectively, which are *performance tasks* and have *obligatory links*. The *Quotation Enquiry* task of the End-User is *a performance task*, i.e., it has to initiate an action - to communicate with the *Begin* node of Dickson Computer Systems by sending an *"Enquiry"* message. If this message is not sent, Dickson Computer Systems can still send the quotation. However, when the Purchase Order communicating task does not send a specific order form within a deadline, Dickson Computer Systems can assume that there is no obligation to perform subsequent tasks.

4   Managing E-Contracts

In the previous section, we have described our e-contract model based on workflow views. In this section, we illustrate the processes related to e-contract management in a cross-organizational E-service workflow environment.

4.1   Workflow / View Adaptation During Negotiation

As long as there is no standardized workflow specification at an application level for each trade or service business, we perceive that workflow adaptation is a hard and tedious problem, which must be adequately addressed. When two organizations are interested in making an e-contract for a certain E-service, they exchange an initial workflow view of each other, to disclose their company profiles, and to inform the other party procedures involved in their organization, such as details of service packages of the service provider and the procurement procedure of the end-user. These views contain also the information and coordination requirements of both parties. However, these requirements often vary in different organization, i.e., workflows from different organizations may often have mismatches. The use of workflow views can now offer another advantage of shielding their underlying workflows from the necessary modifications. The following different levels of workflow adaptation may be required for interoperations of different organizations:

1. Workflow views can be modified to accommodate for interface mismatch and minor procedural differences without the need to modify the internal workflow.
2. Internal workflows need minor adaptation to accommodate for missing procedures (e.g., some companies usually do not pay deposit, therefore they need to add this task) and other minor logistic difference. This adaptation can be permanent if the organization believes it is useful for improving the business process (in dealing with other companies or other favorable reasons). This is known as *workflow evolution* [7]. Alternatively, the adaptation can be just a *deviation*, which is only employed in dealing with this particular business partner.
3. Because there may be major difference in workflows of the two parties, one or both of them decide to re-compose their workflows to accommodate for the cooperation. This case may be common, but few are willing to so. Alternatively, especially if

the business relationship is not a long term one, one of the two parties may choose to fall back to a manual mode of cooperative (semi-manual) work-around. Since E-ADOME supports interfacing with human users through a web-based interface, for example, the end-user may designate a staff member to enter the order form manually through the web-page of Dickson Computer System, and subsequent interaction are done through email, ICQ alerts, and further customized generated web pages.

Because an organization is probably making lots of contracts with many other different organizations, different views of a workflow can be presented to different organizations according to different requirements. In addition, workflow adaptations, which are sometimes required, are also well supported in E-ADOME. Thus, interorganization workflows can be developed fast and managed adequately, together with e-contracts, since the E-service arena is very competitive. Otherwise, effective manual interaction through customized web pages is also supported by E-ADOME. However, a methodology for negotiation and workflow adaptation is beyond the scope of this paper.

4.2   Defining an E-Contract

After two parties have decided to make a contract, they have to arrive at an e-contract, which specifies the detail. In this section we present a methodology to define and verify a contract in accordance to our e-contract specification. When two parties want to form a contract, first they have to decide on the contract description set D, like the following example based on Fig. 3:

```
Create Description D
Accept: User
Offer: Dickson Computer Systems
Goal: Internet Startup Service
Schedule: {Start: June 30, 2001,
           Lease line installation: July 14, 2001,
           Server installation: July 16, 2000,
           ...,
       Finish: July 30 2001}
Payment:  {Before June 30, 2001: $1000 (Deposit),
           ...,
       With 14 days after Finish: Balance }
QoS:  Certified_Professions;
Exception_Rules:  {Schedule_delay <=7 days, do_nothing,
       Schedule_delay > 30 days : ...
       Leased_line.not_installable : ...}
Documents: Enquiry, Company Profiles, Order Form, Quotation
Commit: Yes
...
```

The description is the proof that both parties have agreed on the formation of a contract, and the e-contract model depicts the details. Then, each party has to present the view as specified in the e-contract model, in order to allow access to workflows of each other, and to incorporate the contract requirements on the data and control flow. Moreover, each party has to augment the communicating tasks with necessary communication links. In this example, after the End-User has executed the *Set_Communications* algorithm, it augments the communicating tasks with communication links as follows:

node: Quotation enquiry *Message:* send Enquiry message *Other party task:* Begin *type:* simple performance *Order:* none *node:* Evaluate Quotation *Message:* receive Quotation *Other party task:* Replay Quotation *type:* simple *Order:* none	*node:* Purchase Order *Message:* 1. send Order Form *Other party task:* Replay Quotation *type:* obligatory performance Message: 2. receive Domain Name *Other party task:* Domain Name Registration *type:* obligatory *Order:* 1<2.

From the above example, we can see that since there is no centralized control, each party of the contract defines the communicating tasks so that they can receive and send messages appropriately, thus implementing the specified communication. Because the *e-contract communication graph* is very important, an additional check can be executed to capture any accidental inconsistencies. The consistency-checking algorithm verifies that the communication links are defined as specified. For example when a part sends a message the other party has confirmed that it is waiting to receive the message and they both agree on the type of the constraint.

4.3   Enforcing Contracts

With workflow views support, the enforcement of contracts among different organizations can be facilitated. Examples include the following:

Installation Schedule – Dickson Computer System can compute an installation schedule to the end-user according to reported lead-time of the computer vendor and the lease-line provider.   If a vendor changes the lead-time, but the installation schedule can still be completed within the end-user's deadline, the change can be tolerated. Otherwise, another source has to be sought for, or an alternative solution should be employed, subject to the end-user's approval.

Price - If the price for the web-server rises to an extent that there are no more profits, Dickson Computer System may want to request an increase in price, use of an alternate cheaper server, delay the delivery until the price drops, or cancel the order. However, as protected by a contract, the end-user has the right to enforce the contract.

Server Availability - If a certain server, or critical part of the server is stopped from production, Dickson Computer System may request the end-user's approval of using an alternative server or part.

Because all the important information critical to the enforcement of the contract, viz. availability, price, lead-time, etc., are available in various workflow views and noticeable through effective E-ADOME event-triggering mechanisms, contracts can be maintained in an effective inter-organizational workflow environment.

4.4   Discussion

The section has presented an overview of managing view-based E-contracts in a cross-organization E-service workflow environment. The management of E-contracts is greatly facilitated by the workflow view mechanism for security, information hiding, workflow adaptation, providing different interactions with different organizations, and e-contract enforcement.

5   Related Work

While the concept of workflow view is novel, our approach has been motivated by views in object-oriented data models which can be dated back to [8], and in particular by imaginary objects in [1]. [10] discusses federated OODBMS and views for objects in a distributed environment.

Dartflow [2] is one of the first web-based WFMS, using transportable agents, CGI and Java technologies. Eflow [3] is one of the closest commercial systems with features like E-ADOME in handling e-Services. However, Eflow does not address matching of agents directly with tasks. Instead, it uses the concept of generic service node and service selection rules. Currently, several commercial WFMSs such as TIB/InConcert [18] and Staffware 2000 [16] provide web user interface too. In addition, I-Flow [9] has a Java workflow engine. WW-flow [9] provides a hierarchical control scheme over workflows implemented in Java for both the workflow engine and client interfaces. It allows sub-workflows to be executed in different workflow engines across the web. As for standards, Workflow Management Coalition (WfMC) has recently proposed Wf-XML [22], which is an interchange format specification for an XML language designed to model the data transfer requirements for process specification.

It is a new approach to E-service enactment based on an advanced WFMS engine. Besides E-ADOME, other notable systems using related approaches include Eflow [3] and Crossflow [11]. Crossflow models virtual enterprises based on a service provider-consumer paradigm, in which organizations (service consumers) can delegate tasks in their workflows to other organizations (service providers). Virtual organizations are dynamically formed by contract-based matchmaking between service providers and consumers. Though Crossflow includes detailed work for contracts, contract enforcement is also not so straightforward as the support provided by E-ADOME workflow views equipped ECA-rules mechanisms based on cross-organizational events. [19] presents workflow schema exchange in an XML dialect called "XRL".

However, few of the above-mentioned WFMSs support web-based cooperative exception handling. Most of them contact clients based on electronic mail and web forms and does not directly support active paging of clients with Internet message facilities like ICQ [20]. Very few commercial WFMSs provide support for handling exception. Even if they do, they only address very basic problems in a slight extend. It is also a new approach to build E-service agents based on an advanced WFMS engine. Besides E-ADOME, other notable systems using related approaches include Eflow [3] and Crossflow [11]. However, E-ADOME has the richest features in coordinating distributed agents than other systems close to us. Further details in the novelty of ADOME-WFMS, especially in its pragmatic meta-modeling approach and exception-handling features, are presented in [6,7].

6   Conclusions

This paper has presented an advanced cross-organizational workflow environment with novel features in cooperating with other organizations over the Internet for E-service enactment. We have illustrated in the context of E-ADOME, how its ADOME-WFMS engine, a flexible WFMS based on ADOME active OODBMS with role and rule facilities, is extended to accomplish such objectives. Compared with other research on this topic, E-ADOME provides an improved environment for various types of process enactment, which can adapt to changing requirements, with extensive support for reuse. This paper has introduced a novel concept of workflow view for interfacing different WFMSs, possibly belonging to different organizations, and its applications in an e-service environment. We have proposed a contract model based on workflow views, to simplify the process of developing cross-organizational workflow regarding to contracts. We have also illustrated how management of E-contracts is greatly facilitated by the workflow view mechanism for security, information hiding, workflow adaptation, providing different interactions with different organizations, and e-contract enforcement. Further note that, E-ADOME specification of workflows is based on standardized Workflow Management Coalition workflows, many of the techniques presented in this article can be applicable to any WFMSs for E-service enactment.

We are working on further details of process adaptation for interoperability, e-contract negotiation, methodologies for e-contract enforcement (including preventive measures), based on cross-organization workflows and the workflow view mechanism. We consider further research issues on interfacing and interoperability important for extending the applicability of an advanced WFMS engine. We are interested in the application of E-ADOME in various advanced real-life e-commerce environments, such as procurement, finance, stock trading and insurance. We are developing a more unified way to exchange information, including workflow views, with other agents, with XML. ADOME is currently being built on top of the ADOME-WFMS prototype system, with a web-based user interface to accommodate the whole range of activities.

References

1.   Abiteboul, S. , Bonner, A.: Objects and Views. In Proceedings of ACM SIGMOD Conference, 1991
2.   Cai, T., Gloor, P., Nog, S.: DartFlow: A Workflow Management System on the Web using Transportable Agents, Technical Report PCS-TR96-283, Dartmouth College, Hanover, N.H., (1996)

3. Casati, F., et al.: Adaptive and Dynamic Service Composition in eFlow. HP Laboratories Technical Report HPL-2000-39 (2000)

4. Chiu, D.K.W., Karlapalem, K., Li, Q.: E-ADOME: A Framework For Enacting E-services. VLDB Workshop on Technologies for E-Services, Cairo, Eygpt (2000)

5. Chiu, D.K.W., Karlapalem K., Li Q.: Views for Inter-Organization Workflow in an E-Commerce Environment, 9th IFIP 2.6 Working Conference on Database Semantics (DS-9), Hong Kong (2001)

6. Chiu, D.K.W., Li, Q., Karlapalem, K.: A Meta Modeling Approach for Workflow Management Systems Supporting Exception Handling, Special Issue on Method Engineering and Metamodeling, Information Systems, Elsevier Science, 24(2) (1999)159-184

7. Chiu, D.K.W., Li, Q., Karlapalem, K.: Web Interface-driven Cooperative Exception Handling in ADOME Workflow Management System, Information Systems, Elsevier Science, 26(2) (2001) 93-120

8. Dayal, U.: Queries and Views in an Object-Oriented Data Model. In Proceedings of 2nd International Workshop on Database Programming Languages (1989)

9. Enix Consulting Limited: An Independent Evaluation of i-Flow Version 3.5 (2000) (available at http://www.i-flow.com).

10. Gardarin, G., Finance, B., Fankhauser, P.: Federating object-oriented and relational databases: the IRO-DB experience. In Proceedings of the 2nd IFCIS International Conference on Cooperative Information Systems (CoopIS '97), (1997) 2-13

11. Grefen, P., Aberer, K., Hoffner, Y., Ludwig, H.: CrossFlow: Cross-Organizational Workflow Management in Dynamic Virtual Enterprises. International Journal of Computer Systems Science & Engineering, 15(5) (2000) 277-290

12. Kim, Y., Kang, S., Kim, D., Bae, J., K. Ju: WW-Flow: Web-Based Workflow Management with Runtime Encapsulation. IEEE Internet Computing, 4(3) (2000) 56-64

13. Li, Q., Lochovsky, F. H.: ADOME: an Advanced Object Modeling Environment. IEEE Transactions on Knowledge and Data Engineering, 10(2) (1998) 255-276

14. McCarthy, D., Sarin, S.: Workflow and Transactions in InConcert. IEEE Data Engineering,16(2) (1993) 53-56

15. Miller, J., Sheth, A., Kochut, K., Luo, Z.: Recovery Issues in Web-Based Workflow. Proceedings of the 12th International Conference on Computer Applications in Industry and Engineering (CAINE-99), pp. 101-105, Atlanta, Georgia (1999)

16. Staffware Corporation: Staffware Global - Staffware's Opportunity to Dominate Intranet based Workflow Automation (2000) http://www.staffware.com

17. ter Hofstede, A., Orlowska, M., Rajapakse, J.: Verification Problems in Conceptual Workflow Specifications. Data & Knowledge Engineering, Pergamon Press, Elservier Science, 24(3) (1998) 239-256

18. TIBCO Software Inc., which has acquired InConcert Inc., http://www.tibco.com

19. van der Aalst, W.M.P., Kumar, A.: XML Based Schema Definition for Support of Inter-organizational Workflow. In Proc. 21st International Conference on Application and Theory of Petri Nets (ICATPN 2000), Aarhus, Denmark (2000)

20. Weverka,. P.: Mastering Icq: The Official Guide. IDG Books. ICQ Press (2001).

21. Workflow Management Coalition: The Workflow Reference Model. (WFMC-TC-1003, 19-Jan-95, 1.1) (1995)

22. Workflow Management Coalition: Workflow Standard – Interoperability Wf-XML Binding, WFMC-TC-1023 (2000)

BizBuilder – An E-Services Framework Targeted for Internet Workflow

Raja Krithivasan and Abdelsalam (Sumi) Helal

Computer and Information Science and Engineering Department
University of Florida, Gainesville, FL32611
Phone: (352) 392-6833
{rkrithiv,helal}@cise.ufl.edu
http://www.harris.cise.ufl.edu/projects/e-services.htm

Abstract. One of the fundamental requirements for solutions to succeed in the business-to-business e-commerce domain is the ability to integrate seamlessly or inter-operate with diverse systems. In other words, the services offered by a business should be easily accessible by any consumer or business using the Internet infrastructure and standard protocols. A framework is needed by which new E-services can be created, or existing non-Internet services can be converted to E-services. Also, since these E-services are good candidates to be part of business workflows, a facility is needed to make them support and participate in such workflows. This paper describes BizBuilder, our E-services framework used to create these E-services. BizBuilder addresses the issue of transactions in particular and facilitates managing both synchronous and long-running E-services that can participate in workflows. Additionally, BizBuilder provides suitable support to register E-services to a Universal Description, Discovery and Integration (UDDI) enabled brokering community.

1   Introduction

The phenomenal growth of business-to-business (B2B) e-commerce has fueled the development of software systems that would integrate themselves seamlessly into the existing B2B space and provide value-added services. This rise in the growth of B2B e-commerce is a natural outcome of the success of the earlier model, the business-to-consumer (B2C) e-commerce. It was soon realized that the Internet infrastructure could be used by businesses effectively as done by consumers. The focus shifted from business process re-engineering to inter-enterprise process engineering (IPE) [10]. Businesses could use Internet as their communication medium to set-up business deals and utilize the services they need from other businesses, just in time when needed. A supply chain consisting of a manufacturer, distributor and seller can be taken as an example where a business requires the service of another.

F. Casati, D. Georgakopoulos, M.-C. Shan (Eds.): TES 2001, LNCS 2193, pp. 89-102, 2001.
© Springer-Verlag Berlin Heidelberg 2001

1.1   Motivating Scenario

The need for an E-services infrastructure can be realized by considering the following practical scenario.

Imagine a person X, who is involved with document proofreading. He might work for a publishing company or may have his own web-presence with suitable software, where he takes job orders from customers and provides the proofreading service. This form of business can be classified as one under B2C e-commerce, where X's proofreading business essentially provides services to consumers through HTML web pages and forms. In order to obtain more business opportunities, X may decide to upgrade his proofreading service, whereby even business like publishing companies, booksellers and reviewers can inherently utilize his services. In other words, X wants his proofreading service to be a part of as many businesses workflows as possible. On the contrary, X may also decide to host a new publishing service of his own, and may decide to use services like formatting, printing, shipping and handling along with his proofreading service and create a new workflow of services in order to provide a value-added service like one-stop Book-Publishing.

Considering the above requirements, X needs a software infrastructure, where he can provide his services as an "E-service" that is accessible to anyone (customer or business), programmatically, without the need to manually fill-in details in web pages. In addition he also needs a software framework, using which he can compose a new service, by creating/managing a workflow of existing services on the Internet. This ability to provide an E-services platform, support the creation of composite services, and the construction and management of a workflow of services are the primary motivating requirements for BizBuilder.

1.2   E-Services and Workflow

As depicted in Figure 1, the E-services framework will enable the creation of E-services that are accessible on the Internet and those that can participate in workflow. The other modules represented here include the workflow engine [11] that is responsible for creating, managing and executing workflow tasks, brokering communities that are used as the service repository for matchmaking. The brokering community [6] by itself is sophisticated and provides a mechanism for publishing, inquiring and matchmaking of E-services. In this paper, we concentrate only on BizBuilder – the E-services framework.

e-Services on the
Internet

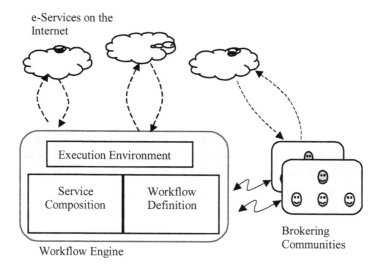

Fig. 1. E-Services and Internet Workflow.

1.3 Related Work

Distributed systems like CORBA offer an efficient way for service discovery and invocation, where the services themselves are physically distributed. However these systems are tightly coupled systems, meaning they need a homogenous framework to be used. Hence they do not lend themselves to being readily usable on the Internet. Architectures like WebTrader [4] and Coyote [7] have taken a different approach by using XML for representing service interfaces or contracts. On the other hand, workflow on the Internet has been dealt in systems like RainMan [5]. Dynamic composition of service components has also been discussed in [8]. Though all of these architectures are closely related to the idea of using services as the participating entities in a workflow, they do not deal with the concept of E-services, in which the focus is on providing services that are accessible using the standard data representation formats and protocols. In other words, these architectures propose a solution based on technologies like JavaBeans or RMI that are not readily inter-operable when considered in the diverse e-commerce space. Various architectures have been currently proposed based on the concept of E-services [1], [2], [3]. We have extended the concept of E-services to be used in conjunction with Internet based Workflow systems.

2   The BizBuilder E-Services Framework

The concept of E-services has become so prevalent that multiple definitions for the term E-service exist. Our framework assumes an E-service as "any service or functionality that can be accessed by a business or a consumer programmatically on the Internet, using standard representation and protocols". By mentioning about the representation and protocols for the Internet, we stress that any E-service should have a representation scheme that is not proprietary and one that is easily understood. Also the service should be accessible using standard Internet protocols like HTTP.

BizBuilder provides the necessary tools and framework using which an E-service can be created and utilized. In specific terms, the framework provides the facility to:

- Take an existing object (or service) implementation and provide an E-service wrapper,
- Provide a XML service description of an E-service (to represent an E-service),
- Provide the facility for advertising an E-service to a UDDI [9] enabled broker,
- Provide necessary tools and APIs to invoke an E-service on the Internet,
- Provide support for executing a "shallow workflow".

The BizBuilder framework targets a service provider who has a web-presence and business services to be provided, but the services not actually being available on the Internet (i.e., as E-services). Using this infrastructure the service provider can enable E-services, thereby making it available to both businesses and consumers. Apart from this primary goal, the service provider can participate in a workflow of another business seamlessly, without having to adapt or build any specific system in order to communicate with the workflow system. Optionally the service provider can also create a workflow of his own that will (re) use existing services on the Internet. Though the E-services infrastructure does not directly support the creation and management of this workflow, it provides necessary support for an E-service to participate in a workflow by providing capabilities to respond to transaction-specific queries. We assume a workflow as a "shallow workflow", which can be viewed as a collection of related activities executed concurrently. In programming parlance, this shallow workflow can be seen as a sequence of functions (or services) invoked in a specific order, with one using the result of another and the end result is seen as a value-added service (like the book-publishing example).

The E-service infrastructure also supports asynchronous long-running services that can be considered to be a part of a workflow. It is quite possible for individual activities in a workflow, to span across organizational boundaries, and take an arbitrary amount of time to execute to completion. Therefore the result of such activities may not be provided synchronously. In this case asynchronous mechanism like event-notification or push, is possible in tightly coupled systems, but is complex in nature when considered in the e-commerce space. This is because the user or the service requestor may wait for the results (asynchronously, without blocking other activities), and hence acts like a server. But the requestors may not be treated as a server anytime in the Internet context, since the requestor can just be a browser client.

Additionally, "callbacks" in HTTP cannot be easily achieved due to the nature of the clients and the HTTP protocol.

3   BizBuilder Architecture

This section details the overall BizBuilder architecture and the important components. Figure 2 depicts the architecture and shows the significant modules that constitute the framework.

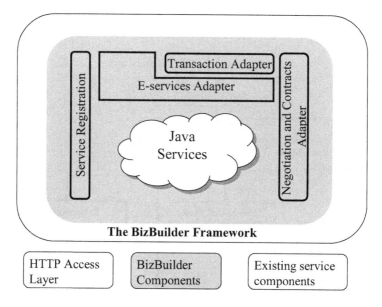

Fig. 2. Components of BizBuilder Framework.

As indicated in the above diagram, the E-service adapter, Service Registration module, the Transaction adapter and the Negotiation and Contract adapter form the core framework architecture.

3.1 Messaging Structure

One of the important requirements for E-services is to provide a messaging mechanism for invocation that is not proprietary, but easy to adopt. This was one of the drawbacks of traditional distributed systems, which required participants to have a homogenous structure as that of the service provider. The Simple Object Access protocol – SOAP, which specifically addresses the issue of RPC over XML, is used in BizBuilder for E-service invocation. Therefore, every E-service request and response is based on the SOAP format. Thus the framework has suitable support to read SOAP coded message, execute the actual services and reply results coded in SOAP format.

3.2   The E-Services Adapter

The E-services Adapter is the core component that allows the underlying services (for example services implemented using java objects) to be accessed on the Internet using the standard protocols and format. This module takes an existing service implementation in the form of a java object and creates the required server side framework, so that the java services can be invoked using a XML messaging structure on the HTTP protocol.

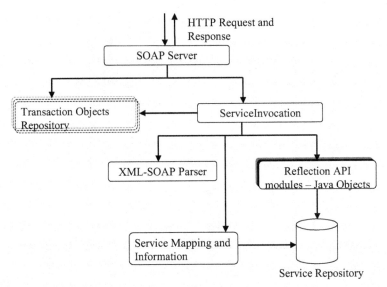

Fig. 3. Depicts the main modules of the E-services adapter and the interactions between them. An arrow from component X to component Y indicates that component X uses component Y.

Service Invocation in E-Services Adapter. The ServiceInvocation module forms the core part of the E-services adapter. This is the module responsible for loading the objects that implement the service and performing method invocation. Service Invocation is done by extensively using Java Reflection, a run-time object introspection facility.

Table 1. List of Modules in the E-Services Adapter and their Purpose.

Module Name	Description
SOAP Server	Servlet based HTTP server that processes SOAP coded requests
Transaction Objects Repository	A repository for storing a collection of service objects that are used to answer transaction probes. This repository does not strictly belong to the E-services adapter but is also accessed by the Transaction adapter
ServiceInvocation	The module that performs the operation of method invocation on native objects, using helper classes like XML parser and reflection APIs and takes care of storing objects in case of long-running services
XML-SOAP Parser	Utility classes that parses XML-SOAP coded messages and provides services to the ServiceInvocation module
Reflection API modules	Modules built based on the Java reflection API, used to perform the actual method invocation on the java objects
Service Mapping and Information	Modules used to provide persistent storage for information regarding services, their associated class files, parameter names and types for service invocation etc.

Apart form doing the basic function of method invocation, the module also takes care of "long-running services". In other words the long-running services are basically asynchronous method calls, which may take an arbitrary time for completion of execution. An example may be a proofreading service, part of which can be automatic like spell checking and part of which can involve manually verification of the document. In such cases it is not desirable to make the client process wait until the operation is complete, in most cases it is not feasible. The ServiceInvocation module handles this appropriately.

3.3 Long Running Services

In order to handle long-running services the E-service adapter executes the asynchronous call as a separate thread. The ServiceInvocation module first gets the information that this is a long-running process by querying the service object using the transaction interface (that must be implemented by the service provider). When it is found that the service under consideration is a long-running service the ServiceInvocation module launches a separate thread to invoke this method. At the same time, it creates and assigns this service a unique transaction id and returns this id to the client. In this way it implicitly tells the client that the result of the current execution will not be available immediately. The result of this long-running service in this case has to be queried by the user using the previously sent transaction id as the key. The Transaction adapter detailed below, processes these transaction queries and the result (if available) will be returned.

The lifetime of these objects that are used to perform method invocation is an interesting issue that should be handled. In case of synchronous services, these objects are destroyed, as the result is available immediately and it is assumed that these objects will not be referenced for anything else apart from the service for which they were created. In case of long-running services, these objects are suitably stored, since transaction probes can be expected at any point during execution. Even if the long-running service under consideration is complete, the objects cannot be destroyed until the result of the service invocation is communicated to the client. So these objects are destroyed only after making sure that the results of these long-running services are communicated to the client.

3.4 Transaction Adapter

The ability to make E-services participate in a workflow is one of the main objectives of BizBuilder. In order to achieve this, the framework has to provide a way for the service inquirers to query about the status of execution of an E-service, so that they can manage and control their workflow. The transaction adapter component is the transaction support interface intended for the service inquirers.

Support for Transaction Probes. An E-service should be able to participate in a workflow in which case it should support transaction specific queries like "how much of an activity is done?" or " What is the expected completion time?" etc. These types of queries can be raised by a workflow engine, which may use the service under discussion to perform an activity or a part of an activity within a workflow. Such queries and their result will help the workflow engine to dynamically modify or manage the execution of workflow. This sort of scenario can be applied to a fault-tolerant and a critical workflow process in which a failure in one service or activity of a complex workflow should not affect the whole workflow as such, instead the workflow should be able to dynamically find and utilize an alternate service.

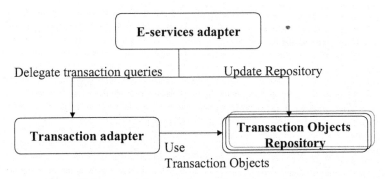

Fig. 4. E-Services Adapter – Transaction Adapter Interaction.

The Transaction adapter (in association with the E-services adapter) provides the necessary functionalities to handle these transaction probes or queries. The Transaction adapter uniquely identifies transaction queries, executes these queries on the corresponding objects in the transaction objects repository and generates suitable responses. It is also important to mention here that all transaction queries have to be ultimately answered by the service objects, since the objects are the ones that actually implement the service and know the status of the execution. BizBuilder provides this messaging infrastructure to query the service objects using the transaction probes.

3.5 Service Registration

The Service Registration modules provide the interface to the broker components, which serves as a central repository for storing details about the nature of services and the corresponding service-provider information. The service provider registers to a broker, all relevant information regarding an E-service that may be used for matchmaking or in search criterion. The broker architecture is based on the UDDI – Universal Description Discovery and Integration, a standard for service publishing and searching in the e-business domain. The UDDI architecture uses web-services description format named WSDL – Web Services Description Language, which in turn is based on XML to describe the interfaces of a service. Since our architecture needs a rich service description language for E-services, we chose to use the UDDI framework and the brokering community is built on top of it.

3.6 Negotiation and Contract Adapter

In order to provide a complete E-services framework, BizBuilder also includes support for Negotiation and Contracts. This module provides a simple negotiation framework, where the service inquirers can negotiate a particular E-service for usage. The Negotiation protocol is a synchronous protocol, in which the negotiating parties use a pre-defined data format to communicate messages. Once an agreement is reached upon the criterion in question (like cost, quantity etc), a contract is established and the service inquirers are bound to the contract. Support to modify existing contracts will be provided by these modules and the contracts once created are stored in persistence storage to be used later during actual service invocation.

4   Implementation

The core components of the BizBuilder framework have been implemented, which allows servlet-based E-services to be accessed using HTTP and XML. Suitable graphical interface tools are provided, using which, a service provider can create E-services from existing service implementation (in the form of java objects). The service provider can also register these E-services to an UDDI enabled broker.

Support is provided to browse the existing service templates with a broker, and register an implementation of the service under a service category of relevance.

4.1 Web-Server Framework

E-services by definition, should be accessible on the Internet using standard protocols and representation format. HTTP is the universally accepted protocol that is used in the e-commerce space. Hence, E-services should also be accessible using HTTP as the transport protocol. In order to enable this feature, BizBuilder uses the Servlet-HTTP framework provided by Tomcat-Apache server. Servlet based HTTP access is a natural choice, since servlets support java objects to be used seamlessly within them. Typically, every E-service that is enabled by the BizBuilder framework runs as a servlet process, when invoked using a Uniform Resource Identifier (URI). The Tomcat-Apache server launches a servlet thread for every request to complete its execution.

4.2 Service Invocation Using Java Reflection API

The ServiceInvocation module acts as an object management tool, because it is responsible for creating objects in memory, managing them by invoking the required methods on them and destroys them when they are not needed. This is the most fundamental facility that defines BizBuilder as an E-services framework.

All service invocations have to be performed on objects that are created or loaded in memory just in time when needed. This is significantly different from the usual client-server paradigm, where the server process knows about the objects to be loaded at compile time or the objects are pre-loaded. In BizBuilder, objects that are used to provide services can be added to the framework any time. This means the framework can be still be used for new objects without recompilation or modification, because using certain user-supplied information the BizBuilder framework will be able to load newly created objects and perform the required method invocation on them. This facility is possible only due to Java Reflection APIs, which are the run-time object introspection feature.

To perform a service invocation, the framework determines the object on which the service has to be invoked. This service to class name mapping is maintained as file information and it has to be constantly updated for new objects and services. Once the class to be used is discovered it can loaded using reflection API's. The service to be invoked and the parameter-values that are needed for the service invocation are obtained from the parser modules that parse the requests.

One crucial piece of information that is needed to perform the object invocation is the order of the parameters, since this is a run-time facility. So the parameter type (optionally) and order information is stored as a Service Signature Description SSD file that can be used by the framework. It is important to create such SSD files for new services or modify SSD files if the actual signature of the methods changes. A simple SSD description file for a service like ProcessOrder looks like the following.

Table 2. Structure of a SSD File.

Parameter Name	Parameter Type
UserID	String
MyOrder	Order

The above-depicted structure indicates that the ProcessOrder service has two parameters; the first parameter is UserID whose data type is String, and the second parameter is MyOrder whose data type is Order. In other words the method signature (without return type and exceptions) is indicated by this information. The parameter names indicated here are the same that are used while describing the service and registering them with the broker. The SSD file provides the semantics of the method, namely, it says how to treat the string (as an UserID in the above case), how to treat the second parameter and so on. The BizBuilder framework provides the necessary user interface for the service provider to take an existing object implementation (as a class file in java) and create the required SSD and other information required for using the new services.

The ServiceInvocation module uses these information to frame the exact method call and performs the invocation using reflection API's provided by Java. This technique of method invocation is not completely safe and secure, since no compile time error checking is possible and any errors would result in run-time exceptions. The ServiceInvocation module suitably handles any run-time errors that can occur, e.g., the user-provided value is not of the correct data type or format.

4.3 Support for User Defined Objects

While performing the actual E-service invocation, user-defined objects can be used apart from the basic data-types supported by java. The BizBuilder API converts this user-defined object into suitable XML representation that can be transported to the service provider. On the other end, the BizBuilder API provides support to construct this java object, from the XML representation and uses it to perform the actual method invocation on the java object. Though this support is provided only for user-defined objects in java, this will be extremely useful in scenarios where user-defined objects are extensively used to represent composite information (like Order, User-Info etc). The XML conversion is provided only for attributes of basic data types in Java and not for Java library data structures like Hashtable, Array etc. In other words, the user-defined objects in this case represent a collection of simple data types. So an order object with attributes {orderno = "O1055", itemno = "A4500", cost = 500} will be converted and represented in XML as follows.

XML representation of a Sample Order Object

```
<order>
  <orderno> O1055 </orderno>
  <itemno> A4500 </itemno>
```

```
<cost> 500 </cost>
</order>
```

4.4 Long-Running Services and Transaction Probes

The BizBuilder framework supports long-running services and transaction probes or queries by providing a transaction interface in java, which every service provider has to implement, in order to support long-running services and participate in workflows. The transaction interface includes methods like the following:

- *GetStatus* provides the current status of execution of the task or service; typical return values include status like expected completion in 2 hours,
- *IsComplete* queries whether the service has completed executing or returns the percentage of task completed; typical return values are 80% completed,
- *Query* is a general-purpose query message intended for the task (e.g., can the task be finished in 1 hour). These types of messages can be used to interact with a service during execution to perform activities like re-negotiation,
- *Tell* is a one-way notification message to the activity or the task,
- *Commit* is used to commit the execution of the current task or service,
- *Abort* stops the execution of the current task or service,
- *GetResult* provides the result of the current execution of the service or activity,
- *IsSynchronous* provides information on whether a service is synchronous or long running.

All of the above mentioned queries depend on the implementation and the current execution status of the service or the task. Only the actual service objects that implement the service can respond to these queries. Hence, all the above-mentioned queries are provided as a Java interface and the service provider is required to implement these interfaces in order to support or participate in workflows.

4.5 Support for E-Service Providers

The BizBuilder framework provides the tools and user-interface, using which the service provider can utilize existing java objects and create E-services. The process of creating the E-services is automated and is guided by the BizBuilder user-interface. The E-service creation process involves creating a set of files (like service-mapping, SSD files) to be used by the framework for service invocation. Apart from the BizBuilder tool, the service provider has to run a web-server (like Tomcat-Apache), to provide access to the E-services and register this URI (through which the services can be accessed) with the broker. A set of Java APIs is provided in order to programmatically utilize these E-services individually or within a workflow.

4.6 Brokering Interactions

The framework allows the service provider to register the E-services with a UDDI enabled brokering community. The service provider typically registers his business and identifies a business category and service template within which an E-service can be published. Once the template is identified, the E-service can be registered within the selected template. The templates maintained by the brokering community serves as a categorization mechanism for services. The framework provides suitable user-interface to facilitate the above process.

4.7 Overall Scenario of Operations

The various components that participate in a workflow scenario are the service providers (using the BizBuilder framework), the service inquirers and the service brokers. The workflow engine and the processing modules can be located in all or any or even none of the service provider and enquirers. The typical sequence of operations that occur in identifying and invoking a service is depicted in the following diagram.

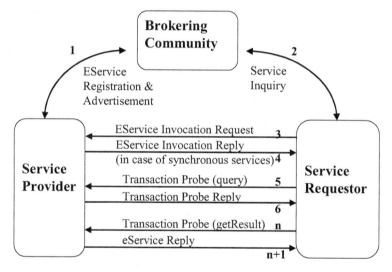

Fig. 5. Overall Sequence of Operations in BizBuilder Framework.

5 Conclusions and Future Work

The need for businesses to interoperate seamlessly has been well understood and E-services is a simple and powerful concept that can enable businesses achieve this goal. In this paper, we proposed the BizBuilder architecture, which enables the creation of these E-services that are based on XML and HTTP. The framework enables creating these E-services from existing non-Internet adaptive systems. These E-services are represented and utilized using SOAP, which is based on XML and hence are interoperable. The framework supports the E-services to explicitly participate in inter-organizational workflows seamlessly. Support for advertising the E-services to a UDDI enabled broker is also provided in the architecture.

The BizBuilder framework currently supports only Java objects; this support can be extended to include legacy systems and other object implementations like CORBA, COM etc. Also service description can be extended to include service constraints to enable better matchmaking of services. Licensing and usage tracking of services is another useful feature that could be supported.

References

1. Kuno, H., "Surveying the E-Services Technical Landscape", HP Labs, 2000
2. Casati, F., Ilnicki, S., Jin, L., Krishnamoorthy, V., Shan, M., "eFlow: a Platform for Developing and Managing Composite e-Services", HP Labs, 2000
3. Web Services, IBM, http://www-106.ibm.com/developerworks/library/w-ovr/
4. Vasudevan, V., Bannon, T., "WebTrader: Discovery and Programmed Access to Web Based Services, Object Services and Consulting Inc., 1998
5. Paul, S., Park, E., Chaar, J., "RainMan: A Workflow System for the Internet", IBM T.J. Watson Research Center, 1997
6. Helal, A., Wang, M., Jagatheesan, A., Krithivasan, R., "Brokering based Self Organizing e-Service Communities", Proceedings of the Fifth International Symposium on Autonomous Decentralized Systems with an emphasis on Electronic Commerce, Dallas, 2001
7. Dan, A., Dias, D., Nguyen, T., Sachs, M., Shaikh, H., King, R., Duri, S., "The Coyote Project: Framework for Multi-party E-Commerce", Proceeding of the 7th Delos Workshop on Electronic Commerce, Greece, 1998
8. Mennie, D., Pagurek, B., "An architecture to support Dynamic Composition of Service Components"
9. Jagatheesan, A., Helal, A., "Architecture and protocols for Sangam Communities", Internal Report accessible from http://www.harris.cise.ufl.edu/projects/e-services.htm
10. Fingar, P., Kumar, H., Sharma, T., "Enterprise E-Commerce", Meghan-Kiffer Press, ISBN 0-929652-11-8, 2000
11. Meng, J., Su, S., Lam, H., Helal, A., "Achieving Dynamic Inter-organizational Workflow Management by Integrating Business Processes, Events, and Rules," Internal Report accessible from http://www.harris.cise.ufl.edu/projects/e-services.htm, 2001

Peer-to-Peer Traced Execution
of Composite Services

Marie-Christine Fauvet[1][*], Marlon Dumas[2],
Boualem Benatallah[1], and Hye-Young Paik[1]

[1] School of Computer Science & Engineering
The University of New South Wales, Sydney NSW 2052, Australia
[2] Cooperative Information Systems Research Centre
Queensland University of Technology, GPO Box 2434, Brisbane QLD 4001, Australia
{mcfauvet,boualem,hpaik}@cse.unsw.edu.au,m.dumas@qut.edu.au
http://www.cse.unsw.edu.au/~{mcfauvet,boualem,hpaik}
http://www.fit.qut.edu.au/~dumas

Abstract. The connectivity generated by the Internet is opening unprecedented opportunities of automating business-to-business collaborations. As a result, organisations of all sizes are forming online alliances in order to deliver integrated value-added services. Unfortunately, due to a lack of tools and methodologies offering an adequate level of abstraction, the development of these integrated services is currently ad hoc and requires a considerable effort of low-level programming, especially when dealing with coordination, communication, and execution tracing issues. In this paper, we present a framework through which business services can be declaratively composed, and the resulting composite services can be executed in a fully traceable manner. The traces of a composite service executions are collected incrementally through peer-to-peer interactions between the involved providers. Once collected, these traces are stored as linked objects in distributed repositories, which are made available for auditing, customer feedback and quality assessment.

1 Introduction

The rapidly growing number of organisations that are making their services accessible through the web, has resulted in a paradigm shift that is gradually transforming the Internet from a repository of information into a vehicle of services. This phenomenon should in turn generate a shift in focus away from the well-known issue of information integration, to the largely unexplored one of service integration. In particular, as new kinds of business intermediaries emerge, it is expected that the practice of developing new services from existing ones (i.e. service composition) will gain a considerable momentum, both as a means to facilitate Business-to-Consumer interactions, and as a foundation to foster Business-to-Business collaborations.

Unfortunately, due to a lack of tools and methodologies offering an adequate level of abstraction, the composition of services is currently done through

---

[*] On leave from LSR-IMAG, University of Grenoble, France.

F. Casati, D. Georgakopoulos, M.-C. Shan (Eds.): TES 2001, LNCS 2193, pp. 103–117, 2001.

ad-hoc assemblages of manifold technologies, which often require a considerable effort of low-level programming. As a contribution to the development of higher-level abstractions for service composition, we present in this paper a platform (namely Self-Serv) through which Internet-accessible services provided by different organisations can be declaratively composed, and the resulting *composite services* can be executed in a fully *traceable* way, following a *decentralised* paradigm, and within a *dynamic* environment. By decentralised paradigm, we mean that the providers participating in a composite service orchestrate the overall execution through peer-to-peer interactions, instead of being dependent on a centralised scheduler, which could constitute a bottleneck. By dynamic environment, we mean that a composite service is not bound to a particular set of service providers. Instead, an organisation participating in the provisioning of a composite service, is free to interrupt its participation without blocking the availability of the composite service. Similarly, new organisations may decide to provide a particular constituent of a composite service in future executions of it.

Tracing past and ongoing executions is an essential requirement in the area of business process management. Organisations need to track down their activities in order to ensure explainability in case of failure or auditing, and to revise also their practices both for increasing their efficiency, and for improving their customers' satisfaction. Similarly, as organisations form alliances to deliver composite services, the need for tracing the executions of these services will become an increasingly important issue. Traces of service executions can be queried for the following purposes (among others):

Performance Evaluation: to make a report on past service executions. A typical query for this purpose would be *"Retrieve the constituents of a composite service whose execution takes the most time in average"*.

Customer Feedback: to explain specific failures. A query for this context would be *"Retrieve the traces of all the service executions that have been triggered for a given client"*.

Quality Assessment: to detect services whose executions tend to fail, like for example in *"Retrieve the executions of a given service that were frozen at some point for more than 30 minutes, and were cancelled after this period of inactivity"*.

More generally, the question of knowing who did what, is central in a dynamic environment. By querying the traces, the provider of a composite service can audit executions of its constituent services, in order to check, for example, the validity of the bills that are issued by their providers.

Given that in Self-Serv the executions of a composite service are carried out in a decentralised manner, it would be inconsistent to collect their traces through direct communication between the providers of each constituent service and a centralised entity: an approach which creates a potential bottleneck. Instead, in Self-Serv, the collection of traces is carried out through peer-to-peer exchange of partial traces between the providers participating in a composite service. The resulting traces are then stored in a decentralised manner: each provider being responsible for storing the traces of its own activities. These distributed traces are connected through universal references (e.g. URLs), in such a way that upon request, it is possible to retrieve all the details of the execution of a composite service.

The remainder of the paper is organised as follows. In section 2 we describe our approach to service composition using statecharts. Section 3 discusses the collaborative execution of services, which is then extended in section 4 to cater for tracing. Finally, section 5 gives an overview of related work and Section 6 provides some concluding remarks.

2 Composite Service Specification

This section introduces the composition model of Self-Serv. We begin with some definitions, before overviewing the statechart formalism and discussing how it is applied to composite service specification. Finally, we conclude with an example.

2.1 Description of the Approach

Each service within Self-Serv, provides an interface enabling its instantiation and the subsequent execution of the resulting *service instance*. In other words, the interface of a service defines operators such as *instantiate, start, freeze, cancel*, etc., and describes the protocol for invoking each operation, passing its input parameters, and collecting its outputs. This protocol can be based on remote method invocation (e.g. Java RMI [15]) or message exchange (e.g. SOAP [13]).

Self-Serv distinguishes *elementary services* from *composite services*. Elementary services are pre-existing (e.g. legacy) services, whose instances' execution are entirely under the responsibility of an entity called *service provider*. The provisioning of an elementary service may involve a complex business process, but its internals are hidden behind the composite service's interface: the user of an elementary service has no information about how it is implemented.

A composite service on the other hand, is an aggregation of elementary and other composite services, which are referred to as its *constituents*. The semantics of this aggregation can be described from at least three perspectives: (i) The *control-flow perspective* establishes the order in which the constituents are invoked, the signals that may interrupt their execution, etc. (ii) The *provider perspective* gives an organisational anchor to the composite service by establishing which entity is responsible for performing which service. (iii) The *data exchange perspective* captures both the flow of data between services, and the conversion of these data between the potentially heterogeneous data models used by the services participating in the composition.

We have chosen to model the control-flow perspective of composite services through statecharts [5], since they provide the basic constructs found in business process modelling tools (e.g. Workflow Management Systems [8]) while still possessing a formal semantics, which is essential for reasoning about composite service specifications. Moreover, statecharts are becoming a standard process-modelling language as they have been integrated into the UML [11].

A statechart is made up of states and transitions. Transitions are optionally labelled by ECA rules. The occurrence of an event fires a transition if (i) the machine is in the source state of the transition, (ii) the type of the event occurrence matches the event description attached to the transition, and (iii) the condition of the transition holds. When a transition fires, its action part is executed and its target state is entered. The event, condition and action part of a transition are all optional. A transition without an event part is said to be *triggerless*. States can be simple or compound. In our approach, a simple state corresponds to the execution of a service, whether it is elementary or composite. Accordingly, each simple state is labelled by a description of a service offer, and the set of parameters that are to be passed to this service upon instantiation. When a basic state is entered, the service that labels it is invoked. The state is normally exited through one of its triggerless transitions, when the execution of the service is completed. If the state has outgoing transitions labelled with events, an occurrence of one of these events provokes the state to be exited, even if the corresponding service execution is ongoing (i.e. this execution is cancelled). Compound states on the other hand, are not directly labelled by a service invocation. Instead, they contain one or several entire statecharts within them. A compound state that contains two or more statecharts (separated by dashed lines), is called an AND-state. The statecharts within an AND-state are intended to be executed concurrently.

The reader can find a comprehensive description of statecharts in [5]. The example in section 2.2 provides a few intuitive notions about statecharts.

The provider perspective is modelled by associating an organisational entity to each service offer. In other words, the concept of service offer in Self-Serv encompasses both: what has to be done? and who has to do it? The organisational entity associated with a service can be either an individual provider or a community of providers. In the former case, the designated provider is responsible for executing all the instances of this service. It may eventually partially or totally delegate the execution of these instances to another provider, but this delegation is hidden to the users of the composite service. On the other hand, a community of providers will systematically and *transparently* delegate the execution of a service to its members. This delegation is carried out by the *representative* of the community. The means by which a community's representative chooses a member to execute a request, is specified via a *selection policy*. It can be based on a 1-N negotiation protocol (e.g. an auction), or on any ranking algorithm involving parameters such as the customer's profile, the provider's reliability, etc., as discussed in [2,1].

2.2 Example

As a working example, we consider the composite service "Travel Solutions" described in Figure 1. This composite service aggregates several independent services like flight booking, car rental, event attendance planner, etc. It starts with an invocation of a flight booking service (FB) followed by an invocation of an accommodation booking service (AB). A service that searches for tourist attractions (AS) is executed concurrently with the former two. After all these services (AS, FB and AB) are completed, and based on how far the selected accommodation is from the major attractions, either a car rental service (CB), or a bicycle hire service (BB) is executed. Upon completion of either of these two services, a service which searches for special events occurring during the stay of the user is invoked. This service is itself a composite service aggregating a services that searches for special events, and another that prepurchases tickets for these events.

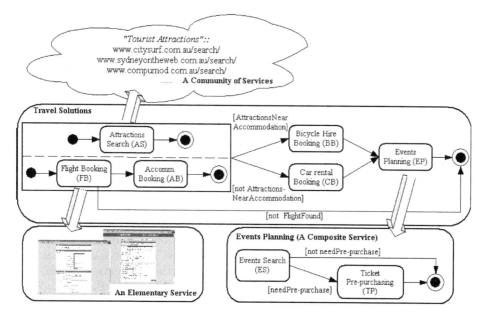

Fig. 1. The "Travel Solutions" Composite Service.

A constituent of a composite service can be assigned to an individual provider, or to a community of providers. For example, in Figure 1, the flight booking is assigned to a web site, that does not delegate its task to any other entity. Meanwhile, the service that searches for attractions is assigned to a community of providers. This community federates entities such as public tourism offices, and private tourism information sites. When an execution request is addressed to the community, its representative forwards it to one of its members.

3   Composite Service Execution

In Self-Serv, the coordination between the constituents of a composite service is ensured through peer-to-peer collaboration between software components, hosted by the providers participating in the composition. This approach provides greater scalability and availability than a centralised one where the execution of a service depends on a central scheduler. In this section, we introduce the two basic concepts of Self-Serv's execution model: service wrappers and state coordinators, and we discuss how they are integrated into Self-Serv's architecture.

3.1   Description of the Approach

Service Wrappers. Each service, whether elementary or composite, is *wrapped* by a software component hosted by its provider. A service's wrapper provides an implementation of its interface, that is, it implements functions such as *instantiate, start, cancel,* etc., and it handles conversions between the data model of the service's interface (based on e.g. SOAP [13]), and that of its implementation (based on e.g. a proprietary C++ API). A service's wrapper therefore acts as its entry point, in the sense that it handles requests for executing the service.

State Coordinators. Each state ST in a composite service's statechart is represented at runtime by a *coordinator*, which is responsible for: (i) Initiating the execution of the service labelling ST whenever all the preconditions are met. (ii) Notifying the completion of this execution to the coordinators of the states which potentially need to be entered next. (iii) While state ST is active, receive notifications of external events, determine if ST should be exited because of these event occurrences, and if so, interrupt the service execution if it is ongoing, and notify the interruption to the coordinators of the states which potentially need to be entered next.

In other words, the coordinator of a state is a lightweight scheduler which determines: (i) when should a state within a statechart be entered?, (ii) What should be done after the state is entered?, (iii) When should it be exited, and (iv) What should be done after it is exited. The coordinators of a composite service are hosted by the providers of its constituents. The provider of a service is responsible for hosting as many coordinators as there are states which are labelled by it. For instance, in figure 2 service A is associated to three coordinators named Coord.A.1, Coord.A.2 and Coord.A.3 because it is involved in three different service compositions.

Peer-to-Peer Service Execution. When the wrapper of a composite service CS processes a request for executing CS (i.e. when it receives a message CS.run(...)) it sends a message to each of the coordinator(s) of the state(s) which need to be entered the first, as indicated by the service's statechart. For the sake of simplicity, let us assume that there is only one such "first" state. The coordinator of this state performs the service invocation which labels its state by sending an invocation message to the corresponding service wrapper. Once the invocation induced by this invocation is completed, the coordinator of the first state sends a notification of completion to the coordinator(s) of the states which need to be entered the next, which in turn perform the service invocation(s) labelling its/their state(s). This peer-to-peer interaction continues until eventually the coordinators of the states which need to be exited the last, send their notifications of completion back to the wrapper of CS, thereby signalling the completion of the overall execution.

Service Description. The knowledge required by each coordinator participating in a composite service execution, is statically extracted from the service's statechart by the *service description module* of the Self-Serv system. Specifically, the composite service designer (or service composer) assembles service offers advertised in a repository of services through the service description module. This module then generates and deploys the corresponding composite service state coordinators. Once the service is deployed and assigned to a provider, users, application programs, and even state coordinators belonging to other composite services, can invoke it through its wrapper. Figure 2 summarises this process.

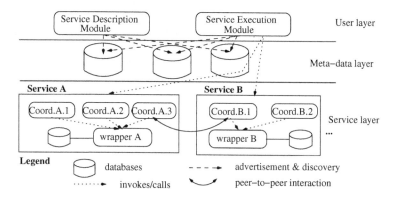

Fig. 2. Partial View of Self-Serv's Architecture for Composite Service Management.

Extracting the knowledge required by a state coordinator from a composite service's statechart, involves answering the following questions: what are the preconditions for entering a state?, When the execution associated to a state is completed or interrupted by a signal?, Which are the states that may need to be entered next? The process by which a coordinator notifies that its state is being exited to the relevant peer coordinators is called *postprocessing*.

The preconditions for entering a state ST are represented by a table whose elements denote rules of the form E[C] such that: (i) E is a conjunction of events of the form ready(ST), meaning that a notification of completion has been received from the coordinator attached to state ST and (ii) C is a conjunction of conditions appearing in the labels of the statechart's transitions. When one of the elements of the preconditions table is triggered, and that its condition evaluates to true, the state is entered, and the service that appears on its label is invoked.

The postprocessings that have to be undertaken when a state is exited are presented as a table whose elements denote rules of the form [C]/A where: (i) C is a conjunction of conditions appearing in the labels of the statechart's transitions and (ii) A is a term of the form notify(ST), meaning that a notification of completion has to be sent to the coordinator associated to the state ST.

The following examples of preconditions and postprocessings tables refer to Figure 1.

- Preconditions(EP) = { ready(CB)[true], ready(BB)[true] }, meaning that the state is entered when a message is received from either the coordinator of the state CB or that BB.
- Preconditions(CB) = { ready(AB) ∧ ready(AS)[not attractions near accommodation] }.

- Postprocessing(ES) = { [need pre-purchase]/notify(TP), [not need pre-pur-chase]/notify(wrapper) }.
- Postprocessing(AS) = { [true]/notify(CB), [true]/notify(BB) }.

Notice that the condition "attractions near accommodation" is not evaluated before undertaking the postprocessing action notify(BB). This is because evaluating this condition requires the coordinator to know where is the selected accommodation located, and this is only known once the accommodation booking is completed.

Algorithms for deriving the preconditions and the postprocessing for state coordinators of a composite service are detailed in [1].

3.2   Example

To illustrate how the coordinators and the wrappers are deployed, and how they interact, we consider the "Travel Solutions" service described in Figure 1. We assume that this composite service is provided by a company named "Full Tours". The life-cycle of the service starts when a service designer within this company defines the structure of the service using Self-Serv's service description module. This module configures a set of software components implementing the coordinators required to run the composite service. It also assists the designer in deploying the wrapper in one of the servers of "Full Tours", and the coordinators in the dedicated servers provided by the companies referenced in the composite service definition. Once the deployment is completed, the composite service is advertised and can be invoked through its wrapper.

When the wrapper of the "Travel Solutions" service receives an execution request, it sends a message to the coordinators of the states labelled FB and AS (see Figure 1). Upon receiving these messages, these coordinators invoke the services labelling their states. When the service that books a flight completes its execution, the coordinator of the state FB sends a message to that of the state AB. This latter invokes the service that books an accommodation, waits for its completion, and sends a message to the coordinators of the states CB and BB. In the meanwhile, the coordinator of AS sends its completion message to the co-ordinators of CB and BB too. These completion messages contain the data that must be exchanged between these services, as per the data exchange perspective of the "Travel Solutions" specification. Using these data, the coordinators of BB and CB evaluate the condition "attractions near accommodation" appearing in the labels of their incoming transitions, and accordingly, they decide which state has to be entered. Assuming that the attractions are far from the accommodation, it is the state CB that has to be entered, so the corresponding coordinator invokes the service for renting a car. Once this service completes its execution, the same coordinator sends a message to the coordinator of the state EP, who sends an execution request to the wrapper of the composite service responsible for searching events. This wrapper initiates the execution of the service that it provides, by sending a message to the coordinator of the state ES, which invokes the service that searches events, waits for its completion, and assuming that tickets for some of the events need to be prepurchased, sends a message to the coordinator of the state TP. This coordinator then invokes the service that purchases tickets, and upon completion, sends a notification to the wrapper of the Event Planning service, which in turn sends a notification to the coordinator of the state EP. Finally, this coordinator sends a message to the wrapper of the "Travel Solutions" service, thereby concluding the overall execution.

4 Service Execution Tracing

In this section we introduce the mechanisms provided by Self-Serv for keeping trace of past executions of composite services. This functionality is essential for customer support and feedback (i.e. retrieving a given service execution) as well as for detecting deficiencies in the constitution of a composite service (i.e. analysing the past executions of a service in order to retrieve repetitive malfunctionings). First (section 4.1), we describe a model for representing the service execution traces. In section 4.2 we introduce the mechanisms for collecting and storing traces. Section 4.3 illustrates our approach.

4.1 Modelling Service Execution Traces

Simplifying Assumptions. For the sake of simplicity, we assume in the sequel that the local coordinators and the wrapper of a composite service share a common time line. This can be achieved using classical clock synchronisation protocols such as NTP [6]. We also assume that all temporal values (instants, durations and intervals), are expressed at the same level of granularity (e.g., the Second or the Minute). Under this assumption, instants and durations are unambiguously designed using integers, while an interval is fully represented as a pair of integers corresponding to its bounds.

Life-Cycle of a Service Instance. At a given instant, an instance of a service can be in one of the following statuses: *running, frozen, completed, cancelled* and so on. The life-cycles of a service instances are controlled by a statechart which describes possible statuses and allowed transitions between them. Transitions are only labelled by events. Life-cycle statecharts are hosted by wrappers and may be customised in order to capture particularities of the service. This customisation is operated by the "service composer".

Status History. A status history is a trace of the life-cycle of a service instance, that is, the statuses through which this instance went, and the times of the transitions. At an abstract level a status history is defined as a function from a set of instants to a set of status values. At a concrete level a status history can be effectively represented by an ordered set of interval-timestamped statuses.

Service Execution. A service execution models the information about a particular service instance that is made persistent by the wrapper of the service after the instance has been executed (i.e. after it has attained its "completed" or its "cancelled" state). Concretely, a service execution is composed of (i) a status history, (ii) a set of effective input and output parameters, and (iii) the individual provider to whom the instance's execution was assigned. This last information is essential when the provider specification of a service refers to a community.

In addition to the above three properties, a composite service execution is associated with the set of references to the other service executions that it triggered. For example, if a composite service CS involves the execution of two services S1 and S2 one after the other, then each of the service executions of CS is associated with a service execution of S1, and a service execution of S2.

The information above is modelled by a class named ServiceExecution with two sub-classes ElemServiceExecution and CompServiceExecution. For each execution of an elementary (resp. composite) service, an instance of ElemServiceExecution (resp. CompServiceExecution) is created. For a full description of these classes see [1].

4.2   Collecting and Storing Execution Traces

The responsibility of tracing the executions of a composite service CS is distributed across the wrapper and the local coordinators of this service.

The coordinator of a state ST belonging to the statechart describing CS, is responsible for:

- Receiving information about ongoing executions of CS in the form of collections of references to objects of the class ServiceExecution. The actual content of these objects are stored in repositories managed by the providers participating in the composite service.
- Obtaining a reference to an object of the class ServiceExecution from the wrapper of the service labeling the state ST. This reference is an URL containing both the address of the repository where the value of the object is stored, and the identifier of this object.
- Adding this new reference to the collection of references received from the other coordinators.
- When the state is exited, passing the new collection of references to the coordinators of the states that need to be entered next, or to the wrapper of CS if no state needs to be entered next.

More precisely, when an instance of a composite service CS starts its execution, the wrapper of CS sends the identifier of this instance to the coordinators of the states that need to be entered first. Let us suppose here that there is only one initial state that we call ST, and that this state is labelled by an invocation to a service called S. The coordinator of ST then contacts the wrapper of S, asking it to perform the required invocation. The wrapper of S performs the invocation, and collects information about the parameters passed, the start and end time of the execution induced by this invocation, and the identity of the *individual* provider that carried out this execution (in the case where the service is offered by a community). With this information, the wrapper of S creates an object of the class ServiceExecution that it stores in a repository maintained by the provider of service S (or the representative, if S is provided by a community). A universal reference (e.g. an URL) to this newly stored object is then created, and passed to the coordinator of ST, which then adds it to an empty collection and passes this collection (with one reference) to the coordinator(s) of the state(s) that need(s) to be executed the next (which is determined using the postprocessing table as discussed in section 3). The coordinator(s) to which this reference is passed, perform(s) a similar operation. On the end, the coordinator(s) of the final states of the composite service, pass(es) its/their collection of references to the wrapper of CS, which stores this collection in a repository maintained by the provider of CS. When a user wishes to query the traces of a composite service, (s)he send her/his query to the wrapper of CS. Should the query need some of the universal references to be resolved, the wrapper of CS will contact the repositories where the data is stored, and poll the actual values of the referenced objects.

As an optimisation aiming at reducing the number of messages exchanged for collecting traces, when an AND-state needs to be entered, the data about the execution trace *before* entering this state is not sent to all the initial states of all of the concurrent threads, but rather to the coordinators of the states that will be entered after the AND-state is exited. Indeed, duplicating this partial execution trace is useless, since when this AND-state will be exited, the traces collected by all its threads will be merged anyway. Let us consider the composite service described by the statechart depicted in figure 3. When S1 finishes, instead of passing the partial trace to each initial state of the AND-state, it sends it straight to S2.

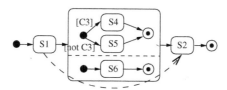

Fig. 3. S1 Sends Its Partial Trace to S2.

4.3   Back to the Example

To illustrate how traces are collected, let us consider the composite service "Travel Solutions" described in Figure 1. We show in Figure 4 one execution of this service. We only show the sequence of statuses through which the service instance goes during its execution, thereby omitting details about their actual parameters and providers. Without loss of generality, we assume that the execution TS_e starts at instant 1.

The following notations are used in Figure 4. TS_e denotes a particular execution of the composite service "Travel Solution" (TS), AB_e a particular execution of service "Accommodation Booking" (AB), and so on. In other words, for each service TS, AS, FB, AB, CB, BB, ES and TP, the suffix _e is added to its name in order to denote one of its executions. A double-arrow ⟷ is used to denote the interval during which the associated service was running, and finally completed.

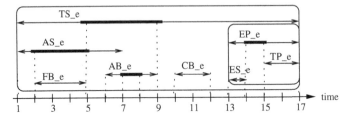

Fig. 4. Execution Details of One Instance of the Service "Travel Solutions".

A thicker part of the arrow means that during the underlying period, the service is frozen.

A detailed view of the messages exchanged during the execution of TS_e is given in table 1. Each line in the table contains the time at which message was sent, the sender, the recipient, and the content of the message as well.

Table 1. Messages between Coordinators During the Execution of TS_e.

Time	From coordinator of	To coordinator of	Content
5	FB	AB	{FB_e}
7	AS	BB and CB	{AS_e}
9	AB	BB and CB	{FB_e, AB_e}
12	CB	EP	{FB_e, AB_e} ∪ {AS_e} ∪ {CB_e}
17	EP	wrapper	{FB_e, AB_e, AS_e} ∪ {EP_e}

For the sake of simplicity, we assume that there is no delay between the moment when a service finishes and the moment when the associated coordinator sends the partial trace to the next one. A symbol of the form X_e (X ∈ {FB, AS, AB, CB, EP}) denotes an instance of the class ServiceExecution, that describes an execution of service X. X_e is created by X's coordinator at the beginning of X's execution.

The 2nd and 3rd lines of the table 1 can be read as follows. At time 7 (resp. 9) AS's coordinator (resp. AB) sends the partial trace to both BB's coordinator and CB's coordinator. Because the boolean expression [Attractions near from accommodation] is evaluated to false, BB is not required to be executed, so the coordinator of the state that it labels discards the partial traces that were sent to it by the coordinators of AS and AB. Because the state labelled by the EP is the last one to be entered, at time 17 its coordinator sends the whole trace to the wrapper of the service TS.

5   Related Work

The issue of service composition, and the related field of inter-organisational workflows, have been the subject of intensive attention in the last years. Here, we focus on those efforts dealing with the aspects addressed in this paper, that is, coordination between services, and execution tracing.

CMI [12] and eFlow [3] are two pioneering systems for specifying, enacting, and monitoring composite services. In both of these systems, the underlying execution model is based on a centralised process engine, responsible for scheduling, dispatching, and controlling the execution of all the instances of a composite service. Clearly, this centralised approach leads to potential bottlenecks, that are avoided in Self-Serv through the use of a peer-to-peer coordination paradigm.

Closer to the decentralised spirit of Self-Serv is CPM [4]. This platform supports the execution of inter-organisational business processes through peer-to-peer collaboration between a set of workflow engines. The major difference between CPM's and Self-Serv's execution models, is that in CPM, the number of messages exchanged between the workflow engines is not optimised. Instead, each time that a process terminates a given task, it must send a notification to all its other peer processes. Moreover, CPM requires that all the players participating in an inter-organisational process, deploy the same workflow engine, since they all need to interpret a single global process specification. Meanwhile, in Self-Serv the inter-service coordination is entirely handled by the state coordinators.

Self-Serv's execution model has also some similarities with that of Mentor [10], although this latter proposal is targeted to intra-organisational workflow management. Specifically, the problem addressed in [10] is that of distributing the execution of workflows expressed as state and activity charts. Mentor's approach differs from Self-Serv's, in that it is only applicable when the assignment of activities to their executing entities is known at the definition of the workflow, which is a restrictive assumption in the context of service composition. Moreover, as in CPM, Mentor imposes that each organisation participating in a distributed workflow deploys a full-fledged execution engine.

None of the above proposals explicitly addresses the issue of tracing the executions of a composite service. Actually, we are not aware of any concrete proposal in the area of composite service execution tracing, except for [7] and [9] which address a similar issue: that of tracing the executions of a workflow. [7] assumes that the workflows are executed in a distributed environment, and that each node within this environment (in our context: each provider), maintains the history of its task executions (in our context: its service executions). Within this context, the authors present several strategies for evaluating queries such as "retrieve the history of a given process instance". Unlike our proposal, the set of entities participating in the execution of a workflow is assumed to be fixed.

Our approach also differs from the above in that in Self-Serv, universal references are used to link the abstractions of the trace maintained by the composite service wrapper, and the actual details of these traces which are maintained by the providers participating in the composition. Meanwhile, in [7], there are no equivalent concepts to those of "composite service wrapper" and "universal reference". Consequently, the traces are entirely distributed among the entities participating in a workflow, and they are only linked through logical references (i.e. foreign keys). This imposes a considerable overhead during query evaluation, since the resolution of these logical references requires the distributed computation of expensive joins.

In [9] the context is that of centralised workflows expressed as statecharts. The authors focus on demonstrating that the process of tracing a workflow's execution can itself be seen as a workflow. Consequently, by merging a workflow **W**, with the workflow dedicated to maintaining the history **W**'s executions, one obtains a "self-traceable workflow". Contrarily to our proposal however, [9] does not discuss how these results can be extended to a distributed and interorganisational workflow, neither does it address the issue of distributedly storing the execution traces.

6   Conclusion and Future Work

We presented an approach to model service composition, in which a composite service is defined as an aggregation of other composite and elementary services, whose dependencies are described through a statechart. The provider of a service, whether elementary or composite, can be either an individual entity, or a community of entities. In this latter case, the choice of the individual entity within the community which is in charge of executing a given instance of the service, is delayed until run-time, thereby supporting dynamic provider selection.

We then proposed an execution model for composite services, in which the providers of the services participating in a composition, collaborate in a peer-to-peer fashion in order to ensure that the control-flow dependencies expressed by the schema of the composite service are respected. Specifically, the responsibility of coordinating the providers participating in a composite service execution, is distributed across several lightweight software components hosted by the providers themselves. In this way, the execution of a composite service is not dependent on a central scheduler, which could constitute a potential bottleneck.

The above collaboration model has been extended so that the state coordinators are able to incrementally collect the execution trace of each composite service instance. These traces are then stored as distributed objects linked through universal references, in such a way that each participant in a composite service is responsible for storing the trace of its own activities, while the provider of the composite service stores an abstracted view of the overall execution. We plan to extend this first attempt to model and query traces in order to address issues such as querying ongoing execution of e-services (i.e., querying the traces of service instances while they are still running).

We are currently developing an implementation of Self-Serv in which the service wrappers and the state coordinators generated by the service description module are packaged as Enterprise JavaBeans (EJB) [14], which interact through a communication layer based on SOAP [13]. Execution traces will be stored and queried as XML documents. References between the execution trace of a composite service and the traces of its triggered constituents can be modelled through URLs.

Our next step will be to examine how modifications in the constitution of a composite service can be smoothly handled in Self-Serv. We also plan to investigate how to augment state coordinators with data integration mechanisms so as to handle explicit data-flow dependencies.

References

1. B. Benatallah, M. Dumas, M.-C. Fauvet, and H.-Y. Paik. Self-coordinated and self-traced composite services with dynamic provider selection. Technical report, The University of New South Wales, School of Computer Science & Engineering, 2001. Available at `http://www.cse.unsw.edu.au/~mcfauvet/selfserv.ps.gz`.
2. B. Benatallah, B. Medjahed, A. Bouguettaya, A. Elmagarmid, and J. Beard. Composing and maintaining web-based virtual enterprises. In *Workshop on Technologies for E-Services*, Cairo, Egypt, September 2000.
3. F. Casati, S. Ilnicki, L.-J. Jin, V. Krishnamoorthy, and M.-C. Shan. Adaptive and dynamic service composition in eFlow. In *Proc. of the Int. Conference on Advanced Information Systems Engineering (CAiSE)*, Stockholm, Sweden, June 2000. Springer Verlag.
4. Q. Chen and M. Hsu. Inter-enterprise collaborative business process management. In *Proc. of the Int. Conference on Data Engineering (ICDE)*, Heidelberg, Germany, April 2001. IEEE Press.
5. D. Harel and A. Naamad. The STATEMATE semantics of statecharts. *ACM Transactions on Software Engineering and Methodology*, 5(4):293–333, October 1996.
6. Internet RFC-1305. Network Time Protocol Specification Version 3. `http://www.landfield.com/rfcs/rfc1305.html`.
7. P. Koksal, S.N. Arpinar, and A. Dogac. Workflow history management. *SIGMOD Record*, 27(1):67–75, January 1998.
8. F. Leymann and D. Roller. *Production Workflow: Concepts and Techniques*. Prentice Hall, Upper Saddle River, NJ, USA, 2000.
9. P. Muth, J. Weissenfels, M. Gillmann, and G. Weikum. Workflow history management in virtual enterprises using a lightweight workflow management system. In *Proc. of the Workshop on Research Issues in Data Engineering (RIDE)*. IEEE Press, March 1999.
10. P. Muth, D. Wodtke, J. Weissenfels, A.K. Dittrich, and G. Weikum. From centralized workflow specification to distributed workflow execution. *Journal of Intelligent Information Systems*, 10(2), March 1998.
11. J. Rumbaugh, I. Jacobson, and G. Booch. *The Unified Modeling Language reference manual*. Addison-Wesley, 1999.
12. H. Schuster, D. Georgakopoulos, A. Cichocki, and D. Baker. Modeling and composing service-based and reference process-based multi-enterprise processes. In *Proc. of the Int. Conference on Advanced Information Systems Engineering (CAiSE)*, Stockholm, Sweden, June 2000. Springer Verlag.
13. SQLData. Simple Object Access Protocol. `http://www.soapclient.com`.
14. Sun Microsystems Inc. Enterprise JavaBeans Specifications. `http://www.javasoft.com/products/ejb/`.
15. Sun Microsystems Inc. Java RMI. `http://java.sun.com/products/jdk/rmi`.

Supporting Reliable Transactional Business Processes by Publish/Subscribe Techniques*

Christoph Schuler, Heiko Schuldt, and Hans-Jörg Schek

Institute of Information Systems
Swiss Federal Institute of Technology (ETH)
ETH Zentrum, 8092 Zürich, Switzerland
{schuler,schuldt,schek}@inf.ethz.ch

Abstract. Processes have increasingly become an important design principle for complex intra- and inter-organizational e-services. In particular, processes allow to provide value-added services by seamlessly combining existing e-services into a coherent whole, even across corporate boundaries. Process management approaches support the definition and the execution of predefined processes as distributed applications. They ensure that execution guarantees are observed even in the presence of failures and concurrency. The implementation of a process management execution environment is a challenging task in several aspects. First, the processes to be executed are not necessarily static and follow a predefined pattern but must be generated dynamically (e.g., choosing the best offer in a pre-sales interaction). Second, deferring the execution of some application services in case of overload or unavailability is often not acceptable and must be avoided by exploiting replicated services or even by automatically adding such services, and by monitoring and balancing the load. Third, in order to avoid a bottleneck at the process coordinator level, a centralized implementation must be avoided as much as possible. Hence, a framework is needed which supports both the modularization of the process coordinator's functionality and the flexibility needed for dynamically generating and adopting processes. In this paper we show how publish/subscribe techniques can be used for the implementation of process management. We show how the overall architecture looks like when using a computer cluster and publish/subscribe components as the basic infrastructure to drive the enactment of processes. In particular we describe how load balancing, process navigation, failure handling, and process monitoring is supported with minimal intervention of a centralized coordinator.

1 Introduction

E-services are, in general, complex sequences of individual steps needed to achieve some business task. They are not necessarily restricted to be executed within

---

* Part of this work has been funded by the Swiss National Science Foundation under the project INVENT.

F. Casati, D. Georgakopoulos, M.-C. Shan (Eds.): TES 2001, LNCS 2193, pp. 118–131, 2001.

a single system but may rather be distributed, both physically and organizationally. Such complex e-services can be found in b2c (business-to-customer) as well as in b2b (business-to-business) interactions, thereby even allowing to cross corporate boundaries by combining existing e-services.

Processes have increasingly become an important design principle for complex intra- and inter-organizational e-services since they seamlessly allow to encompass the individual constraints that can be found in e-services by means of control and data flow dependencies between single process steps. Most existing process coordinators require that the individual steps of a process have to be defined at built-time. E-services being characterized by such static processes can be found, for instance, in e-commerce payment interactions [CST95,PSS00]. However, a considerable class of e-services is characterized by the lack of a pre-defined structure [MWW98], e.g., pre-sales interactions.

Consider, as an example for the management of processes which are dynamically generated at run-time, the supply chain of a car manufacturing company United Cars (UC). UC uses an automated management system to manage parts stored on stock. In case this system detects that the number of screws of a particular type, say *SG-H 37 ZC**, has fallen below a certain threshold, a process ordering new screws has to be triggered. In order to optimize costs, standard parts like screws are dealt with a fixed, single supplier, but they are rather ordered from the supplier offering the best price currently available on the market. To this end, UC first has to gather current offers for 10'000 screws of type *SG-H 37 ZC** from all potential dealers. According to the results of this phase, an order can be placed by the purchasing department. The purchase order will be performed and the screws of the type *SG-H 37 ZC** will be inserted into stock. In order to guarantee that the production of UC cars will never be stopped due to some missing screws, the order process has to terminate correctly and as fast as possible by using clustered services, hence needs dedicated execution guarantees.

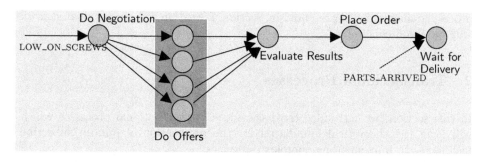

Fig. 1. *Sample Process: Automated Order Processing for Parts Stored on Stock.*

While the example depicted in Figure 1 focuses on execution guarantees and dynamic assignment of services, other applications may introduce additional requirements. Consider, for instance, business processes in the area of multimedia object management which gather image data and finally maintain a search engine on them [WS99]. These processes feature a high need of replicated services in order to speed up execution. To support this, the running components have to be monitored in oder to optimize load balancing. Moreover, this application shows the need of sophisticated resource management at coordinator level: e.g., processing 100'000 images and inserting them into an index will result in 100'000 processes running at the same time which leads to a potential bottleneck of a centralized process manager. Therefore, we see a need to decouple the functionality of a process coordinator and to distribute the individual run-time services to different components, thereby minimizing the intervention of a centralized coordinator and avoiding a bottleneck at coordinator level. In summing up, in order to achieve execution guarantees we must monitor the availability and the load of services. Based on monitoring we must dynamically select the best available service. The implementation must avoid a centralized implementation of the process manager whenever possible.

In this situation — and this is the contribution of the paper — we have come up with a solution for the implementation of a sophisticated process manager that combines the advantages of publish/subscribe techniques with transactional process management. The key feature we are using repeatedly is the following: Systems providing certain services can register (*subscribe*) for the service they offer. Whenever an event like, for instance, the termination of a process step is evoked (*publish*), the process coordinator is able to dynamically chose the next service among all that have been subscribed, thereby considering only those services that are currently available. Based on this publish/subscribe communication infrastructure, many features like process navigation, failure handling, load balancing, and monitoring can be implemented in an elegant and flexible way.

The paper is organized as follows: in Section 2, we briefly introduce the process model we are relying on while Section 3 introduces the idea of publish/subscribe techniques. The application of publish/subscribe techniques to process management is presented in Section 4. Section 5 discusses related work and Section 6 concludes.

2   Transactional Processes

In this section, we introduce the basic ideas of transactional processes which will form the theoretical foundation for the application of publish/subscribe techniques to implementing complex e-services.

2.1   Process Model

A process is a partially ordered collection of activities. In particular, processes introduce flow of control and flow of data between activities as basic semantic elements. Activities, in turn, correspond to invocations of application services. In order to take into account that certain steps within a process are irreversible, activities can be characterized in terms of their termination guarantees: they are either *compensatable, retriable*, or *pivot* — according to the flex transactions model [MRSK92,ZNBB94]. Compensatable activities can be semantically undone after they have committed, pivot activities are those which are not compensatable (when no appropriate compensation is available or when compensation is too expensive and thus has to be avoided), and retriable activities are the ones that are guaranteed to terminate successfully. Due to the special characteristics of processes which are in general long-running and complex, it is not feasible to encompass all activities of a process within a single distributed transaction. Each activity is required to commit immediately after it has been completed — which is even required for pivots. Hence, additional effort is required to handle failures correctly within processes. To this end, the regular order between activities (the *precedence order*) is complemented by an additional order, the *preference order*, indicating alternative executions that can be taken in case of failures [SAS99].

Based on the different termination properties of activities and the precedence and preference orders, it can be validated whether a single process is defined correctly. This is the case when all possible failures of process activities can be handled correctly by either undoing all completed activities (when only compensatable activities have committed) or by executing a safe alternative consisting only of retriable activities (thereby, also failures can be handled which occur after a pivot activity has been committed). Processes for which these structural constraints hold are called *processes with guaranteed termination* [SAS99]. This inherent correctness property of transactional processes is an important and powerful generalization of the "all-or-nothing" semantics of traditional ACID transactions since it ensures that one of eventually many valid executions (specified by alternatives) is effected, thereby ensuring that the system in a consistent state after process completion.

2.2   Process Execution

The execution of transactional processes is controlled by a process coordinator. Starting with the correct specification of single processes having guaranteed termination property, the process coordinator's task is to enforce the correct execution of transactional processes even in the presence of failures and concurrency, i.e., when different processes simultaneously access shared resources. The key aspects of the transactional process coordinator can briefly be summarized as follows: it acts as a kind of transaction scheduler that is more general than a traditional database scheduler in that it

i.) knows about semantic commutativity of activities,
ii.) knows about the termination properties of activities,
iii.) exploits the regular precedence order of processes when executing activities and knows about alternative executions paths in case of failures, and
iv.) optimizes execution costs of processes by choosing the best alternative among the set of alternatives specified by the preference order [Sch01] at each state.

3   Publish/Subscribe Techniques

In this section, we introduce the basic concepts of the publish/subscribe paradigm and give a brief overview of the different applications of this technique.

3.1   Introduction to Publish/Subscribe

Message-oriented middleware (MOM) loosely couples individual systems by replacing the commonly exploited synchronous, RPC-like invocations with the asynchronous transfer of messages. The publish/subscribe (pub/sub) paradigm is a special form of MOM which allows to further decouple a sender and the receiver(s) of messages [OHE99]. The key characteristics of pub/sub interactions is an additional indirection in the communication between sender and receiver(s): rather than addressing a message directly, a sender associates it with a certain topic, i.e., a description of the message content, and does not have to have any information about who will be the recipient of this particular message. Yet, *publishing* a message just requires transferring it to a dedicated *message broker*. The latter is then responsible for distributing this message, according to meta data indicating who has previously shown interest of messages of that particular topic. The procedure of registering an individual client profile of topics with the message broker is referred to as *subscription*. An alternative to the description of messages by means of predefined topics is to use filter predicates specified by recipients to analyze whether or not publications are of particular interest (consider, for instance, an electronic car auction where a client is interested in any offer of a VW New Beetle for less than $10.000). Filter predicates increase flexibility by allowing arbitrary publications, thereby avoiding the restriction of the publisher to the usage of a common topics schema. Moreover, when given the capability to persistently store messages together with the associated description, the message broker may even allow to distribute messages to receivers which did not exist at the time the message has been published. Persistent queuing functionality also allows to guarantee correct message transfer. A message is first inserted into the publisher's local queue. The publication, which then corresponds to the transfer from this local queue to the queue of incoming messages located at the broker's site, is implemented as a two-phase commit (2PC) [GR93] coordinated distributed transaction. In a similar way, also the transfer of messages from the broker to the subscriber is treated, yet in an independent transaction, thus achieving asynchronous publisher/subscriber interactions. An additional degree of freedom in pub/sub interactions, depending on the individual semantics of a concrete application, is whether or not it is sufficient to forward a message to exactly one subscriber, to a certain set of subscribers, or to all of them.

While most commercial pub/sub implementations (e.g., IBM's MQSeries [MQS00] or the implementations of the CORBA Event Service [OMG]) follow the broker approach, certain products even avoid the centralized broker. In TIB/Rendezvous [TIB99] of TIBCO, for instance, a publisher distributes messages via broadcast to all potential subscribers which then have to filter locally the messages they are interested in.

3.2   Applications of Pub/Sub Techniques

The pub/sub idea was originally introduced in the context of mailing lists for Internet newsgroups where a customer explicitly has to subscribe for a couple of predefined topics so as to receive an e-mail whenever a message to one of these topics is published. A generalization of this first application can be found in systems where the recipients of messages are no longer human beings but arbitrary application programs (e.g., electronic stock brokers logging each significant change in the stock value of the shares of United Cars). The usage of pub/sub techniques can even be further generalized, leading to loosely coupled distributed information systems, when the receiver actively reacts on a message. The rationale behind this approach is that a message corresponds to an event that has been evoked by some application (the publisher) and requires certain response by another program (the subscriber).

4   Processes Support by Pub/Sub Technologies

Our PM^{PS} approach relies on the above mentioned idea of loosely coupled distributed information systems and addresses the event-driven execution of business processes (process management, PM) by pub/sub (PS) techniques. By this, core system functionality can be mapped to the underlying pub/sub infrastructure without having to deal with dedicated components for various runtime services such as, for instance, distribution of load information for load balancing purposes. Activities of a process correspond to services provided by one component of the system (in certain cases, services are replicated and thus can be provided by different component systems). In order to avoid that components drive the execution of processes in a bilateral way by explicitly invoking the subsequent service at another host by remote procedure call once a local service has terminated, pub/sub techniques are used. To this end, components offering services which are used within processes have to register the service they offer (subscription). After an event is published —via an appropriate message, i.e, the completion of some task— that triggers another task, the service corresponding to the latter is invoked. Consider, for example, a component C_1 offering a service s_1 which corresponds to activity a' of some process P. C_1 can subscribe this service for events $"s_1.start"$ which, in turn, are generated after the event $"s_0.terminated"$ has been raised where s_0 is a service corresponding to an activity a^* that directly precedes a' in process P with respect to the precedence order. Hence, the component S_0 executing the service corresponding to activity A_0 does not have to be aware of where process execution will be continued; server S_1 is contacted by the PM^{PS} system rather than by S_0. While control flow is initiated by means of messages, data to be shipped between tasks is also encompassed within these messages. A crucial aspect for driving the execution of processes in a reliable way is to exploit persistent queuing mechanisms to avoid the loss of messages.

We use pub/sub techniques also to distribute the implementation of our process coordinator. This helps to improve load balancing, process navigation,

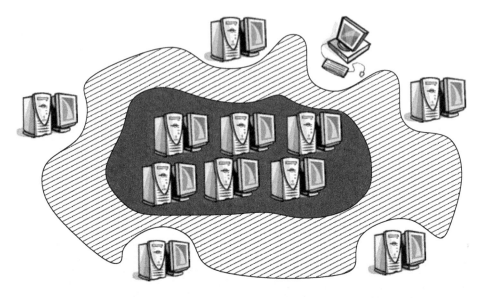

Fig. 2. *Different Types of Components: KER for Process Execution (Inner Part) and APPS for Individual Process Steps (Outer Part).*

failure handling, and monitoring. The implementation of these features are discussed in the following subsections.

4.1 System Model

The PM^{PS} approach is designed to run in a heterogeneous and distributed environment. We distinguish two types of components participating in the system. The first type, called *KER* consisting of a set of dedicated servers, builds the PM^{PS} kernel (depicted in Figure 2 as the machines belonging to the inner, dark-shaded area). These components have to feature high availability since they are exploited to drive the execution of transactional processes and to add services at run-time, e.g., providing load balancing, or monitoring functionality for the states of processes. The second type, called *APPS*, is made up of the components providing application services which will be combined by processes (depicted in the outer part of Figure 2). Hence, these components are used for the execution of single process steps rather than to control the actual process execution. In particular, these components can dynamically change the set of services they provide, and they can themselves dynamically join and leave the system. The overall system should not be affected, even if *APPS* components crash and never rejoin the system.

Since all communication in the system is based on asynchronous messages and pub/sub techniques, no *APPS* component has to be aware of the network address of any another component. The communication layer connecting all components of either type just has to know how to contact the central pub/sub directory which is hosted at one of the *KER* components (and which is, according to the requirements imposed for these components, highly available and/or redundant). This directory lookup service maintains information on pub/sub topics and all subscriptions to these topics. In the PM^{PS} approach to process management, topics coincide both with the different events that are raised by *APPS* components so as to signal the state of service invocations (whether they are successfully completed or whether they have failed) and with the events generated by the *KER* components, reflecting relevant changes in the meta data of the system.

Whenever a new component of the *APPS* type joins the system (note that all components of the *KER* type are static and thus can neither dynamically join nor leave the system), it registers itself at the pub/sub directory by specifying the different services it provides.

4.2   Load Balancing

In order to the increase the performance and availability of *APPS* components, services can be configured to run on more than one component. In this case, the pub/sub run-time infrastructure has to provide a special component implementing a dedicated load balancing service. This service routes incoming message to exactly one subscriber of a subscribed group, where the service corresponding to that particular message can be executed. Since the load balancing component can decide freely —but based on load information it dynamically gathers— where to route a specific task, the result of an execution has to be independent of the location where the service is executed, i.e., the services among which the load balancing component chooses have to be (semantically) identical.

To allow for the implementation of sophisticated load balancing services, each *APPS* component has to publish its actual load. To prevent a high system load, due to heavy load update information, PM^{PS} implements an event-based mechanism that notifies the load balancing service whenever significant changes in the local load occur (i.e., when the deviation of the load exceeds a pre-defined threshold). Hence, the load balancing service acts as a subscriber for load information published by the *APPS* components.

4.3   Process Navigation

In addition to transparent service invocation provided by the meta information maintained at the pub/sub directory allowing to link two subsequent steps of a process, the overall navigation within processes has to take place on top of this infrastructure.

Therefore, a process description lookup service must be hosted at a *KER* component. This service maintains information about all defined processes, following the model of transactional processes (c.f. Section 2.1). For process modeling purposes, we are using a graphical process modeling and simulation tool, IvyFrame of IvyTeam [Ivy], which we have extended in PM^{PS} in order to export process models in the format used by the process description lookup service (i.e., in the form of pairs of consecutive activities and the corresponding services that have to be invoked to execute these activities). In particular, the process description lookup service has to map events raised by some $APPS$ component like $s_0.terminated$ to events that trigger control flow and that start the subsequent activity by invoking its associated service: $s_1.start$. To this end, the process description lookup service needs both information on the correlation between process activities and the associated services as well as on the control flow of a process (which includes both the precedence order for regular execution and the preference order for alternative execution which have to be effected in case of failure).

In general, this mapping is realized by a centralized service which is a subscriber for all $?.terminated$ and $?.failed$ events, i.e., events that signal the successful completion or failure of services. But this navigation by mapping events can also be de–centralized: in this case, the local pub/sub daemon which anyway resides on each $APPS$ component to provide transparent communication by means of pub/sub , i.e., to publish events after a service has terminated, takes over this task. To do this, the daemon has to locally cache global information maintained by the process description lookup service. Based on this cached information, the daemon can decide locally which event to publish after the termination of a service. The prerequisite for this is, however, that the local cache is kept up to date such that dynamic changes in the process description are immediately propagated to all local daemons. Again, this is realized via pub/sub techniques in that each daemon subscribes for process description lookup data which is published by the centralized service whenever changes are performed. This allows to distribute meta data of the process lookup service for cache update purposes.

4.4   Failure Handling

Following the model of transactional processes, the failures of single activities are handled by either re–invoking the service (retry), executing alternatives, or by compensation. In all cases, the strategy is present in the control flow of the process (preference and precedence order, respectively) and the termination characteristics of the activity. To this end, the failure of some local service s_1 corresponding to an activity A_1 is published "$s_1.failed$" and can be handled by the process navigation similar to the successful treatment (However, in this case compensation is required or alternative execution are effected rather than continuing with the regular control flow).

The failure of individual $APPS$ components, however, requires additional effort. In particular, it must be guaranteed that all events that have been published will be processed by some subscriber. Hence, appropriate support by the underlying pub/sub infrastructure of PM^{PS} is required. Essentially, following the ideas of queued transactions [BN97], persistent queuing technology can be applied in order to guarantee not only that a message corresponding to an event arrives at the subscriber but also that it is actually processed there by some service s (before a new event signaling the state of s is raised). To this end,

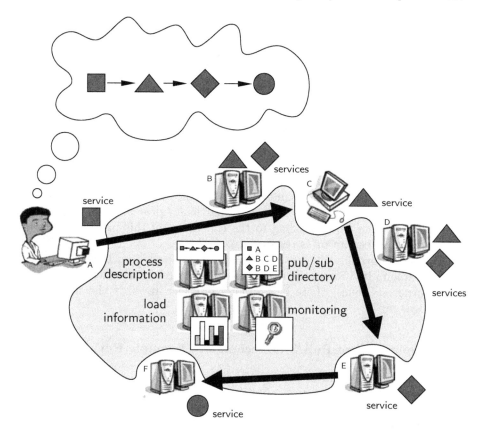

Fig. 3. *Dynamic Process Execution by the PM^{PS} System.*

the delivery of a publication which corresponds to a dequeue operation from a persistent queue maintained by the PM^{PS} system, the service itself, and the enqueue of the event signaling the state of the service (success or failure) have to be encompassed within a single transaction. This is the task of the local daemon which not only provides the basic pub/sub communication facilities but which also relates the invocation of local services to the events being published and consumed.

In case some *APPS* component having subscribed for the execution of a service cannot be reached, three corrective strategies exist:

i.) if there are other components having subscribed for that particular service, they can be chosen instead (in an order imposed by their current load), or
ii.) if alternative services are defined in the process (by means of preference orders, c.f. 2.1), these services can be invoked, or
iii.) in case a particular service is not replicated and no alternative is defined, process execution has to be frozen until either that component is available or until another component has subscribed for this service.

4.5   Monitoring

Meta data on the state of the overall system is very important, both in terms of individual components (what is their current load, what services they are currently executing, etc.) and in terms of individual processes (what is their current state). To this end, an additional run-time service, *monitoring*, located at one of the *KER* components, gathers all information about components connected to the system, active processes, and so forth. By subscribing itself as consumer of all types of system state messages, the monitoring component is seamlessly kept up-to-date without requiring any interception mechanisms on the invocation of services. By using appropriate filter predicates associated with the subscription, the granularity of monitoring can be tailored to the individual needs of processes or users. When, for instance, the state of particular process P_1 has to be monitored, only events corresponding to the enactment of this process have to be gathered, i.e., subscription is restricted to P_1.? .

In order to graphically depict the state of processes in a user-friendly way, PM^{PS} exploits IvyFrame, the same tool that is already used for process modeling purposes. Hence, there is a unique interface towards the users of the PM^{PS} system.

4.6   Application of Pub/Sub Techniques: Example Revisited

Coming back to our initial example, the supply chain management of United Cars, a message *low_on_parts* is published after the stock management system detects the need of screws. This message contains information about the exact type of the parts needed: (screws, *SG-H 37 ZC*).

After the message is published, the pub/sub directory process description service checks whether subscriptions to this message exist. In this case, it is detected that the message corresponds to an *order_parts* process —according to the process description stored in the repository— which has to be executed by copying information from the *low_on_parts* message to the context of the new process. In order to execute the first activity, it sends a message with the topic *do_negotiation.start* to the system. The system routes this message to the *APPS* component offering this service and having subscribed for this particular topic before. In this case, subscriptions consist of suppliers announcing the availability of screws in their catalog. In order to process the initial message published by UC (which corresponds to a call for bids), each subscribed supplier is contacted. The implementation of the *do_negotiation* service uses the pub/sub infrastructure to publish a *get_offers* to reach all suppliers currently connected to the system. The services executed at the supplier sites generate bids for the number and type of screws requested by UC. In addition to the individual bids, they send back the service name and execution parameters specification (which would be required when the bid is chosen for the execution of the ordering service). According to this information, a decision can be made about which dealer will be selected.

After the bidding step is completed, the *do_negotiation* service terminates which results in a *do_negotiation.terminated* message. First, this message is mapped to the start message of the next step with respect to the control flow (*place_order.start*). Second, this message is also consumed by additional *KER* components, for instance for monitoring purposes.

The "place order service" compiles the information for the order and calls the order service at the dealers place. After the execution of this purchase order, the next step in the process is an activity that waits for the message indicating that the parts are shipped and inserted into the stock. In case that this does not take place within a given time–frame, a timeout occurs and an alternative branch of the process is executed so as to perform additional activities like the sending of reminder or the cancellation of the order and the placement of an order using a different supplier. As a last activity, the payment will take place.

Using transactional processes, it is guaranteed that all possible failures of services are handled correctly and the system always terminates in a consistent state. In this case, whenever the screw ordering process is terminated, the stock is refilled with *SG-H 37 ZC∗* screws, either stemming from the initially contacted supplier or from the supplier chosen alternatively in case the initial one could not proceed its order.

5   Related Work

There are many different approaches to realize dynamic process management systems. In general, there are two possibilities to handle dynamic changes during process execution. First, this can be achieved by changing the process definition at run–time. This requires a migration of running instances to the new schema. $ADEPT_{FLEX}$ [RD98] and rule–based approaches as they can be found, for instance, in HEMATOWORK [MR99], handle this migration while preserving consistency of the process instances.

A second method to deal with dynamic aspects is to define a static process definition, but assign services at run–time and therefore achieve dynamic process execution. CrossFlow [GALH01] and *e*Flow [CDS01] focus on negotiation and service discovery. CrossFlow [GALH01] uses an electronic market to support the dynamic assignment of services by advertising and searching for compatible business partners. Other approaches like *ADEPT* [BD00] realize a similar effect by dynamically assigning process managers. The *e*Flow [CIJ+00,CDS01] approach handles changes on process programs as well as on process instances.

The PM^{PS} approach uses a static process program and dynamically resolves available *APPS* servers to decide where to execute activities, while focusing on execution guarantees, using a transparent communication layer to describe and to invoke services by pub/sub.

Commercially available products like IBM's MQSeries Workflows [MQS00] are using persistent queues in order to call activities on remote systems. The MQSeries family also includes publish/subscribe functionality but with a slightly different focus than PM^{PS}, namely to loosely couple applications rather than controlling the execution of processes.

All previously discussed approaches rely on a central process coordinator, while PM^{PS} decouples this functionality in order to distribute process navigation as well as other run–time services.

6   Conclusion

Transactional process management can be used to integrate existing e–services seamlessly into new business processes by plugging existing components together.

This paper has shown how to realize a distributed implementation of a process management system by dividing the functionality into a bunch of decoupled services. Focused on process navigation, failure handling, load balancing, and monitoring, we have described how to map process management to the pub/sub communication primitives.

Our modular framework, supporting transactional process coordination as well as dynamically adapting the execution of processes, can deal with the different particular problems of e-commerce scenarios. Steps of a process program are not hard–wired to application servers. By this, processes can even be executed in a highly dynamic environment. The PM^{PS} system determines the server of a certain service at run–time, so that availability as well as load balancing is taken into account. Yet, the deferment of process execution as a result of unavailable or overloaded components can be avoided.

Using the ideas of transactional processes, the consistent termination of every business process is guaranteed, such that key transactional properties are fulfilled.

As future work, a concurrency control service will be integrated into the system by using a second indirection in the control flow. The goal is that exploiting a locking protocol for processes, e.g., [Sch01] at process coordinator level, allows for the correct parallelization of concurrent processes can be guaranteed, by seamlessly intercepting service calls within the pub/sub infrastructure.

References

BD00.   Th. Bauer and P. Dadam. Efficient Distributed Workflow Management Based on Variable Server Assignments. In *Proceedings 12th Conference on Advanced Information Systems Engineering*, pages 94–109, Stockholm, Sweden, S., June 2000.

BN97.   P. Bernstein and E. Newcomer. *Principles of Transaction Processing*. Morgan Kaufmann Publishers, 1997.

CDS01.   F. Casati, U. Dayal, and M. Shan. E–Business Applications for Supply Chain Automation: Challenges. In *Proceedings of the 17th International Conference on Data Engineering*, Heidelberg, Germany, April 2001.

CIJ$^+$00.   F. Casati, S. Ilnicki, L. Jin, V. Krishnamoorthy, and M. Shan. Adaptive and Dynamic Service Composition in eFlow. In *Proceedings 12th Conference on Advanced Information Systems Engineering*, Stockholm, Sweden, S., June 2000.

CST95.   J. Camp, M. Sirbu, and D. Tygar. Token and Notational Money in Electronic Commerce. In *Proceedings of the 1st USENIX Workshop on Electronic Commerce*, pages 1–12, July 1995.

GALH01.   P. Grefen, K. Aberer, H. Ludwig, and Y. Hoffner. CrossFlow: Cross–Organizational Workflow Management for Service Outsourcing in Dynamic Virtual Enterprises. *IEEE Data Engineering Bulletin*, 24:52–57, 2001.

GR93.   J. Gray and A. Reuter. *Transaction Processing: Concepts and Techniques*. Morgan Kaufmann Publishers, 1993.

Ivy.   IvyTeam, Zug, Switzerland. http://www.ivyteam.com.

MQS00.   MQSeries Publish/Subscribe User's Guide. IBM Red Book, No. GC34-5269-05, 2000. IBM, International Business Machines Corporation.

MR99.   R. Müller and E. Rahm. Rule-Based Dynamic Modification of Workflows in a Medical Domain. In *Proceedings of Datenbanksysteme in Büro, Technik und Wissenschaft (BTW'99)*, Informatik Aktuell, pages 429–448, Freiburg, Germany, March 1999. Springer Verlag.

MRSK92.   S. Mehrotra, R. Rastogi, A. Silberschatz, and H. Korth. A Transaction Model for Multidatabase Systems. In *Proceedings of the 12th International Conference on Distributed Computing Systems (ICDCS'92)*, pages 56–63, Yokohama, Japan, June 1992. IEEE Computer Society Press.

MWW98.   P. Muth, J. Weissenfels, and G. Weikum. What Workflow Technology can do for Electronic Commerce. In *Proceedings of the EURO-MED NET Conference*, Nicosia, Cyprus, March 1998.

OHE99.   R. Orfali, D. Harkey, and J. Edwards. *Client/Server Survival Guide*. John Wiley & Sons, 3rd edition, 1999.

OMG.   OMG. Object Manegement Group. http://www.omg.org.

PSS00.   A. Popovici, H. Schuldt, and H.-J. Schek. Generation and Verification of Heterogeneous Purchase Processes. In *Proceedings of the International Workshop on Technologies for E–Services (TES 2000)*, Cairo, Egypt, September 2000.

RD98.   M. Reichert and P. Dadam. *ADEPT$_{flex}$* – Supporting Dynamic Changes of Workflows Without Losing Control. *Journal of Intelligent Information Systems*, 10(2):93–129, 1998.

SAS99.   H. Schuldt, G. Alonso, and H.-J. Schek. Concurrency Control and Recovery in Transactional Process Management. In *Proceedings of the 18th ACM Symposium on Principles of Database Systems (PODS'99)*, pages 316–326, Philadelphia, Pennsylvania, USA, May/June 1999. ACM Press.

Sch01.   H. Schuldt. Process Locking: A Protocol based on Ordered Shared Locks for the Execution of Transactional Processes. In *Proceedings of the 20th ACM Symposium on Principles of Database Systems (PODS'01)*, Santa Barbara, California, USA, May 2001. ACM Press.

TIB99.   TIB/Rendezvous. White Paper, 1999. TIBCO Software Inc.

WS99.   Roger Weber and Hans-J. Schek. A distributed image-database architecture for efficient insertion and retrieval. In *Fifth International Workshop on Multimedia Information Systems (MIS'99)*, Indian Wells, Palm Springs Desert, California, October 21–23 1999.

ZNBB94.   A. Zhang, M. Nodine, B. Bhargava, and O. Bukhres. Ensuring Relaxed Atomicity for Flexible Transactions in Multidatabase Systems. In *Proceedings of the ACM SIGMOD International Conference on Management of Data (SIGMOD'94)*, pages 67–78, Minneapolis, Minnesota, USA, May 1994. ACM Press.

User Action Recovery in Internet SAGAs (iSAGAs)

Kaushik Dutta[1], Debra VanderMeer[1],
Anindya Datta[1], and Krithi Ramamritham[2]

[1] Georgia Institute of Technology, Atlanta, GA
{kaushik,deb,adatta}@chutneytech.com
[2] University of Massachusetts-Amherst and IIT-Bombay
krithi@cs.umass.edu

Abstract. With the expansion of Web sites to include business functions, a user's typical interaction with a Web site is a multi-step process. The loss of connection, or other system failure, can result in the loss of work accumulated before the disruption. This work must then be repeated – often at significant cost in time and computation. In some environments, such as wireless scenarios, these costs can include battery power as well.

This paper presents a protocol for recovering from such scenarios. We first describe Internet-based interactions using the familiar concepts of transactions and recovery. Using these abstractions, we then describe a protocol for recovering users to valid states in Internet interactions.

1 Introduction

Web sites are increasingly making use of dynamic scripting techniques which allow greater interactivity than static HTML. Here, users interact with dynamic sites to achieve specific goals, typically through a sequence of actions. A disruption in the sequence due to the failure of one of the participating or intermediary systems typically results in the user restarting the sequence, often at significant expense to both the user and the Web site.

Consider a scenario in which a user is buying an airline ticket over his wireless Internet connection. He first logs on to the airline site with his frequent flier number, then checks his frequent flier mileage. He then enters his preferred travel dates and destination, and chooses among the itineraries offered by the site, selects his seat, enters his credit card information, and receives a confirmation of the purchase.

If his wireless connection drops (as occurs frequently in wireless systems [17]) during the purchase step, he must reconnect to the Internet, re-login to the airline site and resubmit all the pertinent information in order to reach the state where he can again attempt to purchase a ticket. Restarting this sequence costs the user time and battery power, both valuable commodities. Resources are also wasted on the server, affecting performance, since (potentially) large amounts of work must be redone.

F. Casati, D. Georgakopoulos, M.-C. Shan (Eds.): TES 2001, LNCS 2193, pp. 132–146, 2001.

The main problem in this scenario is that the user must restart the sequence of actions from the beginning, including expensive steps, such as processor-intensive login and authentication steps, I/O intensive database lookups, as well as consume valuable connections to the database. Significant amounts of time and effort are wasted in redoing previously completed work, and, in the case of a wireless environment, there are additional costs in battery resources and airtime.

The purpose of this paper is twofold: (a) to propose ways for users to "recover" from interaction failures by minimizing the amount of work that must be redone upon reconnection; and (b) to demonstrate that this user "recovery" problem differs significantly from the classical recovery problem in database systems. Here, rather than redoing the entire sequence of steps completed before failure, a user would, upon restart, be placed at a much later stage in his sequence of actions (ideally the last action before failure). This problem encompasses several interesting subproblems:

How Can We Characterize a Sequence of User Actions with a Site? A user interacts with a Web site through a sequence of actions aimed at achieving a specific goal. Upon preliminary considerations, this appears to resemble a long transaction (such as a SAGA [8]). Thus, we model user interaction with a Web site using the long transaction metaphor, and refer to a user's action sequence as an *Internet SAGA (***iSAGA***)*. However, there are significant differences between long database transactions and **iSAGAs**, due to the differences between the highly constrained context of a database system and the loosely constrained context of the Internet. These differences require a rethinking of the basic properties of long transactions in the context of the Internet. We describe these differences in detail in Section 3.

Given the **iSAGA** *Characterization, What Is a Good Protocol for Allowing Users to "Recover"?* Given a means of describing user interaction with a Web site as a long transaction, we need a protocol for actually recovering a user to a previous state after a disruption. The main question is: How can we describe user states in the context of Internet long transactions? We present such a method in Section 4.

To Which State Should a User Be Recovered? Given a set of user states produced by a user's **iSAGA**, how can we decide which state to use for recovery? Ideally, we would simply choose the user's last state before failure. However, this is not always possible. For instance, the data in the underlying database may have changed during the time between failure and reconnection. Thus, user states may become invalid.

Another complexity that arises is the potential for multiple objectives in an **iSAGA**. Here, the sequence of user actions as seen by the server may not correspond a linear sequence of actions toward a single objective, but rather may consist of multiple interleaved objectives. Consider, for instance, the airline ticket purchase example. Here, before purchasing a ticket, our user might check his frequent flier mileage. Effectively, in the same interaction session, the user is performing two tasks: (a) mileage checking, and (b) ticket purchase. The mileage-checking action is not directly related to the ticket-buying action. Thus, our user might express, in the same **iSAGA**, more than one objective. We present a detailed discussion of these complexities in Section 5.

Given that a User Might Express Multiple Objectives, Which Objective Should Be Considered by the Recovery Protocol? Given that our user may have more than one objective, which sequence of actions should we consider when recovering from a failure? We expand our recovery protocol in Section 6 to encompass this possibility.

To summarize, the objectives of this paper are as follows:

1. To model an **iSAGA**, i.e., a user's interaction with a Web site.
2. To demonstrate that **iSAGAs** give rise to issues not relevant in the context of database transactions.
3. To describe how to determine valid states in an **iSAGA**.
4. To find ways of extracting different user objectives and the corresponding sequences of user actions from a single **iSAGA**.
5. To propose a user action recovery technique to handle failure.

The remainder of this paper is organized as follows. Section 2 describes related work. Section 3 presents our model of Internet interactions using a transaction metaphor, and distinguishes **iSAGAs** from SAGAs. Section 4 describes a simple recovery protocol that illustrates the basic ideas of recovering a user's state. Section 5 expands the notion of an Internet transaction to model multiple user goals in a single transaction. Section 6 expands the recovery protocol to include recovery in the context of multiple user goals. Section 7 concludes the paper.

2   Related Work

The theory and application of transaction-based processing in the context of database systems are well-researched topics. Early work, such as [1] and [10] describe the basic tenets of transaction processing and compare the performance of transaction processing protocols. In [12], the authors describe a comprehensive recovery protocol for database systems.

The metaphor of transaction processing has since been extended to other application areas. The ACTA framework [3] describes a formal language for extending the idea of a transaction to other areas. For example, [2] describes workflow processing using transactions, while [18] utilizes transactions to model mobile interactions. The notion of transactions has even been applied to electronic commerce, as in [15] and [16].

The works cited above all have one idea in common: the activity modeled as a transaction is a self-contained activity, with a single goal. This paper describes a user's interaction with a Web site using the metaphor of a transaction, while relaxing the restriction that the transaction model an interaction with a single goal. For this, we draw on the idea of a long transactions [8] and [3].

We also draw on work in recovery. Database recovery is described clearly in [12]. In [13], the authors describe a protocol for mobile recovery. Here, the authors consider basic transaction recovery; our work differs from this in that we consider the validity of stored user states, as well as multi-objective transactions.

3   Internet SAGAs (iSAGAs)

The ideas presented in this work revolve around the notion of an **iSAGA**. Thus, we first define formally what an **iSAGA** is. We then discuss how users interact with Web sites using the notion of an **iSAGA**. Finally, we discuss the ways in which **iSAGAs** differ from SAGAs.

3.1   What Is an iSAGA?

Definition 1. *An* **iSAGA** *I is a sequence of user actions $\langle A_1, A_2, \ldots, A_n \rangle$ (called* component actions*) on a particular Web site to achieve at least one, possibly multiple, user objectives.*

In order to make clear these notions, as well as others in this paper, we now describe an example scenario. We utilize this scenario as a running example through the remainder of this paper to illustrate various properties of **iSAGAs** as well as our proposed recovery protocol.

Example of an iSAGA. Consider an online airline ticket purchase scenario. Here, our example user logs on to the airline site with his frequent flier number, enters his desired travel plan, and checks his frequent flier mileage. He then returns to the reservation page, and re-enters his travel plan, chooses among the available itineraries, chooses a seat, and submits credit card information to complete the purchase. This **iSAGA** I consists of a sequence of several component actions: the login component action A_1, the plan-entry action A_2, the mileage-checking action A_3, the return-to-reservations action A_4, the plan-reentry action A_5, the itinerary-choosing action A_6, the seat-choosing action A_7, and the ticket-payment action A_8. More formally, we denote the **iSAGA** I as the sequence $\langle A_1, A_2, A_3, A_4, A_5, A_6, A_7, A_8 \rangle$, as shown below:

I: A_1 (login);
A_2 (travel plan entry);
A_3 (mileage check);
A_4 (return to reservation form);
A_5 (repeat travel plan entry);
A_6 (itinerary choice);
A_7 (seat selection);
A_8 (ticket payment);

It is worthwhile to note the interleaving of different objectives in the example above. Here, the user reveals two separate objectives: (a) checking his frequent flier mileage, and (b) purchasing a ticket. Each of these objectives can be represented by a (possibly overlapping) sequence of component actions called a **sub-iSAGA**.

Definition 2. *Consider an* **iSAGA** $I = \langle A_1 \ldots A_n \rangle$. *A* **sub-iSAGA** B *of an* **iSAGA** I *consists of a sequence of component actions* $\langle A_j, A_k, \ldots, A_m \rangle$, *meeting the following conditions: (a) each component action of B is a component action in I; (b) for any two component actions A_a and A_b in B, if A_a precedes A_b in B, then A_a must also precede A_b in I; and (c) B semantically represents a single user objective.*

For instance, the **sub-iSAGA** representing the mileage-checking objective consists of the sequence $\langle A_1, A_3 \rangle$, while the **sub-iSAGA** for the ticket-purchase objective consists of the sequence $\langle A_1, A_2, A_4, A_5, A_6, A_7, A_8 \rangle$. Clearly, **sub-iSAGAs** can be arbitrarily interleaved within a single **iSAGA**.

3.2   Web Site and User Views of an iSAGA

The essential intuition needed to understand **iSAGAs** is that the user and the Web site perceive user actions differently. Let us first consider how the site perceives user actions. Effectively, the Web site observes a sequence of HTTP requests coming from the user. Since the HTTP protocol is stateless[7], *the Web site sees each user action as an independent task, rather than as part of a larger transaction.* For instance, in the **iSAGA** of Section 3.1, the Web site has no knowledge that the seat-choosing action A_7 is logically followed by the ticket-payment action A_8. Rather, it observes A_7 and A_8 as independent transactions. Consequently, both before and after each component action of an **iSAGA**, the state of the Web site components (e.g., the associated database systems) are all consistent.

From the perspective of the user, however, each component action is part of a sequence (i.e., a transaction) aimed at reaching a specific goal. To achieve his goal, the user must complete the **iSAGA** entirely; partial executions provide no benefit. Consider the airline example in Section 3.1. After completing the sequence of component actions $\langle A_1 \ldots A_8 \rangle$, the ticket-buying **iSAGA**, is complete.

iSAGAs differ significantly from long database transactions (which, generically, we will henceforth refer to as SAGAs) in several ways: (a) evolutionary growth; (b) view updatability and validity; and (c) potential for multiple objectives. We discuss each in turn.

3.3   Evolutionary Growth

An **iSAGA** is created through user interaction, one component action at a time, and lack the notion of a predefined sequence and well-defined end. Since each of the component actions of an **iSAGA** is an individual transaction from the perspective of Web sites the user interacts with, the Web site must treat each user action as if it were the last in the user's **iSAGA**. The user's **iSAGA** ends if the user *explicitly* disconnects, e.g., by closing the browser, or *implicitly* disconnects, e.g., if his connection fails.

Even if the user's **iSAGA** ends unexpectedly, the database states of the Web sites he interacts with, as well as his own user state, remain consistent with (i.e., they will continue to reflect) the updates, if any, made by the actions completed up to the point of failure. Since the iSAGA has terminated, any needed compensatory actions should be implicit in the Web site, i.e., compensation must be (and in practice, is) built into the site's business logic where required. That is, *no explicit compensating transaction is required from the user*, i.e., the user need take no action to ensure the web site state is consistent after failure recovery. We illustrate this via an example.

Consider the airline ticket purchase **iSAGA** in Section 3.1. Suppose that our user has completed component action A_7 (seat-choice), and that his connection drops while he is in the process of action A_8 (payment-submission). Here, the database at the Web site has allotted a seat for the user on his preferred flight, but the corresponding ticket has not been purchased. Moreover, since the user's connection, and therefore his session on the Web site, has been lost, he *cannot* purchase the ticket for the seat he has reserved, since the site (most likely) persisted his session with a cookie, which disappeared on disconnection. Had the site used a disk-based cookie, to persist his session, he would likely be able to re-establish his session upon reconnection. However, most sites refrain from this practice, since it would require writing the cookie to disk with every user click, adding I/O and storage overhead on the user's browser.

The airline site has a mechanism to handle such scenarios; here, the user's seat selection is simply a reservation for the seat selected, a reservation that expires after some site-specific amount of time if the ticket corresponding to the reservation is not purchased. The important point to understand here is that Web sites (and their associated database systems) are designed to handle such scenarios, and *no explicit action is required in the interaction between the user and the site to handle such "failures"*. Note that such a design also makes practical sense: An airline reservation site can not rely on a customer to explicitly cancel/undo a reservation he/she made, but chose not to purchase.

The implication of this is subtle, but extremely important: Any failure will be handled by the recovery mechanisms on the database and application servers, rather than requiring explicit compensating action(s) from the user interaction. In other words, a failure does not result in inconsistency in an **iSAGA**, from both the Web site's view as well as the user's. Rather, a failure results in the potential need to redo work (were the user to reconnect to the site), wasting resources. Thus, in this work *we need not worry about database or application server transaction recovery*; rather, we *focus on recovering a user's state*, consistent with the current state of the database at the time of recovery, mitigating the need to restart the sequence of actions in the **iSAGA** from the beginning.

3.4   View Updatability and Validity

Another way in which **iSAGAs** differ from SAGAs is that views in **iSAGAs** can be *updated* at any point in the **iSAGA**, while SAGAs operate in a more restricted view update context. These updates can cause an **iSAGAs** view to become *invalid*. We first describe how views can be updated, and then discuss the consequent invalidation effect. By the term "view", we refer to the classical notion of a tranasaction's view of a system state, i.e., *"the objects and the state of the objects visible to a transaction at a point in time."* [4]

View Updatability. In a SAGA, as in traditional database transactions, a transaction's view is *protected* by some type of concurrency control mechanism (such as a locking protocol) to prevent two transactions from writing over one another's updates. Whenever a view is given to a transaction, it is the database system's responsibility to lock (or otherwise control read/write access to) the appropriate portion of the database. In this way, database systems guarantee that the view given to a transaction remains valid until the end of the transaction. Such protection, however comes at the cost of increased response time. In typical long database transactions, such as CAD design, the relatively low user load (perhaps tens to a few hundred users), and the lack of a requirement for real-time response times make these penalties tolerable.

In the Internet environment, locking (or otherwise controlling access to) part of the Web site is infeasible - doing so would severely impact the performance of the transactions of other users on the site. Here, the site database may be accessed to serve many thousands of users simultaneously, and these users expect real-time responsiveness from the site. In this context, concurrency control mechanisms would place an unbearable burden on the site. Thus, an **iSAGA**'s view is *unprotected*, i.e., the view is open for updates.

For example, return to our airline **iSAGA**. In response to action A_2 (the travel-plan entry action), the airline site offers several itineraries to a user, based on his input preferences. It is not possible to place concurrency control restrictions on those itineraries (which have been offered as a user view on the database) because those same itineraries may be of interest to other users on the site, and controlling access would limit the number of users who can access the information.

Given system loads and response time expectations, concurrency control across component actions of **iSAGAs** is simply not a valid solution. Moreover, since each component action is viewed as an independent HTTP request by the Web site, it is not feasible to control access to particular data items.

View Validity. One consequence of view updatability is that **iSAGA** views may become *invalid*. However, database are not the only cause of view invalidity; a view can also become invalid when it no longer has value to the user. Clearly, view invalidity can occur in one of two ways, either from the user's perspective or the site's perspective. We discuss each in turn.

User-Based Invalidation. A view becomes invalid from the user's perspective when the user no longer needs the data in the view. Consider again the airline **iSAGA** described in Section 3.1. Suppose that our user's **iSAGA** fails during action A_6 (itinerary-selection). Further suppose that our user then (possibly frustrated) called the airline's toll-free number to purchase his ticket. The next time he connects to the Internet (perhaps several hours later), in a system equipped to recover after a failure, he might be offered itineraries matching the travel plans he entered before losing his connection. Clearly, the user's state at disconnection is no longer useful. Thus, we must consider mechanisms for determining the value of user's state at the time of recovery.

System-Based Invalidation. A view becomes invalid from the site's perspective when the data in a view provided to a user has changed. Let us return to the airline **iSAGA** example. Suppose that our user's **iSAGA** fails in the middle of action A_6 (choosing the itinerary) and that, while he reconnects, the site sells out of seats at the user's preferred fare on his preferred itinerary. In this case, the user's state containing the originally offered itineraries is invalid, since it is inconsistent with the database at the Web site, and should not be served to the user.

Both types of validity described above must be considered in helping a user recover from failure. In simple cases, invalidating user-recovery states can be achieved by limiting the temporal validity period of a state through the use of a "time-to-live" (TTL) mechanism. Interestingly, this works in both cases, i.e., for both user-based as well as system-based invalidation.

In the case of user-based invalidation, it is fairly safe to assume that the value of recovery to the user decreases as the time between failure and reconnection increases. For instance, consider the airline **iSAGA**. If the user connection fails after seat selection action A_7, i.e., during the payment phase A_8, and that the user turns to the airline's telephone reservation system to purchase his ticket. The next time our user visits the airline site, a large amount of time is likely to have passed (in comparison to the amount of time that would have elapsed, had the user reconnected immediately), sufficient time for the site to assume that the user is no longer interested in recovery. Thus, a site can set a TTL on user recovery states based on the average time to reconnect among users utilizing the recovery feature. For instance, suppose Web logs show that 90% of recovered users reconnect within five minutes after a failure. Here, a TTL on user states could confidently be set at five minutes – users reconnecting after failure would have a high likelihood of recovery.

In the case of system-based invalidation, a TTL value for a view can be set based on the minimum of average times to update a specific data items in a view. For instance, if the fares in the database are updated every hour, the site could confidently set a TTL value for database views of 10 minutes. While this does not guarantee absolute correctness, sites are typically designed to handle transaction failures that occur when the underlying data values in a user's view have changed. If absolute correctness is required, event-driven invalidation, described next, can be used.

In the more general case, invalidation may be event driven. For example, consider the airline reservation system, and suppose that the fare offered to a user is dependent on the fare classes available for a given flight on a particular day (thus, a user would expect to see some variation in fares over time). Here, if a fare in the database is changed, the views using that fare data become invalid, and should no longer be used to serve user requests. This invalidation can be achieved using active database mechanisms, such as triggers.

3.5   Potential for Multiple Objectives

In database transactions, which represent specific goals, all the actions in a transaction work toward the same goal. Consider the example **iSAGA** in Section 3.1. Here, our user reveals two separate objectives: the mileage-checking objective and the ticket-buying objective, each represented by its own **sub-iSAGA**. Note that only one of these **sub-iSAGAs** can be active at any given time. For example, at component action A_3 (mileage-checking), the user is clearly active in the mileage-check **sub-iSAGA**, and not the ticket-purchase **sub-iSAGA**.

In a multi-objective **iSAGA**, given that the user may be hopping arbitrarily between different objectives, the possibility of failure in any one of the **sub-iSAGAs** of an **iSAGA** gives rise to an important question: to which objective should the user be recovered? Our solution is to postulate that the user should be returned to the objective (i.e., the **sub-iSAGA**) that was active at the time of failure. This places an interesting requirement on a recovery protocol: *in order to return the user to a useful point in the* **iSAGA**, *the user's* **sub-iSAGA** *of interest at the time of failure must be discerned, and all other* **sub-iSAGAs** *filtered out from consideration in the recovery protocol.* For example, in the airline **iSAGA**, recovery from a failure at action A_7 (seat selection) should not place the user at the mileage-checking action A_3. Similarly, failure at component action A_3 (mileage-checking) should not recover the user to the travel-plan entry action A_2.

Clearly, other schemes for choosing the **sub-iSAGA** for recovery are possible, e.g., offering the user a choice among all **sub-iSAGAs** in his **SAGA**, or choosing the **sub-iSAGA** with the largest number of actions. Note, however, that the scheme for choosing the **sub-iSAGA** to which a user should be recovered is independent of the recovery protocol, i.e., once the **sub-iSAGA** for recovery has been chosen, the protocol for recovering the user (in Section 6) remains the same.

Having described **iSAGAs** and how they differ from database SAGAs, we move on to describe a simple recovery technique for **iSAGAs**.

4   A Simple Recovery Technique

Recovering a user after a failure in an **iSAGA** requires (a) the ability to describe what a user has done, i.e, to model and capture a user state, and (b)the ability to bring the user back to a useful state upon reconnection after failure. We first provide a formal description of a user state, and then present our protocol.

4.1   What Is a User State?

Intuitively, a user state comprises all the information the Web site knows about a user at a given time. More formally,

Definition 3. *In an* **iSAGA***, a user's state changes from action to action. After each component action A_i in an* **iSAGA***, the user state S_i is a 3-tuple $\langle K_i, Q_i, P_i \rangle$, where*

- K_i *is the set of cookies valid for the user after action A_i,*
- Q_i *is the user's HTTP request corresponding to action A_i, and*
- P_i *is the site's HTTP response to Q_i.*

After every component action the user arrives at a specific state, and the subsequent component action is done over this new state.

In our airline site example in Section 3.1, the user submits the details of his travel, and the site gives back a set of itineraries to the user. After receiving the itineraries, the user's state is composed of his cookie information (which includes his login information), the HTTP request for the itineraries (containing his travel plans) and the site's HTTP response to his query (the page containing a set of itineraries). The itineraries given to the user are dependent on the state of the airline database at the time the query is processed. Thus, the user's state is dependent on the view of the database the site used to generate its response to him, i.e., the projection of the database that contains the itineraries related to user's travel details. Here, the user has a view V_i on the database. After execution of a component action A_i, the user's state S_i will be a function of the view V_i.

Given that a user's state is dependent on the state of the database and, (as noted in Section 3.4), might lose its value to the user over time, we associate a validity period with each user state. In simple cases the validity can be a TTL period. More complex cases might utilize a flag associated with a boolean expression, where this expression represents predicates over the underlying database.

For example, consider the seat-selection action in our airline site example. Suppose only a single seat is available on a particular flight, and that the Web site has offered that seat to two users. Further suppose that, in the process of selecting the open seat, one user's connection is lost. While he is reconnecting, the second user succeeds in reserving the final seat on the flight. When the first user reconnects, the Web site attempts to recover him to a recent valid state. However, as now there is no seat available in the flight the previous response as given to the user would be invalid. If a short TTL period (less than the average time to reconnect after failure) had been associated with the seat-selection user state, this state would likely have been invalid at the time of recovery, and the user recovered to a prior valid state in his **iSAGA**.

4.2   Recovery Protocol

Our proposed recovery protocol has two phases: (a) a *preparatory* phase, in which users' states are saved as they interact with the Internet; and (b) a *recovery* phase, in which the saved states are used to bring the user back to a valid recent state.

Preparatory Phase. In the preparatory phase, subsequent to each component action, a state is saved in a state log. In other words, upon the completion of a component action A_i, a state log records the user state S_i corresponding to A_i. The location where these saved states are stored is dependent on the system architecture, since wired and wireless scenarios present different challenges and opportunities for recovering users.

In a wireless scenario, for example, many client devices usually connect to the Internet via a single system called a gateway, which serves to bridge the protocol gap between wireless and wired systems (in a manner similar to dialing via modem to an ISP). Our recovery protocol can be deployed at a wireless gateway by enabling the gateway to store the users' states locally. Upon the need to recover, the gateway can check the recovering user's state set for the most recent valid state. If such a state exists for the user, the gateway can bring the user back to that state by replaying the response in the valid state to the user. In a wired network, the state-caching function of the gateway in the wireless scenario described above might be served by the site itself, or perhaps a proxy server or even an ISP.

Recovery Phase. The recovery phase ensues when an **iSAGA** fails. More formally, we can recover a valid state for the user on restart by following these steps.

1. **Check log for saved states:** The recovery system first checks the log for saved states for the restarting **iSAGA**.
2. **Check validity of the saved states:** For any saved states retrieved from the log, check the states' validity and remove any invalid states from consideration.
3. **Replay the most recent valid state:** Resend the response in the most recent valid state to the user.

Let us see how this recovery scheme works in our example **iSAGA**, described in Section 3.1. Suppose that our user was disconnected after action A_5, i.e., after receiving a choice of itineraries corresponding to his preferred origin and destination. The recovery system will recover the user differently, depending on when he restarts. If he reconnects within a very short time, say δt, and the validity time t of the user's state containing the itineraries is more than δt (assuming use of TTL based invalidation), then we can recover the user from the itinerary page. However, if the user reconnects after t, then the user cannot be recovered at that page, and would need to be recovered to a prior valid state.

The above scheme of recovery will work well if the component actions are related. However, unlike database transactions, this is not always the case. In an **iSAGA**, a user may be diverted to various unrelated actions while working toward his main goal. Consider the airline reservation **iSAGA**. Here, while purchasing an airline ticket, our user might check his frequent flier mileage (action A_3) in the middle of the **iSAGA**. If his **iSAGA** fails, say after action A_7 (seat-selection), the recovery system need not consider the mileage check, since it does not affect the ticket-buying process. In this type of scenario, the system should consider a subset of the user's sequence of the user's actions, rather than all actions, during recovery. In order to handle this aspect of **iSAGAs**, we modify our simple recovery technique. However, before embarking on a description of this more complete recovery technique, we first describe a means of identify different active **sub-iSAGAs** within an **iSAGA** using the notion of *dependency*.

5 Dependency of iSAGA Actions

A user's **iSAGA** consists of a sequence of actions $\langle A_1, A_2, ..., A_n \rangle$, not all of which are necessarily related to the same goal. The question of interest here is as follows: given a sequence of actions, $\langle A_1, A_2, ..., A_n \rangle$, which might contain different **sub-iSAGAs**, how we can extract the different **sub-iSAGAs** within it?

Extracting this information is possible due to the widespread use of dynamic page generation technologies. In sites using this type of technology, the response given to the user is a not a file residing in the web server, but rather the output generated by the execution of a program (called a *script*), based on parameters in the user request. There are several technologies, such as JSP [11], ASP [5], PHP [9], and Perl [14], that support dynamic page generation. These technologies have become popular because they dramatically increase the potential for interactivity with a user – a dynamic site composed of few scripts can potentially generate an infinite number of different pages based on information retrieved from an underlying database.

When a user interacts with a dynamic site, each component action A_i corresponds to running some script C_i. Consider the airline reservation system example. Here, when the user submits a request with his travel details (e.g., component action A_5), the site runs a program using the user's travel details as input parameter of the program. This program accesses the airline database, which returns a set of suitable itineraries. The program takes the itineraries returned from the database, adds an HTML presentation layer, and serves the itineraries back to the user as the site's response.

In sites built with these dynamic page generation technologies, it is possible to determine the **sub-iSAGAs** *in an* **iSAGA**. Each component action is carried out by dynamic scripts that run on an application server. Since HTTP is inherently a connectionless protocol [7], each of these dynamic scripts runs independently. However, quite often, a script may be dependent on information obtained or generated in another script. Consider, for example, the scenario where our traveler has selected his preferred itinerary on the airline site (component action A_6), and is then presented with a seat selection. The script that generates the itinerary choice list executes independently of the seat-selection script, but the seat-selection script must somehow know which flights are in the user's selected itinerary. Clearly, some method of passing information from one script to another is required. There are several ways to achieve this: (a) hidden fields in forms, (b) cookies, (c) session variables, and (d) explicit parameter passing through the HTTP get/post call.

Since there is a clear data dependency inherent in such parameter passing techniques, we can derive dependent sequences within an **iSAGA**. In particular, if $\langle A'_1, A'_2, ..., A'_n \rangle$ indicates an **iSAGA**, then to achieve a particular goal, we will require running of scripts $\langle C'_1, C'_2, ..., C'_n \rangle$ in sequence. These scripts will pass information from one script to the next using one of the methods described above. For example, C'_i will pass information to C'_{i+1}. In this case C'_{i+1} can be said to be dependent on C'_i (symbolically $C'_{i+1} \rightarrow C'_i$). Since the the number of ways scripts can pass information is limited, and decided at site design time, the site designer can statically describe the dependency list among scripts. Many commonly-used site analyzer/designer tools, e.g., Visual Interdev [6] can automatically determine the dependencies among scripts.

Let us assume that a user has completed a sequence of actions $\langle A_1, A_2, ..., A_n \rangle$. Corresponding to this sequence we have a sequence of scripts that has been executed for these actions, $C = \langle C_1, C_2, ..., C_n \rangle$. From this sequence of scripts we will be able to find a sequence $C' = \langle C'_1, C'_2 ..., C'_m \rangle$ such that $C'_i \in C$ and $C'_{i+1} \rightarrow C'_i, \forall C'_i \in C'$. From C we can identify all such C'.

Note that several variations on this theme are possible. For instance, a C_i such that $C_i \in C'$ and $C_i \in C''$, this means same script may be part of two **sub-iSAGAs**. We may also have a script C_i occurring twice in a sequence C'. Formally, there may exist a scripts C_i and C_j such that $C_i \in C'$ and $C_j \in C'$ and $C_i = C_j$.

After identifying all dependent sequences of scripts, we can map these scripts to corresponding component actions in the original **iSAGA** $A = \langle A_1, A_2, ..., A_n \rangle$. This will result in a set of action sequences $A' \subset A$, $A'' \subset A$, and so forth. Each such action sequence will correspond to a **sub-iSAGA** for a user. Formally, we define the notion of dependency, including invalidation requirements, as follows.

Definition 4. *A component action A_i is dependent on another component actions A_j if the script corresponding to action A_i (i.e., C_i) is dependent on a script C_j corresponding to action A_j.*

Axiom 1. *Let $\mathcal{S}_i$ be the state of the user after execution of action A_i. A_i is dependent on A_j and $\mathcal{S}_j$ is invalid indicates that $\mathcal{S}_i$ is also invalid. In other words, the validity period for $\mathcal{S}_i$ should be less than validity period of $\mathcal{S}_j$ if A_i is dependent on A_j.*

6   Complete Recovery Technique

Given the above discussion of multiple user objectives and dependency, we revisit our simple recovery technique. We first describe our more complete recovery technique intuitively. We then formally describe the recovery technique.

6.1   Intuition

When a component action in an **iSAGA** fails, the user may have already initiated multiple **sub-iSAGAs** in his **iSAGA**. The goal of our recovery protocol is to return the user to a state from which he can continue. As mentioned in Section 3.5, in the context of a multiple-objective **iSAGA**, the user will be recovered to the active **sub-iSAGA**. Consider the airline **iSAGA**, in which there are two clear **sub-iSAGAs**, the mileage-checking and the ticket-buying **sub-iSAGAs**. Suppose the **iSAGA** fails before the purchase action A_8 is complete. Clearly, here, the proposed recovery technique should bring the user to a state from which he can continue the ticket buying **sub-iSAGA**, and should not consider the user's mileage checking **sub-iSAGA**. Rather, it would make sense to bring the user either to the itinerary page or the page after login.

The recovery protocol is a two-step process. First, we identify the active **sub-iSAGA**, the one corresponding to the user's most recent completed action. Second, we will recover the user to the last valid recoverable state in the active **sub-iSAGA**. The preparatory phase, in which user states are collected and stored, is the same as in the simple recovery technique discussed in Section 4.

6.2   Recovery Technique

Consider a scenario in which a user has completed actions $\langle A_1, A_2, A_3, ..., A_n \rangle$, and component action A_{n+1} failed. We are interested in recovering the user to a recent valid state.

1. **Identify the active sub-iSAGA:** Let $A' = \langle A'_1, A'_2, ..., A'_m \rangle$ indicate a single **sub-iSAGA** such that $A'_m = A_n$, following the procedure described in Section 4. If there exist two action sequences A' and A'' which satisfy this condition, then we will consider the preceding action A_{n-1} to determine which **sub-iSAGA** was active before the failure occurred.
   Generally, we identify a sequence of actions $A' = \langle A'_1, A'_2, ..., A'_m \rangle$ indicating a single **sub-iSAGA** such that $A'_m = A_n, A'_{m-1} = A_{n-1}, ..., A'_{m-k} = A_{n-k}, A'_{m-k-1} \neq A_{n-k-1}$, where k is the maximum for all such k found among all **sub-iSAGAs** $A^i \in A$. Any tie will be resolved in step 2.
2. **Identify the most recent valid state:** We identify the action $A'_i \in A'$ for which there exists a valid state S_i such that i is maximum. In the case of a tie in step 1, we consider all such A_i's and choose the one with the latest timestamp corresponding to state S_i. We resolve the tie by considering the valid state which has occurred most recently.

7   Conclusion

In this paper, we consider the problem of recovering from failure during Internet transactions. We model user interactions with Web sites using the metaphor of a transaction, and describe a simple protocol for recovering from failure. We then expand our simple protocol to handle the complexity introduced by allowing multiple user goals in a single **iSAGA**.

References

1. R. Agrawal and D.J. DeWitt. Integrated concurrency control and recovery mechanisms: Design and performance evaluation. *ACM Transactions on Database Systems*, 10(4):529–564, 1985.
2. G. Alonso, D. Agrawal, A. El Abbadi, M. Kamath, R. Gunthor, and C. Mohan. Advanced transaction models in workflow contexts. In *Proceedings of the International Conference on Data Engineering*, pages 574–581, 1996.
3. P.K. Chrysanthis and K. Ramamritham. Acta: A framework for specifying and reasoning about transaction structure and behavior. In *Proceedings of the 1990 ACM SIGMOD Conference*, 1990.
4. P.K. Chrysanthis and K. Ramamritham. Synthesis of extended transaction models using acta. *ACM Transactions on Database Systems*, 19(3):450–491, 1994.
5. Microsoft Corporation. Active server pages tutorial. `http://msdn.microsoft.com/workshop/server/asp/asptutorial.asp`, 2001.
6. Microsoft Corporation. Visual interdev. `http://msdn.microsoft.com/vinterdev/`, 2001.
7. R. Fielding, J. Gettys, H. Frystyk, L. Masinter, P. Leach, and T. Berners-Lee. Hypertext transfer protocol – http/1.1. Available via FTP: `ftp://ftp.isi.edu/in-notes/rfc2616.txt`, 1999.
8. H. Garcia-Molina and K. Salem. Sagas. In *Proceedings of the 1987 ACM SIGMOD Conference*, 1987.
9. The PHP Group. What is php? `http://www.php.net/`, 2001.
10. T. Harder and A. Reuter. Principles of transaction-oriented database recovery. *ACM Computing Surveys*, 15(4):287–317, 1983.
11. Sun Microsystems. Java server pages. `http://java.sun.com/products/jsp/`, 2001.
12. C. Mohan, D. Haderle, B. Lindsay, H. Pirahesh, and P. Schwartz. Aries: A transaction recovery method supporting fine-granularity locking and partial rollbacks using write-ahead logging. *ACM Transactions on Database Systems*, 17(1):94–162, 1992.
13. N. Neves and W.K. Fuchs. Adaptive recovery for mobile environments. *Communications of the ACM*, 40(1):68–74, 1997.
14. Inc. O'Reilly & Associates. What is perl? `http://www.perl.com/pub`, 2001.
15. C. Pedregal-Martin and K. Ramamritham. Guaranteeing recoverability in electronic commerce. In *Proceedings of the Workshop on Advanced Issues in Electronic Commerce and Web-Based Information Systems*, 2001.
16. J.D. Tygar. Atomicity versus anonymity: Distributed transactions for electronic commerce. In *VLDB'98, Proceedings of 24rd International Conference on Very Large Data Bases, August 24-27, 1998, New York City*, pages 1–12, 1998.
17. U. Varshney and R. Vetter. Emerging mobile and wireless networks. *Communications of the ACM*, 43(6):73–81, 2000.
18. G.D. Walborn and P.K. Chrysanthis. Pro-motion: Management of mobile transactions. In *Proceedings of the Symposium on Applied Computing*, pages 101–108, 1997.

Security for Distributed E-Service Composition

Stefan Seltzsam, Stephan Börzsönyi, and Alfons Kemper

Universität Passau
Fakultät für Mathematik und Informatik
D-94030 Passau, Germany
{seltzsam,boerzsoe,kemper}@db.fmi.uni-passau.de
http://www.db.fmi.uni-passau.de/

Abstract. Current developments show that tomorrow's information systems and applications will no longer be based on monolithic architectures that encompass all the functionality. Rather, the emerging need for distribution and quick adaptation to new requirements stemming from, e.g., virtual enterprises, demands distributed systems that can be extended dynamically to compose new services from existing software components. However, usage of mobile code introduces specific security concerns which a security system must be aware of. We present a comprehensive security architecture for extensible, distributed systems using the example of an Internet query processing service which can be extended by user-defined operators. Before an operator is actually used in queries for the first time, our `OperatorCheck` server validates its semantics and analyzes its quality. This is done semi-automatically using an oracle-based approach to compare a formal specification of an operator against its implementation. Further security measures are integrated into the query processing engine: during plan distribution secure communication channels are established, authentication and authorization are performed, and overload situations are avoided by admission control. During plan execution operators are guarded using Java's security model to prevent unauthorized resource access and leakage of data. The resource consumption of operators is monitored and limited with reasonable supplementary costs to avoid resource monopolization. We show that the presented security system is capable of executing arbitrary operators without risks for the executing host and the privacy and integrity of data. In the paper we will concentrate on the `OperatorCheck` server, as this server can itself be viewed as an e-service that can be used by developers and independent associations.

1 Introduction

The recent trend towards extensible and distributed systems demands new sophisticated security systems to meet the challenges of mobile, user-defined code. Examples for such systems are Web browsers executing Applets, Web application servers executing Servlets and Java Server Pages, and extensible database management systems implementing, e.g., the SQL99 [22] standard for user-defined functions. Nowadays even more and more wireless devices execute code in form of

F. Casati, D. Georgakopoulos, M.-C. Shan (Eds.): TES 2001, LNCS 2193, pp. 147–162, 2001.

WML scripts [9], e.g., to interact with a mobile e-commerce system. In this paper we use ObjectGlobe [2], a distributed and extensible query processor written in Java, as an example for such a system. To describe it in short, ObjectGlobe can execute a query with—in principle—unrelated query operators, cycle providers (used to execute operators), and data sources.

The openness of a system like ObjectGlobe creates new demands on a security system. The code of external, i.e. user-defined, operators is unknown. Thus, users of operators do not know, if the operator calculates the correct result, crashes, or manipulates data given to it. For this reason quality assurance is necessary, because users of external operators want to feel certain about the semantics and functioning of operators to be able to rely upon the results of a query. As in every distributed system, it is necessary to protect communication channels against tampering and eavesdropping. Cycle providers execute arbitrary external operators, thus cycle providers need a security architecture which prevents external operators from accessing resources like the file system of the cycle provider, monopolizing resources like memory or CPU time, or manipulating vital components of the ObjectGlobe system. Additionally, cycle providers need an authorization framework to be able to determine the identity of a user.

The goal of this work is to provide a security architecture for ObjectGlobe addressing all mentioned challenges, which is generally appropriate for distributed and extensible systems. Due to space limitations we will concentrate on quality assurance. In order to achieve these goals we have to rely upon some basic assumptions about the environment of ObjectGlobe. First, we assume that the operating system which is running ObjectGlobe is secure and that the administrators of the cycle provider are trustworthy, because we cannot protect the system against the operating system. Second, we assume that the code and the Java Virtual Machine (JVM) used to run ObjectGlobe are unmodified. These requirements are enforced in ObjectGlobe by giving the user the possibility to restrict the cycle providers to a set of trusted cycle providers. The last and most serious assumption is, that the security system of Java 2 [19] works as designed. There have been some security related bugs and implementation flaws of Java, but it seems that there are no elementary flaws in the design of the security model.

The remainder of this paper is organized as follows: Section 2 gives an overview of ObjectGlobe. Section 3 points out the security requirements of such an open system. Section 4 gives a survey about the security measures during plan distribution and Section 5 outlines runtime guarding and monitoring measures used to detect malicious or defective operators. Section 6 describes in detail preventive measures appropriate to detect the majority of low quality and malicious external operators before actually executing them in queries. Related work is addressed in Section 7 and Section 8 concludes this paper.

2   Overview of the ObjectGlobe System

ObjectGlobe distributes powerful query processing capabilities (including those found in traditional database systems) across the Internet. The idea is to create an open market place for three kinds of suppliers: *data providers* supply data, *function providers* offer query operators to process the data, and *cycle providers* are contracted to execute query operators. Of course, a single site (even a single machine) can comprise all three services, i.e., act as data-, function-, and cycle provider. In fact, we expect that most data and function providers will also act as cycle providers. ObjectGlobe enables applications to execute complex queries which involve the execution of operators from multiple function providers at different sites (cycle providers) and the retrieval of data and documents from multiple data sources. In this paper we assume that all data is in a standard format (e.g., relational or XML) or wrapped [21]. Furthermore, we assume that there is a meta-schema that can be used to describe all relevant properties of all services.

2.1 Query Processing

Processing a query in ObjectGlobe involves four major steps (Fig. 1):

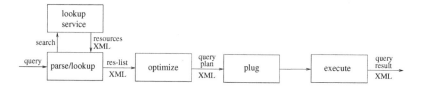

Fig. 1. Processing a Query in ObjectGlobe.

1. Lookup: In this phase, the ObjectGlobe lookup service [16] is queried to find relevant data sources, cycle providers, and query operators that might be useful to execute the query. In addition, the lookup service provides the authorization data—mirrored and integrated from the individual providers— to determine what resources may be accessed by the user who initiates the query and what other restrictions apply for processing the query.
2. Optimize: The information obtained from the lookup service is used by a query optimizer to compile a valid (as far as user privileges are concerned) query execution plan. This plan—represented as XML document—is anno- tated with site information indicating on which cycle provider each operator is executed and from which function provider the external query operators involved in the plan are loaded. Such annotations are used as well for other information, e.g., authentication data and estimated resource requirements.
3. Plug: The generated plan is distributed to the cycle providers and external query operators are loaded and instantiated at each cycle provider. Further- more, the communication paths (i.e., sockets) are established. If necessary, communication is encrypted and authenticated.
4. Execute: The plan is executed following an iterator model [11]. In addition to the external query operators provided by function providers, ObjectGlobe

has built-in query operators for selection, projection, join, union, nesting, unnesting, and sending and receiving data. The execution of the plan is monitored in order to detect failures.

The whole system is written in Java for two reasons[1]. First, Java is portable so that ObjectGlobe can be installed with very little effort; in particular, cycle providers which need to install the ObjectGlobe core functionality can very easily join an ObjectGlobe system. The only requirement is that a site runs the ObjectGlobe server on a JVM. Second, Java provides secure extensibility. Although many people complain about the execution speed of Java programs, we noticed that by avoiding some pitfalls in the Java I/O library the execution speed of the Java Virtual Machine is no bottleneck in wide area distributed systems. Like ObjectGlobe itself, external query operators are written in Java: they are loaded on demand (from function providers). Just like data and cycle providers, function providers and their external query operators must be registered in the lookup service before they can be used. Up to now ObjectGlobe uses a simple classification system for operators: every external operator is associated with a class (e.g., Join). The optimizer chooses the operator actually used within a class considering different aspects, e.g., execution time and time needed to load the operator.

2.2 Example Plan

Figure 2 shows an example of distributed query processing with ObjectGlobe. Suppose you are going on holiday to Nassau, Bahamas, and you are looking for a hotel that is cheap and close to the beach. This task is known as the "maximum vector problem" [20] (actually we are searching for the minimal vectors). Formulated precisely, we are looking for all hotels, which are not dominated by other ones. A hotel dominates another one, if it is cheaper *and* closer to the beach. Dominance imposes a partial ordering on the hotels.

A naive solution for this problem is to compare each hotel against each other and delete dominated hotels yielding quadratic runtime. However, a more sophisticated algorithm with a lower complexity has been developed by [17]. [1] have investigated this algorithm in the context of databases and adapted it to constrained primary memory. They called the operation "Skyline".

The resources used to find the desired cheap hotel near the beach are as follows: two web sites, www.hotelbook.com and www.hotelguide.com, supply hotel data and all external operators are provided by the function provider www.operators.org. Two wrappers, HotelBookWrapper and HotelGuideWrapper, are responsible for querying the two web sites and transforming the data into ObjectGlobe's internal format. They are executed at cycle providers located near the data sources in order to minimize transfer time. As the following equation holds for the Skyline operator, it can be applied to each database directly in order to further reduce data shipping costs:

$$Skyline(Skyline(A) \cup Skyline(B)) = Skyline(A \cup B)$$

---

[1] Currently, the optimizer is written in C++, but we plan to rewrite it in Java.

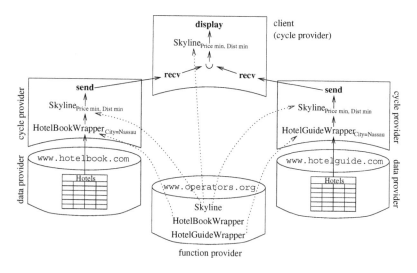

Fig. 2. Processing a Query in ObjectGlobe.

Thus, only the best hotels are passed to the client. The send/receive iterator pairs performing the transmission of data are installed automatically during the plug phase. The client calculates the Skyline of the union of both data sources, and the user can choose a hotel from the result.

3   Security Requirements

We will now analyze the security requirements of users and cycle providers. First, we will concentrate on security issues introduced by external operators: cycle providers want to be able to execute arbitrary external operators in a safe way, i.e., they want to be sure that operators do not monopolize resources, access resources like the file system unauthorized or manipulate vital components of the system. We now demonstrate some attacks and the implications they would have without an effective security system using modified versions of the Skyline operator.

Example. *Resource Monopolization*

```
public class Skyline extends IteratorClass {
  public TypeSpec open() throws CommandFailedException,IOException {
    List l = new LinkedList();
    while(true)
      l.add(new Object());
    ...}...}
```

The example above shows a code snippet which monopolizes the memory by continuously generating and storing new `Object` instances in a `LinkedList`. The execution of this operator would result in a denial of service because there would be not enough memory for other operators. Of course, an external operator could just as well monopolize CPU time, secondary memory, or any other limited shared resource. It would also be possible for an operator to, e.g., access the file system to modify arbitrary files or to steal confidential data.

Apart from security requirements of providers there are requirements of users. They want to be certain about the semantics of external operators to be able to rely upon the results of a query even when they use external operators. Recall the query using a Skyline operator to find the hotels which are cheap and near the beach. And now assume a modified Skyline operator that filters all hotels of the Sheraton hotel chain. The result of a query using this modified Skyline would be all cheap hotels near the beach being not member of the Sheraton hotel chain, which is not the result the user asked for. Privacy is another severe requirement endangered by external operators: an operator could calculate the result as supposed to do, but it could send a copy of the processed data to an arbitrary host in the Internet or leak data to a concurrent query, possibly compromising confidentiality of data. For that reason it is necessary that the security system can guarantee, that data given to an operator can only flow using communication channels which are obvious to and authorized by the user.

In addition to the security requirements induced by external query operators there are some which are common to many distributed systems. First, using our terminology, cycle and data providers may have a legitimate interest in obtaining the identity of users for authorization purposes. It must be considered that users normally want to stay anonymous as far as possible, therefore it must not be mandatory to give authentication data to cycle providers. Second, the communication channels between different collaborating hosts must be protected against tampering to avoid unnoticed modifications of the data. Additionally it must be possible to encrypt confidential data to prevent other parties from eavesdropping. Third, cycle providers need an admission control system to guard themselves against overload situations.

To meet these requirements we use a multilevel security architecture combining preventive measures, security measures during plan distribution, and a runtime security system. Preventive measures take place before an operator is actually used in queries for the first time. They are used to validate the semantics and analyze the quality of the operator. Based upon the validation results, ObjectGlobe could renounce runtime security measures. As preventive measures are optional, untested operators are regarded as malicious and all security measures apply. During plan distribution, common security measures of distributed systems take place including admission control. The remaining security requirements, e.g., protection of cycle providers, are met by the runtime architecture. For length limitations we give a brief overview of the mandatory security levels, i.e., security measures during plan distribution and the runtime security architecture, in the next two sections. Thereafter we present the preventive measures in detail and point out the advantages of validated operators.

4   Security Measures During Plan Distribution

We will now have a look at the common security requirements of distributed systems, as enumerated above. We meet these requirements during plan distribution, where four security related actions take place: setup of secure communication channels, authentication, authorization, and admission control.

Privacy and integrity of data and function code that is transmitted between ObjectGlobe servers is protected against unauthorized access and manipulation by using the well-established secure communication standards SSL (Secure Sockets Layer) and/or TLS (Transport Layer Security) for encrypting and authenticating (digitally signing) messages. Both protocols can carry out the authentication of ObjectGlobe communication partners via X.509 certificates [14], thus ensuring communication with the desired ObjectGlobe server. The security level of network connections can be chosen dependent on the processed data.

If authentication is required for authorization or accounting purposes of providers, ObjectGlobe can authenticate users using one of two possibilities: digitally signed plans or password-based authentication. Of course, usage of X.509 certificates is preferred, but until certificates are widely used, password-based authentication is supported as an alternative. Certificate based authentication requires plans with signatures generated using the secret key of the user. The signature is based on the XML document containing the query plan and a time stamp to avoid reusage of signed plans. The signature of a query arriving at a provider is verified using the user's X.509 certificate and thereafter the originator and the integrity of the query is known reliably. Providers can use this knowledge to enforce their local authorization policy autonomously. Of course, users and applications accessing only free and publicly available resources can stay anonymous and no authentication is required. If a user wants to access a resource that charges and accepts electronic payment, the user can remain anonymous as well (if the electronic payment system supports it) and the electronic payment is shipped as part of the plug phase.

The last security related action during plan distribution, which is needed by all systems offering services to users, is admission control. ObjectGlobe's admission control component determines whether the estimated resource demands of a query—calculated using the cost models of the operators—can be satisfied by the executing host or not. This is done to be able to abort a query as early as possible if any cycle provider executing a part of the query cannot satisfy the resource requirements of the query. Queries whose resource requirements can be fulfilled are scheduled using a FCFS (first come first served) scheduler considering only primary memory usage of the operators. We assume, that a sufficient amount of all other resources like secondary memory is available. This scheduling approach works well, because every query is only allowed to use a small fraction of the primary memory of the server, so a certain degree of parallel execution is guaranteed.

5   Architecture of the Runtime Security System

After plan distribution, all involved cycle providers execute the operators assigned to them to calculate the result of the query. Therefore, they must be protected from damages by malicious or low quality operators as outlined above. To satisfy security interests of users, the security system must also be able to guarantee, that data given to an operator can only flow using communication channels which are obvious to and authorized by the user. These security requirements are met using two techniques: guarding and monitoring.

The guarding mechanisms are realized using Java's security architecture, i.e. security manager and class loaders—to control and restrict access to resources of the cycle provider and components of the ObjectGlobe system.

The class loader's task is to load the bytecode of a class into memory, monitor the loaded code's origin (i.e., its URL), and to verify the signatures of signed code. Additionally, every class loader generates its own name space. To prevent external operators from abusing a connection to a function provider as covert communication channel by requesting classes with data coded into the names of the classes, all (non built-in) classes required by the external operator must be combined into a JAR file. This file is loaded and cached by the class loader during the plug phase, so only one connection to the function provider is necessary. The security manager controls the access to safety critical system resources, such as the file system, network sockets, peripherals, etc. The security manager is used to create a so-called *sandbox* in which untrusted code is executed. Privileges can be granted to code based on the origin and whether or not it is digitally signed. Of course, it would be unreasonable to grant unprotected access to system resources to unknown code. Therefore, all user-defined operators are normally executed in a "tight" sandbox. Furthermore, queries running in parallel are separated from each other to prevent them from exchanging information with each other via, e.g., static class variables. This is done by using a new class loader instance (called `OGClassLoader`) for each query which implicitly separates the name spaces. In this way, external operators are isolated and leakage of data is prevented, because they are only able to communicate with their children and parent operators. Additionally, only selected classes of the name space of the ObjectGlobe system are known to the name spaces of operators, thus protecting vital components of the system. For example, `TmpFile` is a class available to operators and implements a secure interface to the file system to enable operators to use temporary files. The sandbox, the name space separation, and the class loaders are illustrated schematically in Fig. 3.

Monitoring measures are necessary to avoid resource monopolization. We use our own (platform-dependent) resource accounting library which supervises CPU and primary memory usage of external operators[2], because Java does not offer such functionality. Accounting of secondary memory and data volume produced by an operator is done using pure Java. External operators must be endowed with (worst-case) cost models written in MathML [15] for their CPU usage, consumption of primary and secondary memory, number of temporary files in use simultaneously and the number and size of tuples they produce. The last two cost models are necessary to prevent operators from blocking the network and from flooding their parent operators. If an external operator is not equipped with its own cost models, ObjectGlobe uses default cost models, which of course might not be very appropriate. The optimizer annotates query plans with estimated

---

[2] Using our library, accounting results in overheads between 5% and 10%.

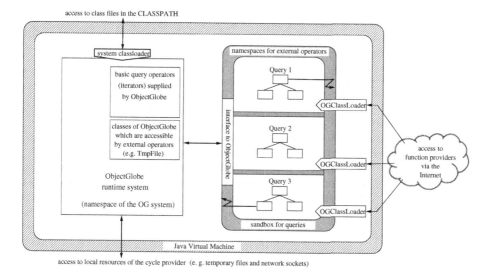

Fig. 3. Protection of the Resources of Cycle Providers.

values for the number and size of the tuples that the different operators will produce. Using these values and the cost models a cycle provider is able to calculate the initial resource limits for an external operator. To be able to keep track of resource consumption, every external operator is executed by a separate thread and disconnected from other operators using buffers, each managed by a send/receive iterator pair.

If there is any limit violation, the monitoring component checks, if the limits have to be adapted dynamically. This is done, if changes to the calculation basis of the cost models occurred, e.g., the optimizer estimated that the underlying operator will produce 100 tuples but it produced 110 tuples up to now. If the newly calculated resource demands of the operator exceed the upper resource limits set by the cycle provider, the plan is aborted. The plan is also aborted, when the newly calculated resource limits are still too low to satisfy the current resource demand of the operator. Otherwise the operator is allowed to resume work until there is another limit violation or the operator terminates normally.

6 Quality Assurance for External Operators

Using the security measures presented up to now, we are able to execute arbitrary external operators without risk for cycle providers and privacy and integrity of data. Nevertheless, it would be advantageous, if the system could in advance verify the semantics of new external operators, examine their behavior under heavy load, and compare their resource consumption with given cost models. If an operator is well-behaved, ObjectGlobe could renounce security measures and execute the code at full speed or it could relax the sandbox of an operator. Several methods of software verification and testing have been developed so far (see [18] for an overview), but it has also been shown that in general the correctness of arbitrary code cannot be proved [13].

6.1   The Goal of Testing

Testing is a verification technique used to find bugs by executing a program. The testing process consists of designing test cases, preparing test data, running the program with these test data, and comparing the results to the correct results. An oracle[3] is consulted for the correct result. This could be a human, a reference implementation, or an interpreter of a (formal) specification of the program. While the design of good test cases requires some ingenuity, test data can sometimes be derived automatically. For automated testing, a test driver is necessary to feed test data to the function and to receive and record the results.

Testing methods, actually methods for deriving test cases, can be divided into two classes, white-box and black-box testing, depending on whether the source code is available or not. [18] provides a detailed description of the most important techniques. We are focusing on black-box testing.

6.2   Methods of Formal Specification

As the correctness of a program depends on what exactly it is supposed to do, a complete and consistent specification is necessary. If testing should be processed automatically, a formal specification is required so that an interpreter can determine whether a calculated result is correct. There are two classes of formal specifications: *Operational techniques* describe a way how the result could be calculated. Their advantage is that the correct result can be determined in advance and compared to the result of the program. However, they will not choose the most efficient way and hence are not a viable alternative to the real program. In contrast to that, *descriptive techniques* specify what the result should look like. Although the correct result cannot be calculated, the result of the program can be checked against them. Moreover, they usually are even more concise than operational specifications.

We have investigated several methods of formal specifications, e.g., SQL, Haskell, Prolog, and mathematical formulae. Table 1 shows these specification methods for the Skyline operator. For our purpose, the best choice is to use a (purely) functional language like Haskell, because coding is quite straightforward and functional languages are Turing-complete and thus (theoretically) every operator can be specified that way. Another advantage of Haskell is that there are interpreters that can execute the specification and thus the correct result can easily be calculated.

Especially in the database context, not only the correctness of the result is important but also the efficiency of its computation. Therefore, the specification of an external operator is augmented with several cost models. For each

---

[3] We think of an oracle in the true sense of the word, not of the commercial DBMS.

Table 1. Specification Methods for Database Operators (Skyline).

	Skyline $(S, \succeq)$	Explanation
Formula	$\{s \mid s \in S \wedge \neg \exists t \in S : t \neq s \wedge t \succeq s\}$	This formula can be derived directly from the definition: "The Skyline of a set S consists of all tuples s that are in S and for which no tuple t exists in S that is different from s and dominates s."
Conditions	Pre $\equiv$ **true** Post $\equiv \forall s \in \mathrm{Skyline}(S)$: $(s \in S \wedge \neg \exists t \in S : t \neq s \wedge t \succeq s)$ $\wedge \; \forall s \in S \setminus \mathrm{Skyline}(S)$: $(\exists t \in S : t \neq s \wedge t \succeq s)$	There is no precondition, i.e., the Skyline operator can be applied to any arbitrary set on which a partial ordering relation is defined. The postcondition describes which tuples may be in the Skyline (cf. the formula above) and which must not be left out, defining exactly the result.

SQL	`SELECT *`
	 `FROM S s`
	 `WHERE NOT EXISTS (`
	 `  SELECT * FROM S t`
	 `  WHERE t`$\neq$`s AND t`$\succeq$`s);`
		This is the naive approach to calculate the Skyline. Each tuple is compared to each tuple and is only selected if it is not dominated by any other tuple. $\neq$ and $\succeq$ must be adapted to the specific scenario.

Prolog	`skyline(S,R) :- skyline'(S,S,R).`
	 `skyline'([],T,[]).`
	 `skyline'([X|S],T,R) :-`
	 `  dominated(X,T),`
	 `  skyline'(S,T,R).`
	 `skyline'([X|S],T,[X|R]) :-`
	 `  not(dominated(X,T)),`
	 `  skyline'(S,T,R).`
	 `dominated(X,[Y|T]) :-`
	 `  dominance(Y,X).`
	 `dominated(X,[Y|T]) :-`
	 `  dominated(X,T).`
	 `dominance(Y,X) :- Y`$\neq$`X, Y`$\succeq$`X.`
		The Skyline of a list S is R, if the result of a function `skyline'` that filters S with itself, i.e., compares each tuple with each tuple and deletes dominated tuples, is also R. If the empty list [] is filtered, the result is also empty.
		 Now consider a list that contains at least one element X. If X is dominated by any tuple of the filter T, the result consists only of the rest of the list still to be filtered by T. Otherwise, X is taken over into the result.
		 X is dominated by a non-empty list, if it is dominated by the first element or by the rest. If the list is empty, X is considered not dominated (closed world assumption).

Haskell	`skyline :: [`α`] → [`α`]`
	 `skyline ss = skyline' ss ss`
	 `skyline' [] ts = []`
	 `skyline' (s:ss) ts =`
	 `  if dominated s ts`
	 `    then skyline' ss ts`
	 `    else s:skyline' ss ts`
	 `dominated s [] = False`
	 `dominated s (t:ts) =`
	 `  dominance t s || dominated s ts`
	 `dominance t s = (t`$\neq$`s && t`$\succeq$`s)`
		`skyline` is a function that takes a list of elements of some type α and returns a list of elements of the same type. Like in Prolog, the Skyline of a list ss is the result of a function `skyline'` that filters ss with itself.
		 Again, there is a distinction between the empty list [] and a list containing at least one element. This element is only taken over into the result if it is not dominated by any element of the filter ts.

supervised resource the user can specify a worst-case cost model, which is a function of the extents of the input relations, namely their number of tuples, their maximum tuple size, and their total data size. If any resource is overconsumed, the operator is considered faulty and aborted immediately in a real application. Nevertheless, the cost models should not be chosen too generous, because then a cycle provider might refuse to instantiate the operator.

6.3   User-Directed Test Data Generation

As stated before, the design of good test cases requires some ingenuity. Thus, in our implementation, it is possible to direct the generation of test data so that they fulfill the preconditions of operators as well as meet the testers' strategies. Testers may want to specify single attribute values, enforce functional dependencies between attributes, establish relationships between relations, and control the order of the tuples. Therefore, the generation is done in three steps. First, the relation is created and the attribute types and the number of tuples are specified. Second, all attribute rows are filled by random values or by referencing other relations. Third, the relation can be sorted or permuted some other way.

For a single attribute column, the values can be generated randomly or deterministically. The latter means that the values are taken one after the other in increasing order. If there are more tuples than different values, the procedure is started cyclically again. Random values can be taken uniformly from their possible values. In order to simulate functional dependencies and primary keys, it is important that unique values can be generated. [7] presents an algorithm that produces random numbers with this property. For Real values, other distributions are possible, e.g., normal distribution, exponential distribution, etc. Foreign key relationships can also be simulated. For 1:1 relationships, the attributes of the other relation can be copied one after the other or be referenced unique-randomly. For 1:N relationships, a uniform random reference should be applied. Occasionally the order of the tuples matters. Thus, the relation can be sorted by the values of an attribute. Moreover, a shuffle operation has been implemented that permutes the tuples of a relation. This is useful to create a slight disorder. A factor between 0.0 (identity) and 1.0 (completely random shuffle) describes how far a tuple can move relative to the cardinality of the relation.

6.4   The OperatorCheck Server

We have implemented a server that checks external operators in ObjectGlobe by performing some tests on them. This server can itself be viewed as an e-service that can be used by developers during development to test the implementation of operators. Trustworthy independent associations can use the server to check external operators and to generate digitally signed test reports. For demonstration purpose, an installation is accessible via a Web interface at

`http://www.db.fmi.uni-passau.de/projects/OG/OnlineDemo/operatorcheck.phtml`

Figure 4 shows the architecture of the server. The tester provides a Java Archive containing the external operator to be tested, a formal specification of the operator in Haskell (for a correctness test) or a cost model (for a benchmark test), and some directives on how the test data should look like.

For a *correctness test*, the server generates test data based on the directives and stores them on the hard disk. A Haskell program is built out of the formal specification and the generic ObjectGlobe query execution plan is assembled. Now the test is performed: The Haskell interpreter and the ObjectGlobe system calculate their results. Afterwards, the results are loaded and compared, and the user receives the result of the test. For comparison, the semantics of the result must be taken into account. If the resulting relation is a list, the order of the tuples and hence their count is important. A multiset is a set where an element may occur several times. The order of the elements, however, is arbitrary. In a set, neither order nor count of elements matters. Furthermore, it is possible to perform a *reference test*. Instead of providing a Haskell specification, the user

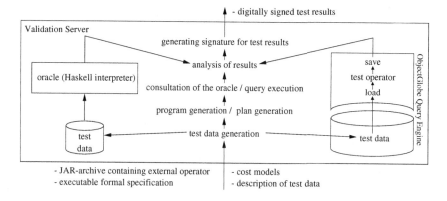

Fig. 4. Architecture of the Operator Check Server.

can also nominate another ObjectGlobe operator that should serve as the oracle. The testing process works in an analogous way.

In a *benchmark test*, no oracle is consulted, but the test operator is executed several times using different sizes of input data. Instead of a formal specification, the user provides cost models for several resources. The consumption of these resources is measured and compared to the cost models. The test result shows the actually consumed resources and the maximum allowed by the cost models. Using large input sizes, a stress test can be carried out that examines the behavior of the operator under heavy load and checks whether its performance degenerates or is still in accordance with the cost models.

6.5   Limitations of Testing

E. W. Dijkstra noted that "program testing can be used to show the presence of bugs, but never to show their absence" [4]. Nevertheless, testing provides a practicable and promising way to find bugs in a piece of code, thus improving the trust in it. Several sophisticated methods of deriving "good" test cases have been developed. Under the hypothesis that the tested program behaves the same way for all test data of an equivalence class, the correctness can even be guaranteed by successful tests with one representative of each class. Malicious operators, however, intentionally destroy the uniformity hypothesis. This can only be detected by a white-box test which can inspect the source code. Therefore, it is still necessary to take some more measures for absolute security.

7   Related Work

There are a lot of extensible database systems allowing the implementation of user-defined functions as predicates or general functions/operators, in C, C++,

or Java. Examples for such systems include POSTGRES [23], Iris [25], and Starburst [12], but there are also several commercially available systems like Informix,
Oracle, and DB2. These systems are all more or less exposed to the same security
risks as ObjectGlobe even if they do not load untrusted code dynamically from
function providers like ObjectGlobe. The security measures of most systems are
not appropriate to guard the database system against attacks from such code.
Thus, only administrators are allowed to augment the functionality and they
have to take care that the extensions are well-behaved and non-malicious. For
example, DB2 implements the SQL99 standard for user-defined functions and
provides the possibility to specify a function as FENCED to execute it in an own
process. In this way, the internal structures of the database system are protected,
but denial of service attacks are still possible. Only recently, with the development of Java as a secure programming language, some new considerations have
been taken into account. [10] have compared the efficiency of several designs
using the PREDATOR database server, namely the naive approach of putting
user-defined functions directly into the server process, running them in a separate process and communicating with the server process via shared memory,
and accessing Java user-defined functions via the Java Native Interface. Their
conclusion is that Java is a bit slower in the average case but a viable and secure
alternative, still facing the problem of denial of service attacks. [5] recommend
to use a resource accounting system like JRes to guard against denial of service
attacks, bill users, and obtain feedback that can be used for adaptive query op-
timization. To neutralize resource-unstable functions, they restrict CPU usage,
number of threads, and memory usage to a fixed limit, which is not appropriate
for complex operators.

Beside database systems, there are, e.g., Java operating systems, which have
to care about security, because enforcing resource limits has been a responsibility of operating systems for a long time. Another task of operating systems is
to separate applications to avoid interference. Using our security system, a Java
operating system could limit the amount of damage that a compromised application could do to the system and other applications on the system as described
in [6]. This paper proposes the usage of Trusted Linux as secure platform for
e-services application hosting, because it adequately protects the host platform
as well as other applications if an application is attacked and compromised.

The OperatorCheck approach is used to validate the semantics and to analyze the quality of operators. Thus, the quality of service of validated operators
is higher than of untested operators. This leads to a more reliable query execution, continuously available cycle providers, and to better result quality. A more
detailed motivation for the importance of these aspects can be found in [24].
Obviously, for upcoming e-service composition frameworks like eFlow [3] and
E-speak [8] those quality considerations will also play a very important role.

8   Conclusion

We presented an effective security framework for distributed, extensible systems
and used ObjectGlobe as an example. We focused on security requirements of

cycle providers and users. The security requirements of users are satisfied by the OperatorCheck server which is used to rate the quality of external operators and test their semantics. Privacy and integrity of data are guaranteed by isolating external operators and by usage of secure communication channels. Cycle providers are protected using a monitoring component which tracks resource usage of external operators to prevent them from resource monopolization and an admission control system to guard providers against overload situations. A security manager and class loaders are used to protect cycle providers from unauthorized resource accesses and to shield the ObjectGlobe system from external operators. Additionally we presented the authorization framework of Object-Globe which can be used by cycle providers to determine the identity of users in a reliable way.

The security system can easily be adapted to other applications, e.g., Web application servers using server-side Java components such as Servlets, Java Server Pages and Enterprise Java Beans to generate dynamic Web content. Nowadays it is common, not to operate an own Web server, but to out source this to specialized suppliers. Using our security system, suppliers of such services can set resource limits to, e.g., Java Server Pages. Of course, there are some necessary adaptions to the security system. For example, server-side components usually do not have real cost models, but in most cases (e.g., primary and secondary memory) it is sufficient to use fixed resource limits. Additionally, the resource monitoring component can be used to establish a "per-resource" instead of, for example, a flat-rate tariff structure.

References

1. S. Börzsönyi, D. Kossmann, and K. Stocker. The Skyline Operator. In *Proc. IEEE Conf. on Data Engineering*, pages 421–430, Heidelberg, Germany, 2001.
2. R. Braumandl, M. Keidl, A. Kemper, D. Kossmann, A. Kreutz, S. Seltzsam, and K. Stocker. ObjectGlobe: Ubiquitous Query Processing on the Internet. *The VLDB Journal: Special Issue on E-Services*, 2001. To appear.
3. F. Casati, S. Ilnicki, L.-J. Jin, and M.-C. Shan. An Open, Flexible, and Configurable System for Service Composition. In *Proceedings of the Second International Workshop on Advance Issues of E-Commerce and Web-Based Information Systems (WECWIS 2000)*, pages 125–132, Milpitas, California, 2000.
4. O.-J. Dahl, E. W. Dijkstra, and C. A. R. Hoare. *Structured Programming*. Academic Press, Inc., New York, 1972.
5. G. Czajkowski, T. Mayr, P. Seshadri, and T. v. Eicken. Resource Control for Database Extensions. Technical Report 98-1718, Department of Computer Science, Cornell University, November 1998.
6. C. Dalton and T. H. Choo. An Operating System Approach to Securing E-Services. *Communications of the ACM*, 44(2):58–64, February 2001.
7. D. DeWitt. The Wisconsin Benchmark: Past, Present, and Future. In J. Gray, editor, *The Benchmark Handbook for Database and Transaction Systems*. Morgan Kaufmann Publishers, San Mateo, CA, USA, 2. edition, 1993.
8. S. Frolund, F. Pedone, J. Pruyne, and A. v. Moorsel. Building Dependable Internet Services with E-speak. Technical Report HPL-2000-78, Hewlett-Packard, 2000.

9. A. K. Ghosh and T. M. Swaminatha. Software Security and Privacy Risks in Mobile E-Commerce. *Communications of the ACM*, 44(2):51–57, February 2001.

10. M. Godfrey, T. Mayr, P. Seshadri, and T. v. Eicken. Secure and Portable Database Extensibility. In *Proc. of the ACM SIGMOD Conf. on Management of Data*, pages 390–401, Seattle, WA, USA, June 1998.

11. G. Graefe. Query Evaluation Techniques for Large Databases. *ACM Computing Surveys*, 25(2):73–170, June 1993.

12. L. M. Haas, W. Chang, G. M. Lohman, J. McPherson, P. F. Wilms, G. Lapis, B. Lindsay, H. Pirahesh, M. J. Carey, and E. Shekita. Starburst Mid-Flight: As the Dust Clears. *IEEE Transactions on Knowledge and Data Engineering*, 2(1):143–160, March 1990.

13. J. Hartmanis and J. E. Hopcroft. Independence Results in Computer Science. In *SIGACT News*, volume 8, pages 13–24, 1976.

14. R. Housley, W. Ford, W. Polk, and D. Solo. Internet X.509 Public Key Infrastructure Certificate and CRL Profile. `http://www.rfc-editor.org/rfc/rfc2459.txt`, January 1999.

15. P. Ion and R. Miner. Mathematical Markup Language. `http://www.w3.org/Math/`, July 1999.

16. M. Keidl, A. Kreutz, A. Kemper, and D. Kossmann. Verteilte Metadatenverwaltung für die Anfragebearbeitung auf Internet-Datenquellen. In *Proc. GI Conf. on Database Systems for Office, Engineering, and Scientific Applications (BTW)*, Informatik aktuell, pages 107–126, New York, Berlin, etc., 2001. Springer-Verlag.

17. H. T. Kung, F. Luccio, and F. P. Preparata. On Finding the Maxima of a Set of Vectors. *Journal of the ACM*, 22(4):469–476, 1975.

18. G. J. Myers. *The Art of Software Testing*. John Wiley & Sons, New York, 1979.

19. S. Oaks. *Java Security*. O'Reilly & Associates, Sebastopol, CA, USA, 1998.

20. F. P. Preparata and M. I. Shamos. *Computational Geometry: An Introduction*. Springer-Verlag, New York, Berlin, etc., 1985.

21. M. Tork Roth and P. Schwarz. Don't Scrap It, Wrap It! A Wrapper Architecture for Legacy Data Sources. In *Proc. of the Conf. on Very Large Data Bases (VLDB)*, pages 266–275, Athens, Greece, August 1997.

22. International Organization for Standardization. Database Language SQL. Document ISO/IEC 9075:1999, 1999.

23. M. Stonebraker and L. Rowe. The Design of POSTGRES. In *Proc. of the ACM SIGMOD Conf. on Management of Data*, pages 340–355, Washington, USA, 1986.

24. G. Weikum. The Web in 2010: Challenges and Opportunities for Database Research. In *Informatics - 10 Years Back. 10 Years Ahead.*, volume 2000 of *Lecture Notes in Computer Science*, pages 1–23. Springer, 2001.

25. K. Wilkinson, P. Lyngbaek, and W. Hasan. The Iris Architecture and Implementation. *IEEE Trans. Knowledge and Data Engineering*, 2(1):63–75, March 1990.

ESTIA-Efficient Electronic Services
for Tourists in Action

Guillermo Fernandez Ortiz, Ana Sofia Caires Branco,
Paz Ruiz Sancho, and José Luis Castillo

SEMA, C\ Albarracín 25, 28037 Madrid, Spain
Tel: 00 34 91 440 88 00, Fax: 00 34 754 35 52
{guillermo.fernandez,anasofia.caires,paz.ruiz}sema.es
joseluis.castillo@sema.es
http://www.sema.es

Abstract. The ESTIA project -Efficient Electronic Services for Tourists in
Action (http://estia.sema.es)- aims to provide the means for mass adoption of
Business-to-Consumer (B2C) E-Commerce in the tourism sector, introducing
value-added services over the next generation access medium of E-Business,
i.e. Mobile Networks. ESTIA is a European project involving 12 partners from
around Europe and partially supported by the European Union.

The main objective of the project is to introduce advanced B2C oriented E-
Services upon intelligent mobile access devices in the tourism value chain and
to attract tourists in active digital marketplaces. To this end, the project will
develop a supportive mediation and brokerage system between product/service
providers and tourists by combining the traditional physical trading activity
with the advanced services of the virtual environment.

ESTIA will develop applications and an intelligent mediation platform that
based on mobile and agent technology and XML standards will link existing &
distributed WEB sites under a common mediation interface and provide the
means for cost efficient trade of tourist products & services.

1 Introduction

As On-line Commerce evolves, services will become increasingly supportive, cost
efficient and consumer-oriented in order to add value to current business practices.
Also in the Tourism industry, suppliers are offering innovative useful services, by
making use of the Internet.

The ESTIA project aims to contribute to the economic development of the
Community by providing the means for mass adoption of Business-to-Consumer
(B2C) E-Commerce in the tourism sector. The project is introducing value-added
services over the next generation access medium of *E-Business i.e. Mobile Networks*,
in order to bring closer and efficiently support, individuals and vendors in the digital
tourism economy.

F. Casati, D. Georgakopoulos, M.-C. Shan (Eds.): TES 2001, LNCS 2193, pp. 163-174, 2001.
© Springer-Verlag Berlin Heidelberg 2001

ESTIA- Efficient Electronic Services for Tourists in Action- is a European project that has started last October 2000 and it will last for 24 months. It involves 12 partners from around Europe and is partially supported by the European Union.

ESTIA, evaluating the potential of Mobile E-Commerce, which perfectly matches with the mobility of consumers in the tourism business framework, will be the initiative for the tourism industry stakeholders to substantiate their competitiveness.

2   Architecture

The concept of the project lays upon the provision of an advanced platform for trading, shopping and reverse auctioning activities to physical Points of Sales (POSs) of tourist products and services accessed by mobile devices while the travel evolves.

On the other hand, ESTIA will support brokers and vendors better target their products and services to the right tourist segment based on pre- or on-line defined characteristics (tourist identity).

The conceptual architecture of ESTIA (depicted in Figure 1) is based on three layers:

- The Data layer referring to the Information Models of ESTIA, including the access and administration modules
- The Functional layer, including the elements that provide the ESTIA functionality and
- The Presentation layer, including the modules responsible for the communication of ESTIA services with tourists and vendors (and their electronic catalogues and services).

The overall conceptual architecture of the ESTIA mediation platform is shown in Figure 1.

The ESTIA platform will be based on a distributed architecture. In particular, the running system will be composed of an ESTIA Vendor Interface for the Vendor Providers and an ESTIA Client Interface for the connected tourists. The core system will provide the basic functionality that is of common interest to both the client and server side interfaces of the system.

The basic concept of ESTIA is based on the efficient gathering of comparable information available in the Internet, about tourism products and services. This information will subsequently be maintained in standardised repositories for brokering purposes. The Offer repository is loaded with standard representations of Tourism resources in the form of "Offers", while the Demand repository is loaded by "Demands" expressed by Tourists, based on the ESTIA tourism service language specifications (XML).

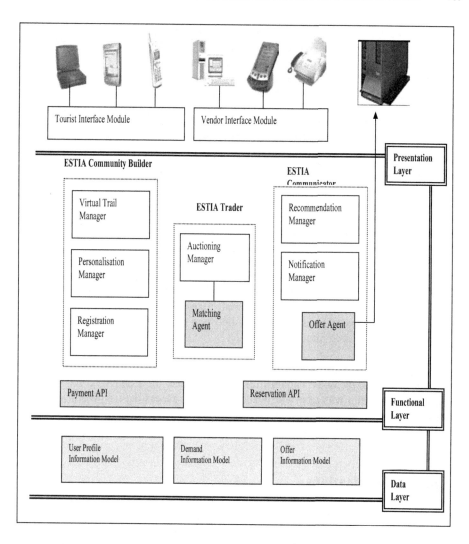

Fig. 1. The Overall Conceptual Architecture of the ESTIA Mediation Platform.

Vendors of tourist services are using the ESTIA standard XML specifications to explicitly define their offers (i.e. the service, its cost, the dates for which the service is valid, the conditions under which there are possible discounts, way of ordering the service, payment method, etc) in their WEB product catalogue.

A component of the 'Trader', the so-called Offer Agent, will browse these catalogues on a regular basis by looking for XML and HTML tags, and store the information in the Offer repository (Offer Information Model - OIM). The vendor himself can also define high priority offers by means of an intuitive user interface, for instance a car rental agency could launch an auctioning event for cars that are not yet rented a couple of days before a weekend. Demands (the conditions tourists require for a service they are looking for, e.g. date, maximum price, quality level, etc.) will be stated to the system and stored in the corresponding Demand Information Model (DIM). Tourists may initiate reverse auctioning events anticipating the active participation of vendors or their agents.

The tourists will mainly access the ESTIA services through mobile access devices during the travelling period, thus satisfying their need for fast and efficient access to information. The lightweight, easy to handle WAP-enabled mobile telephone perfectly suits the needs of the traveller.

The WAP wireless protocol is based on Internet standards that have been optimised for the unique constraints of the wireless environment, which are mainly the low bandwidth of the mobile network, the small size of the telephone screen and the limited navigation possibilities around and between screens when using only one hand as is the case with mobile phones.

Alternatively, tourists may use portable digital assistants (PDA's) with communication and/or WAP capabilities. In every case the ESTIA server will adjust the user interface in a way that will best fit the client access device. We also consider using JINI, so that travellers can not only use their small screen of the telephone, but also make use of devices like the TV-screen and printers of their hotel.

3 ESTIA Applications

The above-mentioned objectives will be realised through the implementation of a multi-layer architecture comprising functional components, WAP based applications, XML, multi dimensional Information Models and underlying technology infrastructure (PDAs, mobile phones, database servers, OLAP technologies & mobile networks).

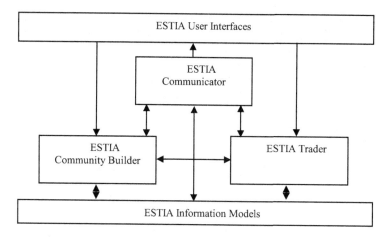

Fig. 2. The ESTIA Applications.

We will design and implement reusable components which we will be configured and integrated to support the functionality of the three main ESTIA applications:

1. The *Trader* is the application responsible for mediating between the market demand and the market offering.

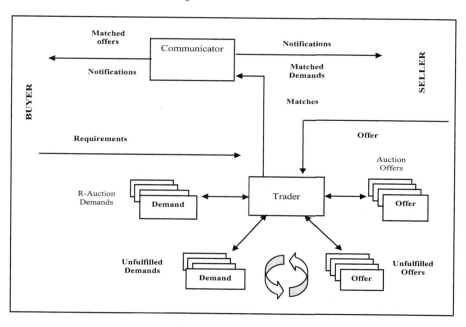

Fig. 3.   The Trader Functionality.

It is the core element of ESTIA, providing the functionality of auctioning and reverse auctioning models, as a black box that receives comparable input by tourists and vendors (demands and offers) and results to efficient matches. Trader can either be launched on demand (when a tourist actually needs a product) or work on the background (acting as a demand and offer repository, illustrating product offering and pricing and operating as a virtual inventory manager). Existing or currently developed payment and reservations systems may be linked with the ESTIA Trader in order to fulfil a commercial transaction. The Trader functionality is mainly based on XML standards elicitation.

2. *The Community Builder* is the application that will develop and administrate virtual communities among tourists. The application will be responsible for monitoring and profiling tourists during their travel (based on GPS technology upon mobile phones and their communication history with the mediator accordingly) and maintaining a virtual trail repository for recommendation and advertising activities. The Community builder is extending existing personalization models and incorporates Consumer Privacy and Rights Protection regulatory schemes.

3. *The Communicator* is the application responsible for the messaging communication among Tourists, Vendors and the ESTIA mediator. The Communicator will be able to apply all communication schemes that are required according to the functionality of the whole system and the business model specification, such as notifications, recommendations, targeted advertising, information collection etc. The application will receive as input, calls and information from the other two applications, and manage all communication flows in a streamlined way.

4   Functional Modules

The ESTIA Functional Modules will be used to build up the three ESTIA applications, above described. We identify the following reusable components:

- Matching Agent (MA). The Matching Agent is responsible to identify matches between demands and offers.
- Auctioning Manager (AM). The Auctioning Manager initiates and administrates auction or reverse auction sessions.
- Offer Agent (OA). This agent "travels" the vendors' WEB catalogues in seeking information about vendor's products and services offerings.
- Notification Manager (NM). This is responsible for the notification of parties involved in an auction and the confirmation – from both sides – of a trader match.
- Recommendation Manager (RM). This module is responsible to provide recommendations derived from the system repositories and the matching process and targeted advertising messages on behalf of the vendors

- Personalisation Manager (PM). This module will be responsible for the update and modelling of the tourist profiles in the TPIM .
- Virtual Trail Manager (VTM). This is the module responsible to monitor and locate travellers during their trip.
- Registration Manager (REM). This will be used for both tourist and vendor authentication and registration purposes. Payment API (PAPI). This will consist of an API to link to existing payment systems.
- Reservation API (RAPI). This will consist of an API to link to existing reservation systems.

The Presentation Modules will be used to provide alternative interfaces in order for tourists and vendors to interact with ESTIA functionality. These will be the modules that will make possible all interaction with PC's, PDA's, mobile phones, Digital Television etc.

These Modules are:

- Tourist Interface Module. This will be responsible for the provision of an easy and intuitive Interface to the Tourist in order to effectively and quickly use the ESTIA system.
- Vendor Interface Module. This will be responsible for the provision of an easy and intuitive Interface to the Vendor in order to effectively and quickly use the ESTIA system.

The ESTIA Information Models (IM) are:

- The "User Profile Information Model" (UPIM). This represents the information regarding the tourist and vendor profile. Information of this type is either entered into the system during authentication or by virtual trail monitoring or modelled by the system through behaviour analysis based on dynamic data ESTIA has gathered for all his/her successful trades and/or auctions.
- The "Offer Information Model" (OIM). This holds all the information concerning the products and services available by tourism vendors. Information of this type is gathered either through the Offer agent by explicitly visiting the Web catalogues or by appropriate interfaces provided by the system for service declarations and launching of auctions for high priority situations.
- The "Demand Information Model" (DIM). This holds the information concerning tourist requirements. In the case of the DIM all the information is entered directly by the tourist through his PC, PDA etc. The DIM also supports "Reverse Auction Demands" submitted by a tourist.

5   ESTIA Innovation

The innovation of ESTIA can be identified in three basic dimensions: Technology Innovation, Business model innovation, and New Marketing Concepts. An initial comparison of ESTIA with other running R&D projects certifies that innovation in multiple layers of the project is clear.

5.1   ESTIA Technology Innovation

- Develop a tourism offer and demand language which will be used for the implementation of the auctioning component, based on XML where tourism professionals can describe the services they offer and tourists describe the services they are looking for. Then, appropriate agents (after tourist's enquiry) try to match supply and demand. XML's capability to specify meta-data models that are processable by multiple applications enables application integration, which eliminates redundant data entry, expedites access to data, increases automation and will make it possible to streamline applications significantly.
- Design of appropriate interface with respect to mobile devices and networks characteristics such as small display and low bandwidth. Furthermore, such characteristics necessitate the introduction of new usage patterns (service instantly available and designed to be used for a few minutes at a time) and their efficient use in essential tasks (handset devices is not the best way for Net-surfing, but is appropriate for small specific tasks)
- Explore data mining and OLAP technologies for clustering market-based information. The research organisation and technology providers will apply data mining and other techniques on the analysis of user navigation and preferences
- Convergence of Mobile devices with JINI technologies.
- Mediation / brokerage technology developments in the field of mobile e-commerce.

5.2   ESTIA New Business Model

ESTIA will introduce a new innovative business framework, in order to sufficiently support the value chain of the tourism sector, exploiting the emerging mobile technology.

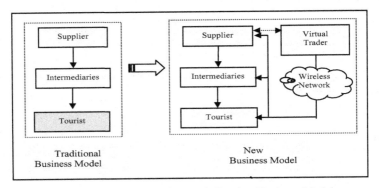

Fig. 4. ESTIA Transforms and Extends Tourism Business Model.

The traditional tourism value chain (depicted in its generalised form in Figure 4), encompasses the supplier of the products/services, the intermediaries (incorporating tour agencies/operators, CRS, etc.) both targeting to the end user, the tourist.

The business model occurring before the trip is already, well facilitated with services offered over Internet, providing an efficient alternative distribution channel for tourist vendors.

If you have supplementary material, e.g., executable files, video clips, or audio recordings, on your server, simply send the volume editors a short description of the supplementary material and inform them of the URL at which it can be found. We will add the description of the supplementary material in the online version of LNCS and create a link to your server.

However, tourists during their travel are bound to time and space restrictions and they can hardly find offers matching their demands in a cost efficient way.

Indeed, current business model does not support immediate access to tourist products and services providers. With the emergence of new mobile technologies, tourists will be able to match their demands through ESTIA's mediation services when they need it, thus resulting to a new business model with the following innovative concepts:

- Tourists will be able to request comprehensive information concerning local services, while smart electronic forms will require only a minimum of information.
- Tourists will be active participants of the value chain, providing feedback to suppliers and intermediaries in an anonymous way, during the trip.
- Tourists will be able to launch reverse auctions through their mobile phones investigating availability and prices of products or services, which they will be able to book and pay through their mobile phones.
- Tourists will be able to receive stock offers from suppliers and participate as bidders in auctioning processes for low-price commodities.

"Tourist identities" which identify tourists in an anonymous way as consumers in the local market in order to gain access to personalised services and at the same time ensure their consumer privacy. In this model, the suppliers and intermediaries can analyse the consumer profiles in clusters to develop target marketing techniques, without directly relating to personal data (align to the EU data protection legislation). Consumer identities can be considered as portable profiles to be used in other related interactive environments.

Moreover, tourists will be able to join communities of people with the same nationality or matching interests. This matching can be realised through the exploitation of GPS technology combined with submitted profiles of ESTIA's registered users. This will lead to the development and maintenance of virtual communities after their trip. Currently, tourists receive personalised offers after their travel, whenever they visit specific Internet sites that eventually hold their profiles. The proposed business framework enables suppliers and intermediaries to submit customised offers using a truly personalised channel, such as mobile phones.

5.3   ESTIA Innovation in Interactive Marketing

Within the project the current state-of-the-art of interactive marketing will be explored and further research will be conducted in the following areas:

- Define new interactive and personalised marketing schemes
- Develop models for consumer profiling (consumer on-line identity) by incorporating Consumer Right Protection principals in accordance with EU data protection legislation, and by incorporating the behaviour of tourists during negotiation.
- Develop techniques for clustering of consumer information, by using multidimensional analysis (OLAP) and data mining techniques to assure target market segmentation on well defined clusters

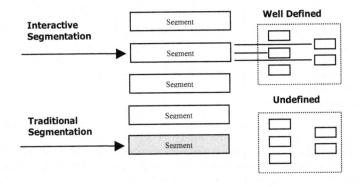

Fig. 5. Interactive Segmentation.

It has to be noticed that all above issues are strongly related to technology advance and innovation, since technology developments enable the new business models and interactive marketing processes to arise.

In the present dynamic business framework, tourist suppliers (and particularly SME's), intermediaries are forced to become more competitive in order to survive, they have to exploit the potential of emerging technologies. Such potential is clearly demonstrated by the new generation of e-commerce: Mobile E-Commerce. According to recent studies, the total number of mobile phone users world-wide is over 300 million, double the number of Internet users. European tourism businesses have to adapt to the changes in the business environment quickly enough and invest more on know-how and skilled employees to be able to increase their competitiveness.

ESTIA, evaluating the potential of Mobile E-Commerce, which perfectly matches with the mobility of consumers in the tourism business framework, will be the initiative for the tourism industry stakeholders to substantiate their competitiveness. Moreover, ESTIA, in the above context, will support the offering of existing tourist services / products, via the new mobile channel, and enhancing the possibilities for the creation of new services and products for tourists.

ESTIA Tools and Services

More specifically, this project will provide the following tools and services:

- Easy and cost efficient access to travel information (and all associated info) during the actual holiday trip
- Brokering tools and platforms for locating, reserving and purchasing domestic products & services better matching their needs
- Personalised services including recommendation and bundling services that best complements their tourist plan and schedule and matches their tourist identity and travel profile
- On line virtual communities of groups of people that belong to their target segment, travelling along them that build virtual trails in order to be easy located from other un-informed travellers and people at home.
- among involved parties for all communication schemes provided in the business model.

ESTIA will develop applications and an intelligent mediation platform that based on mobile and agent technology and XML standards will link existing & distributed WEB sites under a common mediation interface and provide the means for cost efficient trade of tourist products & services.

- ESTIA will offer value-added services such as *on line trading, auctioning, transaction integration, bundling etc integrated with reservation, booking and payment services, and targeted advertising and recommendation services* under a common technology and process infrastructure. Multimedia integration on ESTIA information models is a key aspect, investigating the linkage of XML standard specifications with multimedia content in distributed WEB catalogues upon WML.
- ESTIA will integrate technologies such as Internet and Mobile networks and access devices under common transactional and interface standards i.e. WAP, GSM, HTTP, SMS, GPS, XML, etc. ESTIA will also result to common processes for trading of tourist products & services while at the same time facilitate the emerging need for mobile access and transaction. Main characteristic of the ESTIA services is the personalisation and interactivity (based on tourist profiles) and the combination of alternative communication schemes for all participants.

- ESTIA will identify the optimum processes based on global research and develop best practice guides especially for Small and Medium Enterprises in the Tourism market. Interoperability is a key issue in the ESTIA project while adaptability to other digital infrastructures will also be investigated.

The interface of the mediator with Tourists and Vendors will be provided through a multiple interface management platform compatible with mobile telephones, PDA's and normal computers.

Mobile commerce applications have the potential to be used by consumers in all levels of community, since no hesitation has been observed with respect to the use of mobile phones by people who are not familiar with technology. The development of user interface that is incorporated in ESTIA moves toward the standardisation of m-commerce applications supporting common interfaces and design-for-all systems. ESTIA will be the vehicle for the tourist sector m-commerce as a very comfortable, accessible means of tourist information comparative search and product or service purchasing.

With Europe's Mobile-Commerce in its infancy, so far, most of the mobile data users use only SMS applications, which can provide only limited functionality compared to, for example, Internet services for tourists. However as the mobile industry evolves, mobile applications are fast becoming a reality thanks to adoption of WAP technology, Operating Systems (EPOC) and the integration of mobile devices with Bluetooth or JINI technology.

InfoPipes: A Flexible Framework for M-Commerce Applications

Marcus Herzog[1,2] and Georg Gottlob[1]

[1] Vienna University of Technology, Database and AI Group
Favoritenstr. 9, A-1040 Wien, Austria
{herzog,gottlob}@dbai.tuwien.ac.at
[2] Electronic Commerce Competence Center - EC3
Siebensterngasse 21, A-1070 Wien, Austria

Abstract. M-Commerce applications are E-Commerce applications having at least at one end a mobile terminal. Therefore M-Commerce applications share a number of properties with E-Commerce applications while adding additional burdens on the application developer. In this paper we present a conceptual model of an application framework that provides services at the core of M-Commerce applications. We will also present an implementation of this framework and discuss the properties of the information processing involved.

1 Introduction

The World-Wide Web technology has triggered a new business era. While the web has been invented to share scientific documents the marketing departments soon discovered this technology to communicate the latest product information to potential customers world-wide. The next generation of E-Business solutions included online transaction processing facilities for actually selling those products to customers. With the advent of mobile devices capable to tap into the information universe the installed base of terminals for E-Commerce processing quickly increased.

Although the rising number of access and transaction points is a positive development it has also some hidden drawbacks. The environment gets more complex and heterogeneous. Different operating systems, smaller memory footprints, slower communications and data synchronization, and different data input methods all come into play. The incompatibilities of first releases of assorted standards such as early versions of the WAP — Wireless Application Protocol [9] did not help matters.

We now see a massive trend towards personalized information systems, and mobile devices enable users to access portals that can be configured according to their needs. But since M-Commerce applications are even more platform-specific than conventional E-Commerce applications, systems need additional adaptors in order to integrate with legacy systems or to retrieve specific Web content. Data must be enabled to be sent to different devices without being authored for

F. Casati, D. Georgakopoulos, M.-C. Shan (Eds.): TES 2001, LNCS 2193, pp. 175–186, 2001.
© Springer-Verlag Berlin Heidelberg 2001

each device individually. A scalable and flexible approach uses transformation to generate the content from a single source to fulfil the formatting needs of all clients.

2 Application Scenarios

In the following we will give some application examples that will underpin the need for general architectures of M-Commerce applications that can be configured to fit the specific application needs. In our application scenarios we will concentrate on information mediation services and will spare transaction processing systems for a later presentation.

2.1 Flight Information

Flight information is only one example of all kinds of travel information services that are vital to travelers around the globe. The information domain is quite similar among those including a departure location, an arrival location, and some time and date information at its core.

Although this kind of information is usually available on the web, it is often not available on a central point for all service providers. In the case of flight information, timetables of individual flights are either scattered about different airport information systems or about the portals of individual airlines.

Moreover, as a traveller is out of home by definition, this kind of information is best communicated over mobile devices. The user has the ability to subscribe to specific flights either by providing the flight number or the departure and destination location. The system will send the actual flight status to the user, but only if the status changed between consecutive requests.

2.2 Quoting Service

Another class of typical applications for M-Commerce are all sorts of quoting services that report the price for a certain product or service. The range of tradable goods spawn from stocks to second-hand articles to computer devices. All those share the property of being for sale at a given price, although the price might be determined by different methods and the rate of price building will vary.

If we take for instance the case of an auction site the notification of new quotes for bidding items can be very well communicated over wireless devices. Moreover a bid can be acknowledged instantaneously and at any location. This service can also be easily integrated with existing web services and be offered as an add-on. The integration of a number of source services can be very interesting, especially in comparison shopping applications, where a quote for a specific product is collected from different vendors.

2.3 Tourist Information

On of the disadvantages of wireless applications is the reduced bandwidth and complexity of interaction available. On the other hand the mobility of the device can be exploited for additional request properties such as the location from which the request is made. The location property can be used to provide personalized information such as the closest facility of a certain kind.

Location-based services are best suited for tourist information systems where travelers are searching for services in a given distance to their current location. For instance locating a hotel room in a given price range would be a typical task. Integrating such a service with the actual transaction processing of booking a free resource further enhances the value for the customer.

3 Information Processing

The previous section presented some application scenarios that expose typical properties of the information processing involved. In this section we will present our information processing model for M-Commerce applications derived from these scenarios. We show how to decompose the overall task of information processing into stages that can be used as building blocks for assembling an information processing pipeline which we call INFOPIPES . We will also describe the characteristics that are associated with these sub tasks. The stages are as follows:

- *acquiring* the required content from the source locations;
- *integrating* the content;
- *transforming* the content;
- and *delivering* the content.

3.1 Acquiring the Content

Content can be retrieved from a number of sources with different characteristics. The main characteristics of content feeds are:

- relationship to the originator of the content;
- transport protocol used to transfer the content;
- format of the content feeds;
- access modality;
- periodicity of update.

The relationship to content owners can be somewhere between the two extremes of cooperative and non-cooperative (we are speaking of technical cooperation, not of legal implications, which have to be dealt with separately). In the cooperative case, the content feed is fully transparent to the M-Commerce applications. This is e.g. the case in direct access to databases or to files in the file system, where the structure is known and the access rights are granted. This is often the case when the system and the content feeds are under the same control such as in EAI systems. If the M-Commerce application has to integrate content from different content providers, the interface will often be restricted to access content only from web services. The issue of the relationship actually determines most of the following characteristics.

The transport protocol of choice will be in most cases HTTP, as it is well suited for all kinds of file access, wether remote or local. The access is also nicely abstracted in the URN respectively URL concept, which defines a transport protocol along with a resource identifier. HTTP furthermore allows to tunnel through firewalls, which relieves the problem of connecting to proprietary ports, albeit dodging the concept of assigning ports to specific services to a certain extend.

The format of content ranges from structured (e.g., table rows in a database) to unstructured (e.g., plain text). Semi-structured formats tend to increase in importance with the advent of XML [5]. XML brings together the advantages of the structured and unstructured format, allowing to define the structure to a certain degree while still providing a certain flexibility [1]. XML can be both used for document-based as well as message-based communication. Although XML seems to be the future, we still have to take legacy data into account, especially the myriad of HTML formatted resources. In this case transformation of HTML formatted content into an XML representation is an important subtask.

The access modalities differs according to the transfer protocol and to the formatting of the content feed. In the best case retrieving the content is a single command (e.g., executing a SQL statement or reading a file). Interacting with a web service is more tricky including the complexity of navigating the document structure. In this case the system has to emulate the browsing behaviour of the user to acquire the content.

Finally, M-Commerce applications have to deal with the high volatility of the source content. We can distinguish between pull and push content. While the update rate of push content is under control of the supplier-side, push content is actively fetched by the receiver. The receiver has to decide weather to fetch data on demand or in advance. On demand would fetch data only it data are currently needed, while in advance would fetch data at a given rate independent of an actual request for that data. For most applications both methods have to be supported to be able to trade accuracy of the data against response time.

3.2 Integrating the Content from Various Sources

In our model acquiring data from a number of heterogeneous sources is supported in the integration stage. We assume that the input to this stage is XML based, either by native XML data sources or by translation during the acquiring stage of the processing pipeline. The purpose of the integration stage is two-fold:

- *integrate and normalize the XML element structure*; this is achieved by mapping rules between incoming and outgoing XML document types. The mapping process can be necessary when conceptually similar sources do not share a common document type, although the structure of the domain is related;

- *normalize the content of XML elements*; it is sometimes necessary to map between textual fragments and concepts, e.g., the flight status could be denoted as *delayed* in one web source and as *verspätet* in another — both terms will be mapped to a single concept that can be processed by other stages.

The output of the integration stage is a canonical data structure that can be used as a data source for the subsequently following information processing steps. The integration needs some human intervention for the specification of the various mappings being applied. It is our intention that this mapping is carried out using interactive tools. Furthermore, it is an interesting research issue to apply techniques from various fields such as statistics and information retrieval to support the user in creating those mappings for the individual source structures.

3.3   Transforming the Content According to the User Needs

The purpose of the transformation stage is to enable the application designer to define XML transformations on the content. This is needed to customize the content according to the requirements of the user who is requesting the content. This stage can be compared to defining a query in traditional databases. In fact we are currently evaluating which XML query language can be applied to fulfil this task. In contrast to the classical relational approach there is no definitive standard for query formulation in the XML field. A recent survey of XML query languages is given in [4].

While the previous two stages can be performed independent of the application user, the transformation and also the subsequent delivery of the result will be tailored according to the user configuration. The transformation is composed by the application designer and parameters are submitted by the user. This strategy is well known from so-called publish-subscribe systems [2, 6, 11]. Applying the transformation on XML data allows to generate results independent of platform specific formatting constraints. The formatting of the result is part of the delivery stage.

3.4   Delivering the Content to the User

The final stage of the information processing chain is responsible for delivering the result to the target platform. In M-Commerce applications this can be a number of different clients ranging from mobile phones (usually with different capabilities) to PDAs and other mobile devices. While the basic infrastructure for E-Commerce and M-Commerce applications is pretty equivalent, M-Commerce applications have to face the multi-platform publishing challenge to a greater extend.

In principle the delivery stage can be regarded as the opposite side to the acquisition stage. During acquisition the application has to communicate with a number of different data sources by means of correct requests. In the delivery phase requests from heterogeneous clients have to be answered correctly. It is the challenge not to use only the least denominator of all features exposed by the various clients but to adapt the response according to the features of the client.

The task of formatting the information processing result has to be supported by graphical and interactive tools that are targeted at content managers in contrast to application programmers.

4   System Architecture

In the remainder of the paper we will present our approach towards an system architecture that enables application designers to rapidly build M-Commerce applications. In our system architecture the whole information processing task is split into a number of stages according to the task decomposition as presented in subsection 3. The stages are implemented as software components that can easily be combined to build full-featured information processing pipelines. The construction of these infopipes is supported by a visual tool (see figure 1). The infopipe architect creates and configures the elements of the infopipe by a number of mouse clicks and parameter entries.

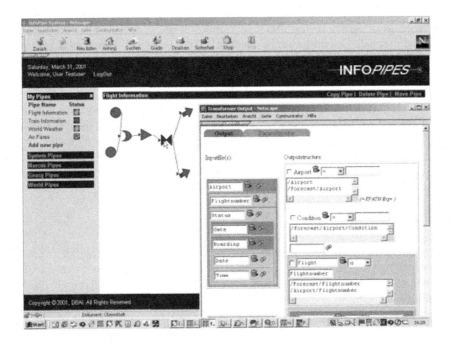

Fig. 1. Main Infopipe Screen and Transformer Configuration Screen.

The actual data flow within the infopipes is realized by handing over XML documents. Each stage within the infopipe accepts XML documents (except for the source, which accepts HTML documents), performs its specific task, and produces an XML document as result. This result is fed to the successor components which in turn will perform the next information processing stages. Components which are not on the boundaries of the network are only activated by their neighbouring components. Boundary components (i.e., source and deliverer components) have the ability to activate themselves according to a user specified strategy and trigger the information processing on behalf of the user. Figure 2 shows an infopipe topology representing the information processing according to the flight information scenario.

Two source components to the left wrap the airport web sites in Frankfurt and Vienna. The output of these source components are data on flight departures in XML format. These structurally differing outputs are fed into an integrator component which normalizes the data. The normalized data are transformed to select flight data based on the flight ID or the departure and destination attributes respectively, which are supplied by users of this information pipe. The deliverer components transform the XML output of the transformer components into formats appropriate for the target devices.

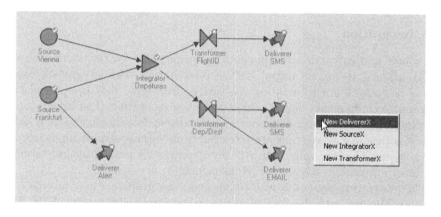

Fig. 2. An Example of an Infopipe Topology.

The topology of an infopipe is determined by the application designer. Once activated the information flow within the infopipe is request driven. In our architecture the activation is spreading from the sinks towards the sources. All stages use local caches to cache intermediate results that can be reused by other connected components. A checksum computed over the input XML document and the configuration of the component is applied to detect whether the cache is still valid.

In the following we will discuss the tasks that are carried out at the different stages of the infopipe information processing model.

4.1   Source

The source component is responsible for retrieving the data from the data sources. Data sources are any kind of machine readable data store that features an access protocol to fetch data over the network. Source components abstract the individual data stores and provide a unified interface for other infopipe components. In a first step the main focus of our INFOPIPES system is on web sources. The task is to emulate the browsing behaviour of a user to retrieve the data from the web by utilizing a crawler engine [10]. The source component implements the HTTP, respectively HTTPS protocol to communicate with web sources. Moreover, it supports Cookies to handle client-side state management.

The source component is configured by the user through observing the interaction of the human user with the web source. The result of the source configuration is a list of HTTP method calls and associated arguments. The aim of the navigation is to locate a web page that holds the information the user is interested in. Once the user arrives at this page, the HTML code is handed over to the extraction component. In the INFOPIPES system we use a novel approach for generating HTML extractor programs. Details on the extraction process are given in [3].

4.2   Integration

The source and extraction components are responsible for retrieving web data and translating it into an initial XML representation. The integration component is responsible for integrating the various fragments that are passed along from source components into a unified XML representation. The integrator will integrate data from information sources in the same domain that share a similar data structure, e.g., data that are retrieved from various airport flight information systems. The incoming data will be mapped to a unified output structure that incorporates all necessary XML elements.

The integration process is also configured via a graphical user interface (see figure 3). The user sees the document type structure of all incoming XML documents. After defining the document type of the output document, the individual incoming document types are mapped to the output structure. Furthermore regular expressions can be defined to perform the concept matching as described in the previous paragraph.

The result of the configuration are XSLT [8] programs that perform the necessary translations between the input documents and the output document. Again the user is not required to know the mechanism of XSLT but can take advantage of the full-fledged capabilities if the automatically generated XSLT does not fully satisfy the users' needs.

The result of the integration component is a normalized view on all integrated web sources that will serve as a data source for the following components in the pipeline. Due to the implicit cache architecture in the INFOPIPES network only those documents have to be reintegrated that changed in between successive request.

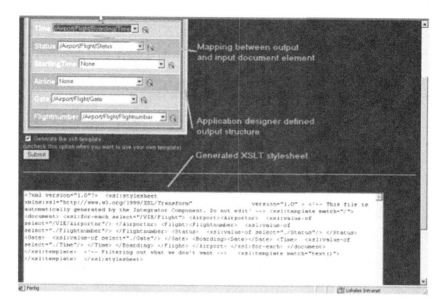

Fig. 3. Integrator Configuration Dialog.

4.3 Transformation

In addition to the expressive power of the query language we have to evaluate how queries can be formulated by graphical means to fit into the overall strategy of a fully visual interface. An example of a visual query language for XML documents is given in [7]. The first impression is that visual representations of queries tend to get rather confusing when complexity is increased. This leads to the assumption that we have to trade complexity for usability. An alternative is to allow the experienced user to formulate queries in the native query language while lay users use the visual interface with reduced expressive power.

Besides query formulation the transformation component will also generate query masks according to the formulated queries where users can submit actual values to arguments in the query. It is important to note that these masks are available for different clients on different platforms, e.g., for HTML and WML clients. These masks are used during the information processing when users can only state their information needs according to predefined transformations.

Figure 4 shows a screenshot of the transformer configuration dialog.

4.4 Delivery

The final stage in the processing pipeline is to deliver the information to the user. An important design principle of the INFOPIPES architecture has been to support clients on various platforms. This implies a multi-platform publishing supporting both *push* and *pull* technology. The responsibility of the delivery component is to:

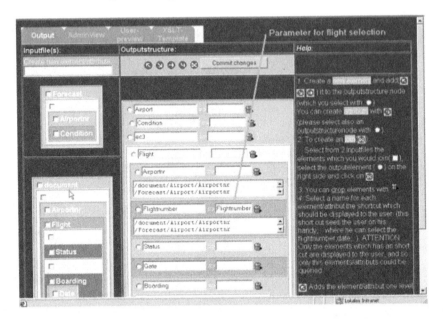

Fig. 4. Transformer Configuration Dialog.

- check on delivery constraints such as time, date, or if the information content has changed since the last delivery;
- transform the information from XML into a format suitable for the requesting client, ranging from simple text formats (e.g., e-mail, SMS) to markup languages (e.g., HTML, WML, or VoxML);
- deliver the content to the client utilizing the appropriate communication channel and protocol.

The delivery component is on the boundary of the network structure and has the ability to activate itself and trigger the processing of the pipeline. The processing takes place through backward chaining to all immediate successor components which in turn activate their successor components. The user can configure at what time or in what intervals the component should activate the pipeline processing. On the other hand the delivery component gets activated if one of the source components in the same pipeline changes its state.

In the case of activation by source components checking delivery constraints is important because otherwise the infopipe would permanently push information to users even when they are not interested in it. Once the user has subscribed to the pipeline and the processing is started the infopipe continuously produces information output. On the other hand activation by delivery component is interesting for infopipes with "lazy" source components which change only infrequent but the user wants to be informed on a specific point in time.

The transformation process is visually configured by selecting elements from the DTD of the input document and assembling an output DTD in case of markup documents or assembling a text document in case of text based output formats. The configuration is then translated into an XSLT program that is executed at run time. Similar to the transformer component the infopipe architect can replace this program with a hand-coded one in case of more complex transformation needs. See figure 5 for a screenshot of the deliverer configuration dialog.

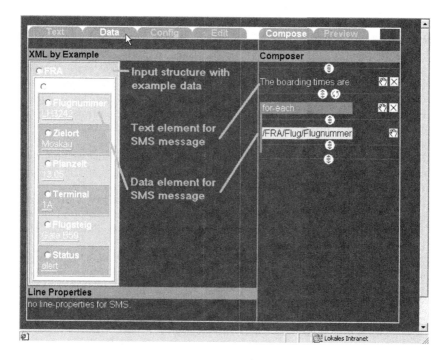

Fig. 5. Deliverer Configuration Dialog.

5   Conclusions

We have presented our novel approach towards an architecture for personalized information channels that feed content extracted from semi-structured information sources to clients on various platforms. The main focus of this paper has been on the presentation of the whole system architecture from a logical point of view and to clearly structure the problem domain. Some of the technical details had to be omitted due to the restricted scope of the presentation.

The INFOPIPES system is currently under construction and is designed as a web-based application. The implementation language is Java and we utilize the J2EE infrastructure to translate the logical components into software components. The project is carried out in cooperation with the Electronic Commerce Competence Center in Vienna, where we realize the airport scenario using the infopipe infrastructure. The prototype has received high attention from the mobile telecom companies that are partners of this center.

Acknowledgement

This work was partly supported by the Austrian Science Fund Project NZ29-INF and by the Electronic Commerce Competence Center - EC3, Austria.

References

[1] S. Abiteboul, P. Buneman, and D. Suciu. *Data on the Web: From Relations to Semistructured Data and XML*. Morgan Kaufmann, 1999.

[2] Guruduth Banavar, Tushar Deepak Chandra, Bodhi Mukherjee, Jay Nagarajarao, Robert E. Strom, and Daniel C. Sturman. An efficient multicast protocol for content-based publish-subscribe systems. In *Proc. of International Conference on Distributed Computing Systems*, pages 262–272, 1999.

[3] Robert Baumgartner, Sergio Flesca, and Georg Gottlob. Visual web information extraction with Lixto. In *Procs. of 27th International Conference on Very Large Data Bases (VLDB)*, Roma, Italy, 2001. to appear.

[4] Angela Bonifati and Stefano Ceri. Comparative analysis of five XML query languages. *SIGMOD Record*, 29(1):68–79, 2000.

[5] T. Bray, J. Paoli, C. Sperberg-MacQueen, and E. Maler. Extensible Markup Language (xml) 1.0 (Second Edition), 2000.

[6] Antonio Carzaniga, David S. Rosenblum, and Alexander L. Wolf. Achieving scalability and expressiveness in an internet-scale event notification service. In *Proc. of Symposium on Principles of Distributed Computing*, pages 219–227, 2000.

[7] S. Ceri, S. Comai, E. Damiani, P. Fraternali, S. Paraboschi, and L. Tanca. XML-GL: A graphical language for querying and restructuring xml documents. In *Proc. of 8th Int. World Wide Web Conference*, pages 1171–1187, 1999.

[8] J. Clark (ed.). XSL Transformations (XSLT) Version 1.0, November 1999.

[9] WAP Forum. Wireless application protocol.

[10] Allan Heydon and Marc Najork. Mercator: A Scalable, Extensible Web Crawler. *World Wide Web*, 2(4):219–229, December 1999.

[11] Radu Preotiuc-Pietro, Joao Pereira, Francois LLirbat, Francoise Fabret, Kenneth Ross, and Dennis Shasha. Publish/subscribe on the web at extreme speed. In *Proc. of ACM SIGMOD Conf. on Management of Data*, Cairo, Egypt, 2000.

Ψ—Pervasive Services Infrastructure

Dejan Milojicic[1], Alan Messer[1], Philippe Bernadat[1], and Ira Greenberg[1],
Olaf Spinczyk[2], Danilo Beuche[2], and Wolfgang Schröder-Preikschat[2]

[1] Hewlett-Packard Labs, MS 3U-18, 1501 Page Mill Road
Palo Alto 94304, California, USA
{dejan,messer,bernadat,iragreen}@hpl.hp.com

[2] Otto-von-Guericke Universität Magdeburg, Fakultät für Informatik, Universitätsplatz 2
39106 Magdeburg, Germany
{olaf,danilo,wosch}@ivs.cs.uni-magdeburg.de

Abstract. Future systems have been characterized as ubiquitous, pervasive, and invisible. They will consist of devices that are diverse in size, performance, and power consumption. Some of these devices will be mobile, posing additional requirements to system software and applications. The focus will move from technology to deployment and ease of use of services. Consequently, traditional paradigms for reasoning about, designing, and implementing software systems and services will no longer be sufficient.

We believe that this future vision will rely on a three-tier infrastructure consisting of back-end servers, infrastructure servers, and front-end clients (mobile or static, handheld or embedded). The critical question for future systems will be how to deliver services on demand from back-end servers to resource-constrained clients. If we can handle the new requirements of these systems, we can enable this computing infrastructure to offer significantly more services to users in a more pervasive way.

1 Introduction

The future of computing has been painted by many visionaries. It was coined as ubiquitous computing by Mark Weiser [37], and D.A. Norman introduced invisible computing [26]. IBM promotes pervasive computing [14], Sybase calls it mobile embedded computing [33], and Sun uses the term Post-PC era [32]. HP Labs' vision is presented in CoolTown [18]. Several umbrella projects in major universities are also exploring these topics, such as Aura at CMU [25], Portolano at the University of Washington [8], Endeavour at Berkeley [11], and Oxygen at MIT [7]. The government is investigating Ubiquitous Computing Figure 6 and Composable High Assurance Trusted Systems [5]. Finally, there are numerous startups in this area, such as StreamTheory [31], Transvirtual [34], and WordWalla [39].

Common to most of these visions are the ideas of blending computers into the infrastructure and providing user-friendly services to non-expert users. The center of gravity is moving from technology to users and services. Mobile and wireless are becoming common rather than the exception. Connectivity and bandwidth are improving, approaching 5-20Mbps for 4G networks in 2005. We believe that the focus of future technology will be in the intersection of the Internet, on-line ser-

F. Casati, D. Georgakopoulos, M.-C. Shan (Eds.): TES 2001, LNCS 2193, pp. 187-199, 2001.

vices, and mobile wireless communication. The environment will consist of globally distributed high-end servers hosting services (e.g., Oceanstore [19]), mid-point servers caching and otherwise complementing service delivery to clients (e.g., Akamai), and a variety of client devices.

Under services, we assume a variety of applications and underlying support (description, look-up, storing state, etc.). Examples include traditional desktop applications, enterprise applications (e.g., project management, expense reporting), personal information management, and various vertical market applications, such as retail, health care, financial, entertainment, and travel.

We are investigating a Pervasive Services Infrastructure (PSI—Ψ in Greek) for delivering Internet services to (wireless) users. The Ψ vision is "Any service to any client (anytime, anywhere)". We envision that in the future it will be possible to deliver services to clients on their mobile, handheld devices in the same way as it is possible at the desktop today. In addition to the traditional challenges of mobile computing [30], we believe that the biggest challenges of this environment are in adapting services to diverse client devices and in delivering services to clients.

Most devices are resource constrained compared to desktop systems. They differ in many ways, such as user interfaces, CPU, memory size, and power constraints, all of which will require service delivery to be adapted in some way. We are investigating how offloading parts of applications to *mid-point servers* can enable and enhance service execution on a resource-constrained device. Dynamic delivery of services to devices is required to eliminate the need for pre-installed services, to enable the downloading of dynamically composed services, and to support system evolution. For Ψ, client devices and infrastructure servers act as caches for delivering services from back-end servers, thereby improving the performance of remote access.

The rest of the document is organized as follows. Section 2 discusses adaptive offloaded services. Services on Demand is described in Section 3. In Section 4, we present some initial results. In Section 5, we compare our project to related work. We summarize the paper and present future work in Section 6.

2 Adaptive Offloaded Services

Pervasive systems bring a proliferation of devices and infrastructure with differing capabilities and capacities. We believe the scale and diversity will lead to several problems in supporting services on these devices. Consider Personal Digital Assistants (PDAs). While fundamentally doing the same task, specifications have varied greatly for screens, processors, and memory capacities. Providing even a simple service to these similar devices presents a complex task for the software manufacturer who must provide software for the lowest common denominator or must provide separate versions. When computing is pervasive or multiple services are run simultaneously, this problem becomes more acute.

We believe such device limitations can be relieved when devices are universally networked. Instead of hitting resource constraints when supporting a service, other parts of the infrastructure could cooperate to offload parts of the service from devices. However, offloading services in a networked environment is difficult because the available device resources and each device's location may change

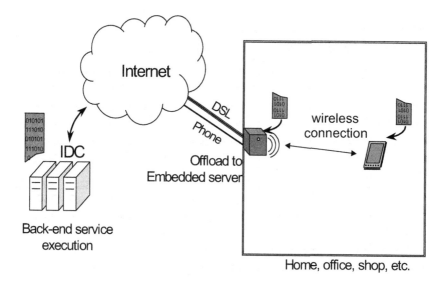

Fig. 1 Adaptive Offloaded Services.

dynamically. Therefore, we believe that if services are to best exploit this environment, they will also need to adapt to changes in it.

Scalability also poses interesting problems when providing services to so many devices. With just three to five networked devices per user and several million users, the problem of running complex services such as multimedia or interactive services can easily outgrow a single central server cluster. Proxy caches and companies such as Akamai have shown that a multi-tier approach can be used for data to overcome this problem of scale. We believe that service provision can similarly benefit by a multi-tier approach for caching and execution, allowing service offloading into the infrastructure.

To illustrate our vision, consider using a PDA to edit a digital photograph sent to you by URL. This poses a problem for your device, because despite having a color screen there is little spare capacity. Yet, you would like to edit the photograph even if you cannot fully execute an editing application, such as Adobe Photoshop. Instead, the device's runtime uses its understanding of the service, its surrounding devices, and back-end servers to allow the device access to the service, independent of the limitations of the device. For example, the main execution may be performed on a nearby server leaving the device to handle performance sensitive operations and I/O (see Figure 1). A more capable device might run the main execution and user interface, and use the server to hold swapped memory and to perform intensive image processing.

We believe that dividing service responsibility can be achieved by borrowing resources from mid-point servers (e.g., memory swapping), or by constructing the service from multiple components that are placed and executed separately. Services developed in compositional frameworks are therefore good candidates for our vision. Unfortunately, except for very coarse granularity, few services have been constructed this way. However, we believe that some automatic decomposition may be possible using additional system support in modular systems (e.g., Java).

We believe that infrastructure support for service offloading and adaptivity will allow scalable, high-performance services for a multitude of differing devices in a mobile environment. However, several questions will have to be answered. What service framework requirements would be needed for such distributed execution? Can existing services be automatically split and efficiently placed? Can placement be performed transparently or should services and runtimes interact? Can services be performant and scalable when distributed across a multi-tier environment? Can service offloading effectively cope with the widely varying characteristics of different devices? Can users roam and still effectively obtain service? What if the service infrastructure decides to migrate parts of the service onto another node, or there are communication errors? If operation is not transparent, it may be necessary to do a service-specific cleanup, such as closing temporary files or restarting, requiring extra application code.

Initially, we intend on investigating the division, placement, and execution support for services. We have started manually offloading part of a service's storage and execution across a two-tier environment (mid-point and client) to study the performance and scalability effects of distributed execution with an educated split in a simple scenario. At the same time, we are examining the characteristics of services (active memory footprint/access patterns, execution paths) to determine whether automatic splitting is appropriate for services. Using these results, we will investigate the effect of roaming in such an environment and the effects of placing the same service on alternative resource-constrained devices.

3 Services on Demand

It is becoming increasingly important to provide services on demand with minimal support from users. In general, users will be less computer savvy and will want to focus on using services, not administering them. Users will connect to the Internet with a wide variety of devices running a diverse collection of system software (e.g. operating systems, browsers). Many services will become available and will be updated frequently. Users will want to access their preferred services and environments from any location and any device.

These trends call for a new system software infrastructure to support services on demand. In this approach, no "a priori" service installation will be required. Instead, desired services will be dynamically located and retrieved, perhaps with service brokers, based on available resources. A trust framework will be needed so that services with an appropriate level of trust can be obtained, and services with different levels of trust can work together. Appropriate billing models will have to be integrated into the infrastructure so that clients can be dynamically billed for the services they use. Because user devices will have volatile storage, user environments and data will have to be securely and persistently stored on storage servers, with support for privacy and integrity. Services, user environments, and data will have to be enabled and loaded on a user's device wherever the user is located, even if the user is moving. The infrastructure should also support disconnected operation for services that can operate in that manner.

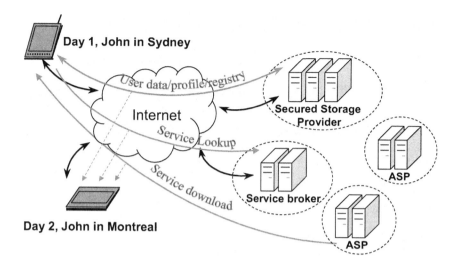

Fig. 2 Services-on-Demand Infrastructure.

Consider the following scenario. While listening to the news, you hear about a new financial service that makes it possible to simulate some investment model. You connect to the Internet, request the service, and start it. The service might also be located by type from a look-up service provided by a service broker. As opposed to a Web-server-based service running remotely, the service may run partially or entirely on your device. In reality, the service can be any type of Java software, and it will be seamlessly installed (or cached) on your device, if it fits. Otherwise, it will be offloaded to a support server.

Assume that the service saves simulation results as files. Your data is managed by a storage provider, and the files are transparently updated there, at reconnection time if required. You decide to move and will either carry your PDA or use another device at your destination (hotel, airport, etc.). When you log in on this new device, you will provide a user key to the storage provider. The service will be downloaded (if it is not already cached), and your private files and environment will be retrieved (see Fig. 2).

Achieving these goals poses several fundamental challenges. How should device resources be characterized (primary and secondary storage, user interface, peripherals, etc.), and how should service resource requirements be characterized? How can services be acquired and composed with appropriate levels of trust? What service look-up strategies make sense, and how should users be billed for services? What service-dependent reconciliation strategies can be used for disconnected operation?

To answer these questions, we modified Java virtual machine to investigate performance and techniques to interpose file system operations. Asking users to switch to system software that noticeably degrades performance is unacceptable. We want to determine the real cost of using a virtual machine, interacting with a service broker, and downloading services on demand, and to see how much caching helps. We will experiment with client devices that are small, portable, resource-con-

Table 1 Java Execution Environment Comparison

Java Environment	Memory Consumption & Score		
	Total initial memory consumption (KB)	CaffeineMark overall score	kB per score point
Sun JDK 1.3 (JIT)	7476	1828	4.1
IBM JDK 1.3 (JIT)	8212	5155	1.6
GCJ-Linux 2.95	1416	3109	0.5
jPure (client+server)	312+800	2167	0.5

strained, and JVM-enabled, such as HP Jornada personal digital assistant. Additionally, we will setup a service broker with a sufficiently large number of services to allow us to experiment with real-life situations. In the long term, we will investigate resource characterization and disconnected operation, and investigate a security and trust framework in this context.

4 Preliminary Investigations

We performed two experiments to investigate whether service offloading is beneficial. The first experiment studied the trade-off between the performance/footprint implications of offloading and its benefits in a static scenario. The goal of the second experiment was to gain insight about the dynamic behavior of objects in a Java virtual machine.

The first experiment uses the jPure system [4] on top of the Pure OS [3] to measure the performance of statically offloading the Java runtime support to a server. The jPure system is designed to bring Java execution to systems that are typically too constrained to run a full JVM. It does so, by manually splitting the Java execution environment into a client (for execution) and a server (for runtime support), thereby reducing the footprint of the client. This system, therefore, represents a simple, static form of offloading from a resource-constrained device. We compared the performance/footprint trade-off of this system against that of a variety of JVMs and Java-to-native compiler-based solutions using the EmbeddedCaffeineMark benchmark. Table 1 illustrates that a fixed offloading of runtime support can offer a good performance/footprint trade-off compared to a traditional Java execution environment, and a similar trade-off to that of a monolithic Java-to-native compiler. The results for the jPure and monolithic Java-to-native compiler show similar performance/footprint trade-offs because they are derived from the same source, but the absolute performance score for jPure is lower because of the cost for remote access of runtime support functions on the server.

For the second experiment, we used the Kaffe [35] JVM to investigate the dynamic behavior of Java execution. The Java memory footprint can often be a limiting concern even with offloaded runtime libraries because applications in large sys-

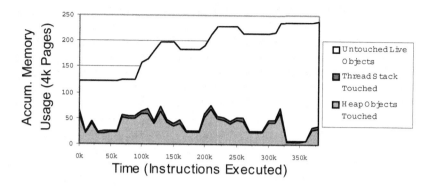

Fig. 3 The Java Heap Page Working Set of 'Hello World'.

tems can dwarf the runtime support. To investigate the execution behavior of JVM, we modified Kaffe to record access to the pages (4kB in size) used to implement the Java thread stacks and the Java heap for every 10,000 bytecodes executed. Figure 3 presents the results for the EmbeddedCaffeineMark benchmark, which uses a 1538-page heap with between 125 and 225 pages of live objects, of which only between 6 and 70 pages are actually accessed during the benchmark's runtime. This simple example indicates that there is an opportunity to dynamically offload memory for services because very few pages are simultaneously used. A similar study of object access would probably show an even smaller working set because of false sharing in the pages being monitored.

To better understand the possibility of offloading parts of applications, a prototype is being built to split Java applications at run-time and offload part of the application to a nearby server. Figure 4 presents early results of splitting an execution of the JavaNote editor application (a Java version of notepad). The figure

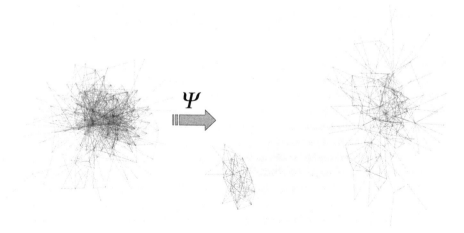

Fig. 4 Partitioning the JavaNote Application.

Table 2 Services-on-Demand (SoD) Loading Overhead

Service	Local Loading (s)	SoD Loading (s)			Loaded URLs		Java Classes	
		Intranet	Wave	Dialup	Cnt	Size (B)	Cnt	Size (B)
calculator	0.1	~0	+0.1	+4.7	2	9520	2	9520
calendar	0.2	~0	+0.4	+4.7	4	12952	4	12952
editor	0.2	~0	+0.3	+5.2	7	15885	7	15885
game	0.2	~0	+0.3	+6.1	9	18739	9	18739
agenda	0.2	+0.1	+0.7	+8.4	1	35360	12	59846
ftp	0.6	+2.1	+3.2	+20.9	3	107725	22	142155
mail	2.5	+2.7	+15.1	+129.4	1	675046	138	365574

shows two graphs of the execution history of the JavaNote application. Each graph is composed of a set of nodes (Java classes) connected by interactions (method invocations, data accesses). The left portion of the figure shows the execution history of the application as a large text file is loaded. At this point, the application would normally run out of memory because of the client's 8-megabyte heap limit. The right portion of the figure shows the execution history after a splitting algorithm split the application state to try to free at least 20% of the memory on the client. The splitting algorithm was based on a run-time analysis of the execution history. Two sub-graphs are now formed, representing local execution on each of the two machines. The interconnections between the subgraphs represent potential RPCs between the machines. As a result, the Java heaps on both the client and the server would have plenty of free space to continue executing, even though the program has grown beyond the client heap's 8-megabyte limit. Work on this prototype is continuing with the aim of better understanding the splitting of applications in general and their performance.

To investigate the cost of downloading services on demand, a prototype system was instrumented to measure the elapsed time until a service is ready. Table 2 shows the performance of various service classes, ordered by download size. All services are downloaded from servers outside of the HP intranet. The reference is measured when the service is fully cached. The download overhead is only incurred when the service is first used. The relative performance (in addition to reference time) is measured uncached for three connection types:

- **Intranet** within HP (with Web proxy side effects).
- **Wavelan** connected to the HP intranet.
- **Dialup** telephone line.

These preliminary results indicate that, on a reasonable network link of the future, the overhead of downloading and installing services on demand is relatively small (a couple of seconds). Even for large applications that can be compressed in the JAR format, performance is not unreasonable. However, we can see that for this application (mail) the code size is only 300KB leaving the rest as documentation and graphics. A service-on-demand version of this application might download these supplemental items incrementally or they may be cached to avoid noticeable delays. Overall, these results point towards the suitability of Java applications coupled with a good infrastructure to effectively present services on demand without adversely affecting performance.

Besides service lookup and download, the SoD prototype demonstrates remote storage handling. Using Java bytecode editing techniques, accesses to local resources such as files are interposed and redirected to a storage provider. The infrastructure is not tied to any protocol for remote file systems; instead, it defines a framework where file storage handlers can be to plugged-in. The prototype also includes basic support for disconnection through the use of caches and a simple file inconsistency detection mechanism. We intend to handle reconciliation through the use of plug-ins, because synchronizing file content often depends on the file-type or application.

The current prototype implementation has been successfully demonstrated on laptop and hand-held devices running various operating systems (Windows, Windows CE, Linux) and virtual machines (JDK, Personal Java, Kaffe, and ChaiVM). The following services are currently supported:

- Basic service brokering
- Transparent download and execution of services in sandboxes
- Interposition of a local resource access (File IO) and redirection to storage provider
- Support for a third party FTP client storage plug-in
- Service and storage caches
- Support for disconnected operation
- Simple disconnection/reconciliation modules

5 Related Work

Due to limited space, we do not discuss related work in detail; instead we just compare it with our project. In addition, we omit some related work, such as Rover [15], Coda [23], and GAIA [29].

The **Odyssey** project defines a software platform for application-aware adaptation of diverse mobile applications [25]. This approach considers agile applications in varying fidelities, adapting to system variations, e.g., in network bandwidth. Our work takes a similar view to adaptability applied to services and the system. We are interested in adaptability in a different scope, such as adaptability using computation and storage placement.

The **Ninja** project (as well as earlier work by Fox [9]) investigates a software infrastructure for next generation Internet services [11]. Services are designed to be composable, customizable, and accessible from a variety of device types. The service components can be executed closer to the client to enable transcoding. Our approach takes locality of computation further by considering mid-point servers as locations for computation and storage used by service providers and service clients.

In addition, our focus is on offloading services rather than altering service fidelity as with proxy transcoding.

The **Oxygen** project studies software environments for composable applications and systems [7]. Their approach is to use abstraction, specification, persistent storage, and transactions to support change through adaptation and customization.

The **Portolano** projects (Active Fabric and ARCaDE) focus on service provisioning for self-organizing, mobile, composable services; service migration; and automatic service management [8]. Oxygen and Portolano take an active networks approach. We instead consider the computation and storage in the infrastructure to be temporary service caches, with services ultimately originating from back-end service providers.

To support nomadic users, HPL's **CoolTown** project offers a model based on a convergence of Web technology, wireless networks, and portable devices [18]. Cool-Town attempts to bridge physical and virtual worlds, whereas Ψ addresses resources and services. CoolTown addresses location dependency and connectivity, while Ψ emphasizes deployment and disconnection.

There are also related industrial standards. Universal Description, Discovery, and Integration (**UDDI**) is a specification that defines a way to publish and discover information about services [36]. Open Services Gateway Initiative (**OSGi**) explores Java platform independence and dynamic code-loading for small-memory devices [27]. Ψ can benefit from either standard.

Coign has investigated the possibilities and merits for the automated partitioning of Microsoft COM applications into client/server implementations [13]. By profiling the interactions between COM components, this work showed that it was possible to construct a tool that could create a good (if not better than human) client/server implementation automatically. Similar work in the **DAP** project at IBM has also considered the importance of caching in these client/server implementations [17]. From a dynamic runtime perspective, the **M-Mail** system has considered runtime offloading decisions for the creation of mail objects on the client or server to improve overall performance and throughput [12]. Our work on Adaptive Offloaded Services extends these approaches to apply offloading at run-time on generic application through the consideration of execution graphs and resource load information.

Finally, there are a number of technologies addressing execution of code on the server rather than on the client. Examples include **Active Server Pages** (ASP) [28], **Java Server Pages** (JSP) [2], and **PHP** [38]. Active Server Pages is a server-side scripting technology that can be used to create dynamic and interactive Web applications. ASP uses scripts which can contain COM components and XML. JavaServer Pages use XML-like tags and scriptlets written in Java to encapsulate the logic of the content for the page. PHP is an HTML preprocessor that enables the creation of dynamic web pages.

ASPs, JSPs, and PHP represent a reverse trend compared to Java applets. Motivation for this server-centric approach is based on software maintenance and administration, security, and performance. Compared to these systems, our work (AOS) addresses the execution of the applications (not necessarily applets) on the clients, as well as the installation and administration of these applications (SOD). We don't think that there is a right answer or optimal solution for all applications. Under some circumstances and for some applications, thin clients will be optimal (the server-centric approach), in other cases, it will be thick clients (the PSI approach). Disconnection, mobility, and the increased deployment of handheld devices will only complicate the trade-offs between these two approaches.

6 Summary and Future Work

We presented our vision of a pervasive services infrastructure. In particular, we addressed the two technologies required to achieve our vision: adapting services to execute on resource-constrained devices and installing services on demand. We believe that both are required to achieve ubiquitous systems. We also presented preliminary results indicating the benefits of offloading and downloading services. If the Ψ vision can be achieved, it may be possible to offer today's desktop services to a variety of resource-constrained devices in a mobile environment.

Our work is equally applicable to traditional wired networks and infrastructures as well as to wireless and mobile systems and services. In the presence of mobility, the traditional requirements for scalability, performance, reliability, and security are enhanced. Nevertheless, we believe that mobility opens up even more opportunities for Pervasive Services Infrastructure support in terms of disconnection, adaptivity to variances in network speed, and support for reliable storage.

We are also interested in investigating service composition. Promising techniques in this area are component-based computing [24] and aspect-oriented programming [16]. The ideal service would consist of a number of components glued together, and would separate placement and configuration from the core functionality, such as in Regis [22]. The service component boundaries would provide points for switching between local and remote execution control of the infrastructure runtime. Java RMI/JavaBeans, Puppeteer [20], and CANS [10] are other examples of component-based systems. Aspect-oriented programming takes a similar approach [16]. A tool called the aspect weaver can be used to connect the components with the implementations of their technical aspects. The result is a loose coupling, which leads to a high degree of configurability at either compile- or run-time. Examples include D Figure 21 and work by Becker [1].

Acknowledgments

We are indebted to G. Candea, C. Karamanolis, K. Keeton, E. Kiciman, M. Mahalingam, D. Muntz, G. Snider, and J. Wilkes for reviewing the paper and/or otherwise contributing to the project. Their comments significantly improved the content and presentation.

Additional Information

For more information on the PSI project, please refer to the following Web site: http://www.hpl.hp.com/research/itc/csl/pss/psi/.

References

[1] Becker, C., Geihs, K., "Quality of Service — Aspects of Distributed Programs," ICSE'98 Workshop on Aspect-Oriented Programming, 1998.

[2] Bergsten, H., "JavaServer Pages", O'Reilly, December 2000 (see also http://java.sun.com/products/jsp/).

[3] Beuche, D., et al., "The PURE Family of Object-Oriented Operating Systems for Deeply Embedded Systems," Proc. 2nd IEEE Symp on OO Real-Time Dist Comp, StMalo, France, May 1999.

[4] Beuche, D., et al., "JPure - Purified Java Execution Environment for Controller Networks," Proc. of the IFIP Workshop on Dist. and Parallel Embedded Systems, Paderborn, Germany, Oct 2000,

[5] Composable High Assurance Trusted Systems (CHATS), www.arpa.gov/ito/research/chats.

[6] DARPA ITO Ubiquitous Computing Program, www.arpa.gov/ito/research/uc.

[7] Dertouzos, M.L., "The future of computing, Scientific American," July 1999. http://oxygen.lcs.mit.edu.

[8] Esler, M., et al., "Next century challenges: data-centric networking for invisible computing: the Portolano project at the University of Washington," Proc of 5th ACM/IEEE Conf. on Mobile Computing and Networking, Aug 15-19, 1999, Seattle, WA. http://portolano.cs.washington.edu.

[9] Fox, A., et al., Adapting to Network and Client Variation Using Active Proxies: Lessons and Perspectives," IEEE Personal Communications, August 1998.

[10] Fu, X., et al., "CANS: Composable, Adaptive Network Services Infrastructure", to appear at proc. of USENIX USITS, 2001.

[11] Gribble, S., "The Ninja Architecture for Robust Internet-Scale Systems and Services," Special Issue of Computer Networks on Pervasive Computing, 2000. http://endeavour.cs.berkeley.edu/

[12] Hai Yan Lom, "M-mail: A case study of dynamic application partitioning in mobile computing," Master's thesis, Dept. of Computer Science, University of Waterloo, May 1997.

[13] Hunt, Galen C. and Scott, Michael L., "The Coign Automatic Distributed Partitioning System, "Proc. of the Third Symposium on Operating System Design and Implementation (OSDI '99), pp. 187-200. New Orleans, LA, February 1999. USENIX.

[14] IBM Pervasive Computing http://www-3.ibm.com/pvc/.

[15] Joseph, A., et al., "Building Mobile Applications with the Rover Toolkit," Proc. 15th SOSP, Copper Mountain Resort, CO, Dec. 1995, pp 165-171.

[16] Kiczales, G., et al., "Aspect-Oriented Programming," Proceedings of the ECOOP 1997, Finland. Also available as Xerox PARC, TR SPL97-008 P9710042, Feb., 1997.

[17] Kimelman, D., Rajan, V. T., Roth, T., Wegman, M. N., "Partitioning and Assignment of Distributed Object Applications Incorporating Object Replication and Caching," 3rd Workshop on Mobility and Replication, European Conference on Object-Oriented Programming (ECOOP), pp. 313-314. Brussels, Belgium, 1998.

[18] Kindberg, T., et al., "People, Places, Things: Web Presence for the Real World. ", Proceedings of the third WMCSA, 2000. see also HPL CoolTown, http://cooltown.hp.com/.

[19] Kubiatowicz, J., et al., "OceanStore: An Architecture for Global-Scale Persistent Storage", Proc. of 9 ASPLOS, Nov. 2000.

[20] de Lara, E., et al., "Puppeteer: Component-based Adaptation for Mobile Computing," to appear at proc. of USENIX USITS, 2001.

[21] Lopes, C.V., Kiczales, G., "D: A Language Framework for Distributed Computing", Xerox PARC, TR SPL97-010 P9710047, Feb. 1997.

[22] Magee, J., et al. "A Constructive Development Environment for Parallel and Distributed Programs," In IEE/IOP/BCS Distributed Systems Engineering, 1(5): 304-312, Sept 1994.

[23] Mummert, L.B., et al., "Exploiting Weak Connectivity for Mobile File Access," Proc. of the 15th ACM SOSP, Dec. 1995, Copper Mountain Resort, CO, pp 143-155.

[24] Nierstrasz, O., Gibbs, S., and Tsichritzis, D., "Component-Oriented Software Development," CACM, v 35, no 9, September 1992, pp. 160-165.

[25] Noble, B.D., et al, "Agile Application-Aware Adaptation for Mobility," Proc of 16 SOSP, St. Malo, France, October 1997. Aura projects at CMU http://www.cs.cmu.edu/~aura.

[26] Norman, D. A., "The invisible computer," Cambridge, MA, MIT Press, 1998.

[27] OSGI Service Gateway Specification, available at www.osgi.org.

[28] Powers, S., "Developing ASP Components", O'Reilly, March 2001. (See also http://msdn.microsoft.com/library/default.asp?URL=/library/en-us/dnasp/html/asptutorial.asp, for tutorial on ASP)

[29] Roman, M., and Campbell, R.H., "Gaia: Enabling Active Spaces," Proceedings of the 9th ACM SIGOPS European Workshop, Kolding, Denmark, September 2000.

[30] Satyanarayanan, M., "Fundamental Challenges in Mobile Computing", Proc. of 15 ACM Symp. on Principles of Dist. Computing, May 1996, Philadelphia, PA, pp 61.

[31] StreamTheory, www.streamtheory.com.

[32] Sun Microsystem, "The .com Revolution Meets Consumer Appliances", available at: www.sun.com/990106/ces/.

[33] Sybase white paper, "Enabling e-Business Anywhere, Anytime: the Sybase Strategy," http://my.sybase.com/detail?id=1003164

[34] Transvirtual, www.transvirtual.com.

[35] Transvirtual, Kaffe (A clean-room, open source implementation of a Java virtual machine and class libraries). Available off of www.kaffe.org

[36] UDDI Technical White Paper, available at www.uddi.org.

[37] Weiser, M., "Some Computer Science Problems in Ubiquitous Computing," Communications of the ACM, July 1993, 75-84.

[38] Welling, L., and Thomson, L., "PHP and MySQL Web Development", SAMS, March 2001. (See also PHP, www.php.net).

[39] WordWalla www.wordwalla.com.

Adaptive Migration Strategy for Mobile Agents on Internet

DongChun Lee[1] and JeomGoo Kim[2]

[1] Dept. of Computer Science Howon Univ., South Korea
ldch@sunny.howon.ac.kr
[2] Dept. of Computer Science Namseoul Univ., South Korea

Abstract. Due on failures of clients (or Internet nodes), mobile agents may be blocked or crashed even if there are available service on the Internet. To solve this situation, we propose adaptive migration strategy with reordering and backward recovery of the paths to guarantee the migration of mobile agents. This paper will provide the extension with the autonomous migration of mobile agents, and it is implemented with the Java Mobile Agent System (JAMAS), which is independent on system platforms, developed by the Java language.

1 Introduction

Mobile agent technology has been interested in the last years as a new paradigm for distributed processing systems. Moreover, this technology has been applied for various application areas such as Internet management, and E-commerce [1,3,4,5,7,8,11]. Mobile agents are autonomous objects that migrate from node to node of Internet and provide to user which have executed themselves using database or computation resources of clients (or Internet nodes) connected by the Internet. To migrate the mobile agent, it will be needed a virtual place so-called the mobile agent system to support mobility [7]. Several prototypes of mobile agent system have been proposed in several different agent systems such as Odyssey [3], Aglet [4], Agent TCL [9], Mole [2], and so forth.
Most systems are little ensured its migration for a fault of Internet nodes or a crash of clients (or hosts), which may happen during migrating after a mobile agent launch. On the faults such as a destruction of the nodes or the mobile agent systems, we may consider that mobile agents may be destroyed, or blocked against the seamless Internet processing. It is no natural attribute to monitor the seamless progress of agent's execution, in a viewpoint to guarantee the autonomy of mobile agents. Therefore, we proposed a strategy with the simple techniques of path reordering and backward recovery to migrate mobile agents. In this paper, we propose adaptive migration strategy with reordering and backward recovery of the paths to guarantee the migration of mobile agents, and it is implemented in the JAMAS, which is a model of mobile agent system based on Java language for system independent platform.
The remainder of the paper is described as follow. We describe related works for

F. Casati, D. Georgakopoulos, M.-C. Shan (Eds.): TES 2001, LNCS 2193, pp. 201–212, 2001.
© Springer-Verlag Berlin Heidelberg 2001

the migration strategy of the existing systems and problems associated with it in Section 2. Section 3 describes the proposed algorithms, which is reordering and backward recovery of the path for a seamless migration on the Internet. Section 4 shows the implementation issue of the proposed strategy in the JAMAS. Finally, we conclude with a brief summary and future direction.

2   Related Work

Most of mobile agent systems provide a virtual place for migrating mobile agents under our basic ideal condition that there are no faults on the systems or nodes, or include relevant protocols. While a mobile agent is launched to specific nodes/clients according to relevant routing schedules [4], it is possible to happen some problems about migration of mobile agent if the host happens an accident within where the agent visits and executes. For example, when the node in the middle of the routing path happens a fault on Internet, the agent may infinitely wait at message queue of the current client in order to connect with the right next node. In other case, even if the agent has migrated successfully in autonomous running process of mobile agent, the agent may not work its own mission when there are no service interfaces among resources that specific host must support, e.g. database. In this situation, it causes low mobile reliability and critical confusing in the E- commerce. This leads to problem of the mobile agent's life span.

Typically, ORB [6], [7] implements distributed garbage collection in order to delete objects having no more references. Voyager [6] provides five policies for mobile agent's life cycle. Mole [2] supports the shadow protocol for orphan detection and successful termination for agents in mobile agent systems. The protocol is for detecting and processing what occurs any fault on migrating mobile agents. However, it does not provide to guarantee migration reliability of mobile agent. There is a simple protocol using transaction message queue [10], which is a procedure that the sender puts messages in the queue and receiver gets messages. There is also the same problem as the process of autonomous mobile agent in that it does not include facilities for monitoring the progress of an agent's execution. For example, assume that there is an agent in input queue of a host and the node's error occurs before the agent moves to queue of next node. Then the agent is blocked until that the node is recovered. This situation differs from problem in client/server. Mole [2], [10] provides a fault tolerant protocol to support effective way for 'exactly once' migration using voting and selecting protocol as copying mobile agent to all nodes.

Nevertheless, inter-monitoring facility and communication between each observer's nodes except worker node is needed and assumed that there is no fault in Internet connection.

3   Adaptive Migration Strategy for Mobile Agent

Mobile agents are autonomously migrated according to the relevant routing schedule, and then accomplished with their goals. We mention an enhanced strategy for the agent system to support adaptive migration of mobile agents even if it may happen a certain failure on nodes or clients on a whole clustering of the Internet. The strategy is adapted 'fault type' such that agents are not able to migrate more continuously.

3.1   Path Reordering Algorithm

The mobile agent may be impossible to migrate to the destination node by the fault of a node or the crash of a client. Figure 1(a) supposes that there is a migration path corresponding with an agent's routing schedule and some faulty nodes, such as N3, N4, and N7. An agent migrates and executes from node N1 to N2 sequentially, but it is blocked at the client of node N2 until the node N3 is recovered. If the node N3 dose not recovered, the agent may be orphaned or destroyed by the particular client. To solve this situation is for the agent to skip the faulty node N3 that includes on the migration path, and to move the address of node N3 back to the last one of the migration path. And then, the node N2 successfully connects the next other node N4 without any fault. Node N4 also has a particular fault. Therefore, node N2 Hop the right consecutive next one of node N4. As the same method is also applied to other nodes, the agent's migration path has reordered. That is, despite of any particular faulty nodes, the agent tries to connect subsequent nodes for the migration touring. This solution changes the previous arranged migration path by connecting with normal nodes except that some nodes have the particular fault. Afterward, the agent retries to connect each certain fault node after it waits for the timestamp assigned by the mobile agent system. If the certain faulty node is recovering by the timestamp, the agent will succeed in migrating to the destination node. Otherwise, the address of the faulty node will be discarded. Since the agent may be apt to loophole, we will give a restriction against the number of reconnection times.

Figure 1(b) shows that a whole re-arranged migration path for the mobile agent be changed by this strategy.

Algorithm 1: Path Reordering

For each agent's routing-table
{
Extract a target address and fail_checked information;
//*multicasting the signal to eliminate that clones if the agent has no more than*
// *the destinations.*
if(no more a target address)
Backward multicasts 'Agent_Fire' signal to successful_target nodes;
//*noticing of the flag to reentering for the failure of some nodes.*

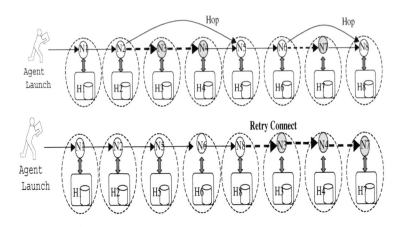

Fig. 1. The Path Reordering before and after Meet with Faulty Nodes.

```
if( exist a fail_checked_address) {
// check whether connect more than two times or not.
Wait the agent during some system_timestamp;
Try to connect Socket to the address;
if(success) {
Call goAgent;
Exit; }
else {
Notify to user the address is unavailable;
Ignore the address; }
}
//trying to connect the destination node the agent starts to migrate.
else if(not a fail_checked_address) {
Try to connect Socket to the destination node;
if(success) {
Call goAgent;
Exit;
}// if the agent does not connecting or migrating, set the flag and notify to user,
// Re-ordering the path in the routing-table at the same time.
else {
Notify to user;
Move the current failed_address to last in the routingtable;
Set the fail_checked information;
} } }
```

The mobile agent system executes the path reordering to connect every nodes of the migration path. If the agent doesn't connect a particular node in the middle of reaching the destination node via the migration path, it will succeed with connecting the right next one of a particular node of the path. After the failed address is pushed to the top one of routing table, it will retry to connect to the node. When it does reconnect each failed node, it does wait as much the timestamp assigned by the mobile agent system to reconnect. If it passes over the timestamp, it does ignore this address, and repeatedly connect the next faulty node. We have a limitation for reducing Internet overhead that mobile agent can just try two times to connect the failed node. That means a mobile agent to occur infinitive looping for just connection. Although it is connected, it applies equally the same as that way if each host of the node errors the mobile agent system. Algorithm 1 offers automatically to reorder the migration path when the mobile agent can not migrated the next host due to the faulty nodes.

3.2 Backward Recovery Algorithm

In Figure 2, we suppose that the migrated agents execute autonomously at the client H5. If the client H5 of node N5 crashes, all agents at that host are blocked or destroyed. To prevent it, the agent copies itself (that is, the clone) in the current client when an agent migrates the next node after it ends its job at the current client. The clone is unconditionally waiting until receiving an acknowledge signal 'ACK' from the next client. If the signal 'ACK' doesn't reach to the current client H4 within the timestamp from the next client H5, the cloned agent at the client H4 has automatically activated to resolve this hindrance. Consequently, it hops to the next node N6. If the agent faults at the client H6 on execution, it will work repeatedly the same method to connect the other next node.

In Figure 2, it happens that the current running agent at a client H5 is destroyed by a particular clash. At the same time, if the current client H4 also happens the succeeding fault, a cloned agent (which has already copied the previous client H3 of the client H4) wakes up and re-runs. This is so-called Backward Recovery.

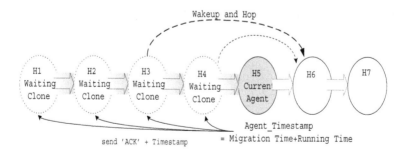

Fig. 2. Backward Recovery.

The backward recovery method is as follows: the agent system copies the clones of its agent on the client before migrating to the right next client. Each

$$TS_i = \text{System\_timestamp} + \sum_{x=1} \text{Agent\_Timestamp}_x$$

clone is waiting by it's own timestamp. Its timestamp of the original clone is maximum at the original host of the migration path, the next clone will be less than the migration and execution time of the previous one, and so forth. From launching an agent, the timestamp accumulates every clone of the previous clients with it's own moving and running time before it depart for the current client. Therefore, clones are waiting by the timestamp. Each clone spontaneously revives and attempts to work the path reordering as soon as regarding as a clashed host when none received any signal from the next host. At the final destination's node of the host, the agent system should broadcast a signal 'Agent_Fire' to all copied clones of the agent excepting the faulty nodes and failed hosts until reaching the destination. When the original agent is at the client Hk, the waiting time TSi of the cloned agent at the i-th client Hi is calculated as follow:

In such method, the algorithm 2 provides a backward recovery method for which mobile agents support adaptive migration from a host to the next one.

Algorithm 2: Backward Recovery

Waiting Clones Check
// *Periodically checking the timestamps of the clones.*
for each sleeped_clone
if (empty a clone_timestamp) {
Notify to user;
Call wakeup Clone;
}
Go Agent // *migrating the agent or cloning it.*
Send the agent;
Wait the agent's 'ACK' signal during send_timestamp;
if ('ACK') {
Clone the agent;
Call sleepAgent;
}
else call wakeupClone;
Arrive Agent
// *if the agent arrives in the JAMAS, noticing the previous node with the signal*
//*and executing.*
Send 'ACK' to the previous_node;
Execute the agent;
Sleep Agent // *Each cloned agent is waiting for the assigned timestamps.*
for each cloned_agent {
Add agent_timstamp to system_timestamp;
Add the agent to the sleeped_list;
Sleep the agent;

}
Wakeup Clone // *re-activating the clone of the agent.*
for the sleeped_list
Find a cloned_agent;
Remove it from the sleep_list;
if ('Agent_Fire') remove the cloned_agent;
else {
Move the current failed_address to last in the routing-table;
Set the fail_checked information;
Call the algorithm 1; // *arranging the path.*
}

4   Implementation

The proposed strategy is implemented in the JAMAS based on Java language,
a model of mobile agent system that we is developed. As shows in Fig. 3, the
JAMAS consists of Graphic User Interface, Agents Mobile Service Component,
Agents Execution Environment Component, and Agents Repository to provide
the naming transparency of agents. In addition, it may be executing one more
systems within a host.

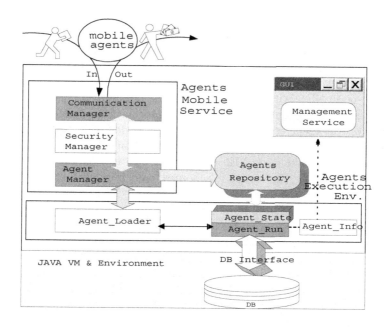

Fig. 3. The Architecture of JAMAS.

We show to launch through the process of an agent which manages some NE*s* (Internet elements). The following figures show that the simple agent as a role of Management Information Base (MIB) browser should be migrated and executed according to the routing schedule. Figure 4 depicts the routing path of the agent such as NE*h* → NE*b* → NE*a* → NE*c*, and we assume to be a fault at the client NE*b*.

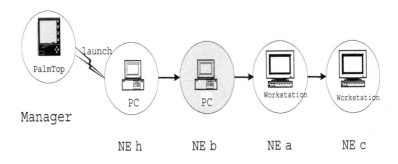

Fig. 4. A Routing Path with a Fault of Clients NE*b*.

The Internet manager fetches the prepared agent and specifies routing addresses of it to migrate. So, clicking the 'Go' button on the manager's window in Figure 5 to launch it, the agent starts on a tour to get the MIB information of each NE on behalf of the Internet manager.

Figure 5 and 6 show screen shots of results of the mobile agent. Figure 5 describes the gathered MIB information for nodes NE*h*, NE*a*, NE*c* which have no faulty, as well as a message of the second trial for migrating to the failed node at the last node NE*c*. Although there are some faults on the routing path, the mobile agent should maintain the own state information persistently.

In Figure 6, the agent tracer GUI shows what nodes have faulty and how to migrate continuously in the Internet. The executed agent at the host IP address 172.16.53.21 of the first node NE*h* does migrate to the second node NE*b*. Due to a particular failure, the agent has hopped and migrated at the third node NE*a*. On completing the execution at the last node NE*c*, it results information of reconnection to the faulted node NE*b* on the reordered path.

Finally, Figure 7 shows executions of the agent at each NE as follows: Figure 7(a), as a screen capture of the host NEh, shows hopping by a failure of connection at the next NEb after the launched agent normally progresses. Due to a failure of the host, the agent passes to next one. Thereafter, Figure 7(b), (c) capture executing of the agent at the hosts NEa, NEc. Then it is adapted to the proposed policy. Therefore, the agent has toured for all nodes having no faults before that it does re-connect with the faulty nodes.

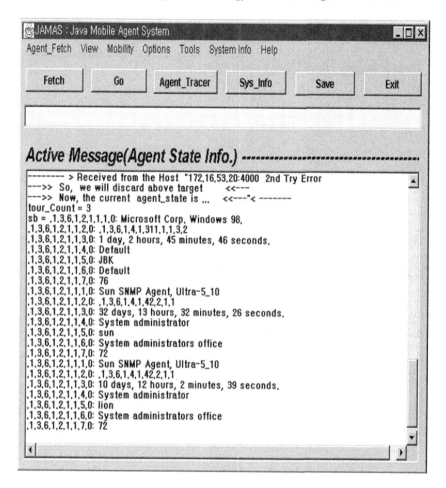

Fig. 5. A Persistent State Information of the Mobile Agent.

Therefore, the adaptive migration strategy for mobile agents ensures the persistency of computation to preserve autonomous mobility and information of state for agents though there are some faults of nodes or clients on the routing schedules of the Internet.

5   Conclusion

In this paper, we introduce the path reordering and backward recovery to ensure adaptive migration of mobile agents on Internet. All presented techniques have been implemented in our system, JAMAS. Therefore, JAMAS can improve effectively the problem of performance and Internet overhead due to the imposed

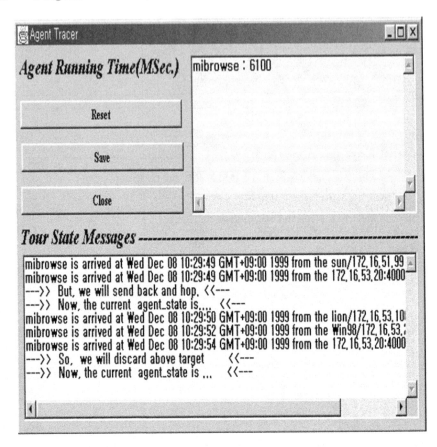

Fig. 6. Agent_Tracer GUI.

characteristics of distributed architecture since a mobile agent offers not only the migration reliability and transparency for mobile agent as autonomously as possible but also computing environment which is capable of distributed processing with mobile objects. Future work will investigate for the agent groups with distributed event services on Internet.

Acknowledgments

This work is supported by Howon University FUND 2001.

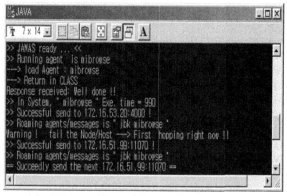

(a) A Screen Shot of Executing at the NE*h*.

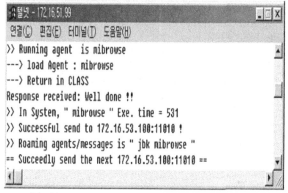

(b) A Screen Shot of Executing at the NE*a*.

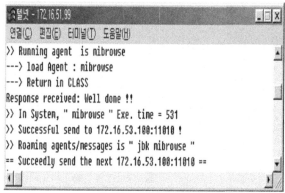

(c) A Screen Shot of Executing at the NE*c* and Attempting Migration of the Second at the NE*b*.

Fig. 7. Executions of a Mobile Agent at Each NE.

References

1. K.A. Baharat, L. Cardelli.: Migratory Applications. Proc. of the 8th Annual ACM Symp. on UISTech., November 1995.
2. J.Baumann.: A Protocol for Orphan Detection and Termination in Mobile Agent Systems. TR-1997-09, Stuttgart Univ. Jul., 1997.
3. General Magic.: Odyssey, URL: http://www.genmagic.com/agents/
4. IBM.: The Aglets Workbench, URL: http://www.trl.ibm.co.jp/aglets
5. D. B. Lange, M. Oshima.: Seven good reasons for mobile agents. Proc. of CACM, Vol. 42(3), Mar. 1999, PP 88-89.
6. Objectspace Voyager, GeneralMagic Odyssey, IBM Aglets.: A Comparison, June, 1997.
7. OMG.: Mobile Agent Facility Interoperability Facilities Specification (MAF). OMG.
8. A. Puliafito et al.: A Java-based Distributed Network Management Architecture. 3rd Int'l Conf. on Computer Science and Informatics (CS&I'97), Mar. 1997.
9. Robert S.G.: AgentTCL: A flexible and secure mobile-agent system. TR98-327, Dartmouth Col. June 1997.
10. K. Rothermel, M. Stra(c)er.: A Fault-Tolerant Protocol for Providing the Exactly-Once Property of Mobile Agents. Proc. of 17th IEEE SRDS'98, Oct. 1998.
11. J. Vitek and C. Tschudin.: Mobile Object Systems: Towards the Programmable Internet. Springer-Verlag, Apr. 1997.

Author Index

Lecture Notes in Computer Science

For information about Vols. 1–2084
please contact your bookseller or Springer-Verlag